# Same-Sex Marriage

Recent titles in
**Historical Guides to Controversial Issues in America**
*Ron Chepesiuk, Series Editor*

Gun Control and Gun Rights
*Constance Emerson Crooker*

The Pro-Life/Choice Debate
*Mark Herring*

Genetic Engineering
*Mark Y. Herring*

# Same-Sex Marriage

Allene Phy-Olsen

Historical Guides to Controversial Issues in America

GREENWOOD PRESS
Westport, Connecticut • London

**Library of Congress Cataloging-in-Publication Data**

Phy-Olsen, Allene.
   Same-sex marriage / Allene Phy-Olsen.
      p. cm. — (Historical guides to controversial issues in America, ISSN 1541–0021)
   Includes bibliographical references and index.
   ISBN 0–313–33516–8
   1. Same–sex marriage.   2. Same–sex marriage—Religious aspects.
3. Homosexuality—History.   I. Title.   II. Series.
HQ1033.P47 2006
306.84'809—dc22          2006015690

British Library Cataloguing in Publication Data is available.

Library of Congress Catalog Card Number: 2006015690
ISBN: 0–313–33516–8
ISSN: 1541–0021

First published in 2006

Greenwood Press, 88 Post Road West, Westport, CT 06881
An imprint of Greenwood Publishing Group, Inc.
www.greenwood.com

Printed in the United States of America

The paper used in this book complies with the
Permanent Paper Standard issued by the National
Information Standards Organization (Z39.48–1984).

10 9 8 7 6 5 4 3 2 1

# Contents

*Preface*                                                                          vii

1   Marriage and Homosexuality in the Religious Traditions
    of the World                                                                     1

2   Homosexuality in History                                                        37

3   The Emergence of a Homosexual Subculture and
    Gay Liberation Movements                                                        63

4   The Argument for Same-Sex Marriage                                              75

5   The Argument against Same-Sex Marriage                                         113

6   Life-style Choices: Alternatives to Traditional Marriage                       149

7   Same-Sex Marriage Today                                                        167

8   The Future of Gay Rights and the Precarious State
    of Matrimony                                                                   179

*Appendix A: Gay Acceptance and the Entertainment Media*                           185

*Appendix B: Selected Motion Pictures*                                             191

*Selected Annotated Bibliography*                                                  203

*Index*                                                                            227

*Photo essay follows page 112*

# Preface

Same-sex marriage is an issue that polarizes the American public like no other. Not even abortion arouses such passion among both its opponents and its advocates. Polls show that the majority of Americans continue to oppose same-sex marriage on religious, historical, and pragmatic grounds, even while the courts are reinterpreting the laws that have in the past limited the rights of gay and lesbian persons.

Same-sex marriage has become a major legal and political concern throughout the Western world. Public opinion can change almost overnight. In one century, Russia was transformed from the most religious country in Europe to an atheistic state; yet by the end of that same century, its people had overthrown communism, and the wife of the last leader of Soviet Russia was buried in the full rites of the Orthodox Church. Such rapid changes are also evident in the Canadian province of Quebec, where I have spent much time. During the early sixties, it was still a "priest-ridden province," with religious supply houses on every city block and clerics in black cassocks on the streets of every village. Ten years later, the quiet revolution was under way, and the city of Montreal had become a secular metropolis. At McGill University, a number of my friends, who were young nuns, were forced to remove the habits of their order when they ventured into the shopping district of the city. Nuns were no longer regarded as brides of Christ, but had become objects of sexual fantasies, to be peppered with crude suggestions by passersby.

It is clear that within the last 20 years throughout North America a revolutionary change in attitude has taken place with regard to homosexuality. The love that once dared not speak its name is now discussed in every publication. Admired entertainers allow themselves to be photographed holding hands with their same-sex partners, and conservative politicians acknowledge having gay sisters and daughters. Still, most Americans, while now willing to live and let live when it comes to private sexual practices, are still strongly opposed to the legal recognition of gay unions. Judging from the protests accompanying Canada's emerging same-sex marriage laws, it would seem that many Canadians agree.

Strong arguments on both sides of the same-sex marriage issue—based on psychology, social welfare, law, public policy, history, tradition, and religion—have been presented by articulate and notable people, many of whom are quoted in this book. In the United States, the controversy highlights questions of equal protection under the Constitution, the operation of the courts, and the validity of community standards of conduct even when they challenge personal liberties. Despite the opposition of the majority, which has been evident every time the matter has been placed before the voters, most books, articles, and Web sites have supported same-sex marriage. This is perhaps not surprising, considering the liberal philosophy that dominates the media and the entertainment and academic professions.

The appeals on both sides of this burning question deserve respectful reflection. These arguments need to be brought together, calmly presented and evaluated, without name-calling or rancor. Opponents of same-sex marriage are often quick to accuse its advocates of disregarding tradition, religion, morality, and public decency to promote what they feel is a sick and degenerate life-style. Advocates reply in kind; they feel their opponents are ignoramuses, bigots, and benighted reactionaries. The assumption in this book is that, generally speaking, both advocates and opponents of same-sex marriage are reasonable, charitable, honest seekers of what is best for their community and country. For this reason, the pejorative terms used by extremists on each side are avoided (except in quotes). For example, opponents of homosexual conduct and same-sex marriage are not here identified as "homophobes." Even though this term is in wide use, it is etymologically inaccurate and offensive. The thoughtful opponents of gay liberation do not *fear* homosexuals and frequently do not even dislike them; they *disapprove* of their life-style.

I have tried, as much as possible, to use terms and labels that each group accepts for itself. In literature by homosexuals, one finds the use of "gay," "queer," "homophile," "lesbian," and "homosexual," and I therefore assume these are acceptable designations when used in their proper contexts. In the literature, "gay" frequently designates the masculine gender, but it is also used with some frequency to refer to both men and women who identify themselves as homosexual. It thus becomes a convenient and respectful shorthand, avoiding the constant repetition of "gays and lesbians," which might otherwise be necessary. If I have inadvertently employed words that needlessly offend either gay rights advocates or their opponents, I apologize in advance and, when informed, will make appropriate changes in subsequent editions.

Before the twentieth century, there was an inadequate vocabulary for objectively discussing homosexual matters. By World War II, homosexuals began using "gay" to describe their inclinations and activities, although the general population did not use the term until the 1960s. Nobody is quite clear about its origin, though a popular belief is that it comes from Avenue de la Gaieté in Paris, a Bohemian quarter where homosexual life flourished. There also may be American associations with "Gay Paree," the "Gay Nineties," and the Earth goddess Gaia. Early usage employed "gay" as a preferred designation for both male and female homosexuals, and this usage is still found in much of the literature supporting the cause. However, in the 1970s, some in the organized lesbian movement, deeply influenced by women's liberation in general, felt that men dominated the gay rights movement to the detriment of their own needs. They preferred to be called "lesbians," although this choice was not that of all women so identified.

Another problematic term is "sodomy," which merits a brief explanation. Because so much of the early literature on homosexuality employs this word, and it appears frequently in descriptive rather than judgmental writings, I have retained it in some contexts, despite its unfavorable biblical connotations. Here, unless otherwise stipulated, sodomy refers not to a particular sexual practice but to male homosexuality in general.

When the discussion of complicated social questions is accompanied by strident accusations and name-calling, the obvious result is that people only become more firmly entrenched in their views and less willing to concede any merit in the opposing opinion. Two examples from personal experience illustrate this.

Several years ago my husband and I were conducting a series of discussions on current social problems for an adult Sunday school class at an Episcopal church in Montgomery, Alabama. Most of the members of the group were teachers, social workers, psychologists, and lawyers. One of the issues discussed was homosexual rights. Calmly and reasonably, the class examined many facets of the subject. Although no consensus emerged from these friendly discussions, everyone left with a fuller understanding of a complex topic and, I think, more empathy for homosexuals as they face their unique problems.

In contrast, a few years later, in a church setting in another state, my husband and I were asked to assist in a series of discussions on homosexuality. The national hierarchy of this denomination had decreed that it was time for the entire church to achieve a vox populi consensus on the issue. Regarding the matter as too important to leave to the discretion of lay people, the rector of the congregation took charge of the discussion, determined to indoctrinate everyone in his own viewpoint. He was an intelligent, eloquent, and compassionate man who felt the gay rights movement was analogous to the Civil Rights Movement of the 1960s. He immediately labeled anyone who disagreed a "homophobe," thus cutting off further discussion in what had been promoted as a free and open airing of ideas. Cowed by such priestly authority, the assembled laity offered no open dissention, although several left whispering to one another their strong disagreement with the views that had been promulgated. Later, it was not surprising when this denomination erupted nationally in turmoil and schism. It was intriguing to observe the irony of the descendants of plantation owners in some Southern parishes withdrawing their allegiance to their national hierarchy and placing themselves under the spiritual oversight of African bishops.

The literature of the gay rights and same-sex marriage movements is voluminous and expanding daily. However, much of this literature has been quickly prepared and is frequently misleading. Even when scholarship is impressive, the preconceptions of the scholars too frequently skew the interpretation of sources. Although a substantial body of material on same-sex marriage is available, most is found in newspaper accounts, periodical articles, and editorials, where there is neither space nor time to provide historical context or philosophical reflection. Many books are little more than propaganda for a particular point of view. The aim of this book is to examine as objectively as possible both sides of the issue. It is hoped that the presentation of salient facts will enable teachers and students to carefully examine the issues that determine public policy.

It is the further aim of this book to go beyond a mere summary of the oft-reiterated arguments on both sides of the topic. To more fully understand the principles involved in the current controversy, it is essential to provide context. What has marriage represented in the past, and what is its role today? What is it about the institution of marriage that makes it so compelling that many gays and lesbians want a share in it? What expectations and social values of marriage have changed through the centuries and have always varied according to geographical location, religion, and economic class, and how do these changes strengthen or weaken the argument in favor of same-sex marriage? Where is the continuity and what is the commonality in this enduring relationship we continue to call, despite its fluctuations, marriage? When gay and lesbian couples are pronounced "married," does the essential nature of a time-honored institution change, or is it merely a shift of semantics?

A substantial annotated bibliography is included at the end of this book. Because I am not writing a polemic and do not present any definitive answers to complex questions, I believe that it is especially important for readers to examine sources for themselves. Each bibliographic annotation identifies the author's point of view and, where appropriate, briefly evaluates the research and logic presented, further commenting on the general usefulness of the work. Currently, more books supporting gay rights are being issued by major publishers than those opposing the agenda. However, the books by Gagnon, Bork, and Bennett more than compensate for this imbalance. Because motion pictures not only reflect but influence our values and ideals, I have included a list of those I feel shed light on the subject at hand. All are readily available on video and DVD. The film library is also large, although slanted on one side of the issue, but I have cited only examples I have had the opportunity to personally scrutinize.

Because this book is designed largely for students researching issues raised by the general topic, each chapter is designed to be coherent apart from its overall context. For this reason, some repetition is found from chapter to chapter. It will be evident that I have relied heavily on a number of excellent historical, sociological, and theological studies. Readers are again urged to consult these directly for the full presentation of arguments which I have summarized.

Years ago I was married in Alabama, in the eyes of God and with the sanction of George Wallace. In the words of the Book of Common Prayer, I was reminded on that occasion that "our Lord Jesus Christ adorned this manner of life by His presence and the first miracle which He wrought in Cana of Galilee." Yet Jesus was a single man, and, as a teacher of Renaissance literature, I concur with Sir Francis Bacon that "the best works, and of greatest merit for the public, have proceeded from the unmarried or childless." In our current obsession with marriage, what it has been in the past, and what we hope or fear it may become in the future, it is well to remember that there are a number of vocations in which humans may flourish. People, both gay and straight, may choose, whether through temperament or circumstances, to remain single. Their rights, too, should not be ignored.

# 1

# Marriage and Homosexuality in the Religious Traditions of the World

Some historical perspective is essential in any examination of current developments in homosexual theory and the activist platform—particularly the demand to be included in the venerable institution of matrimony. Does the perplexity of U.S. society have a historical precedent, or are our attitudes toward gay people unique? Has homosexuality always existed among humans and animals? Has it ever been accepted by society, and, if so, under what circumstances? Homosexual relationships have been widely celebrated in story and song, and gay individuals have been given honored roles as shamans, priests, and entertainers—but they also have been objects of ridicule, persecution, and execution. In the twenty-first century, numerous Western nations are making an effort to achieve the separation of the sacred and secular that Americans so cherish. Yet even when Thomas Jefferson's "wall of separation" between church and state is successfully erected, historical religious doctrines play an important part in the formulation of laws and personal attitudes. This is nowhere more evident than in marriage customs. To understand what same-sex marriage can be or may become, and to comprehend the strength of the resistance to it, a survey of the teachings of major world religions on both marriage and homosexuality becomes instructive.

Later chapters of this book examine specific religious arguments both for and against same-sex marriage, concentrating on the teachings of the Judeo-Christian tradition that has so strongly conditioned Western attitudes. Yet the gay movement is international, despite the strength of the present resistance to it in Asia and Africa; its ultimate goal will be to make same-sex marriage acceptable throughout the world. Some attention must therefore be given to the established religious traditions of India, China, and elsewhere. Around the world, matrimony remains closely intertwined with the historic religions of the local people, even in those lands where religious observance has sharply declined. And, interestingly enough, no matter how removed people's lives become from religious rites and ceremonies, they generally want to be married in a church or temple.

The now-defunct Soviet Union took measures to discourage religious practice, providing secular marriage parlors, as if these could ever adequately substitute for the poetry and splendor of Russian Orthodox Christian liturgies. In France, a country that clearly separates legal marriage from religious observance, the religious ceremony, with its full pomp, still generally follows the required secular ceremony at town hall. Recently Prince Charles was married for the second time; because his bride was a divorcée, he could not be wed in the full rites of the Church of England, of which his mother is the head. Yet a stately compromise was arranged: after the civil marriage in the town hall of Windsor—where some months later singer Elton John would seal his civil union with his male companion—a ceremony of blessing was conducted in the chapel of Windsor Castle by the Archbishop of Canterbury, complete with boy's choir and Russian opera singer.

Most major religions of the world agree on the importance of marriage, though they differ as to its privileges and the obligations of married couples. Even the different denominations within Christianity fail to reach consensus as to the precise meaning of this durable institution. For same-sex couples who desire a share in this "holy estate," it is well to consider exactly what they may be asking to embrace. Are they ready to assume the responsibilities that most societies attach to marriage? Do they wish to partake of an ordinance highly structured by history and religious obligation? Or are they asking to change the very nature of the institution itself?

Throughout the world, marriage is acknowledged as a major initiation ceremony into adulthood, strongly encouraged in most lands, though reluctantly made optional in some. Marriage festivities, in which family and community celebrate, may last for weeks and frequently strain the financial resources of the families involved. Some societies crown newlyweds, proclaiming them royalty for this one day of their lives. In Western countries, quite ordinary young women are elaborately groomed and gowned and escorted to church in stretch limousines. For this day they are surrounded by attendants as if they were celebrities. In every land, this official coming together of male and female is a special occasion that engages the entire community and is treated with an importance that the covenanting parties themselves often do not fully comprehend.

For religious people, a wealth of symbolism surrounds matrimony. In Judaism, Christianity, and some Hindu sects, marriage symbolizes the union of

Divine and human. It is not surprising that those universal emblems of religious mysticism—the rose and wine—feature so prominently in marriage ceremonies and receptions. Marriage vows, even in countries (such as the United States and Sweden) where half the unions are likely to end in divorce, are taken "until death us do part." Mormons venture a step beyond, marrying for time and eternity. Divorce, no matter how common it becomes in a society, is almost always perceived as a failure. Newly divorced people are frequently desolate, and the search for a replacement of the one who has been lost or gotten away may become frantic. "All the world's in love with love," it appears to those who are alone. Are gay people, who as social pariahs have enjoyed unusual freedoms within their own communities, ready to pledge the permanence and faithfulness that traditional marriage requests?

Some critics of same-sex marriage, usually from within the gay community, find the imitative character of many homosexual commitment ceremonies objectionable. To outsiders these ceremonies may come off as parodies of traditional weddings. Two elaborately gowned brides may march down an aisle, or two immaculately groomed young men in tuxedos may join their right hands to take vows. More frequently in lesbian weddings, one partner wears an elegant tuxedo, while the other is the blushing bride in white. There are a number of ways to pronounce the newly united couple: "wife and wife," "husband and husband," "partners for life," "spouses," or some other designation of choice. The wedding cake, the crowning (as in some Eastern weddings), the breaking of a glass (according to Jewish custom), the exchange of rings, the kiss that seals the ceremony—all elements of traditional marriage—may initially seem ironic when two people of the same gender take their vows.

Romance entrepreneurs are making fortunes with online Web sites, and matchmaking is earnest business, serving both the gay and straight communities, particularly in the anonymous milieus of large cities where highly mobile yet rootless masses live. Marriage making is further complicated in modern Western societies by the expectation that young people will choose their own mates at a time in their lives when they are driven by high emotions and uncertainty, lacking the wisdom that experience is supposed to bring (though frequently does not). Young people are further burdened by the myth of romantic love, a concept invented about six centuries ago by Provençal troubadours and idle clerics who neither took it seriously nor considered it a proper basis for marriage. As if heterosexual love were not complicated enough, gay lovers must cope with additional problems.

Not one of the great world religions today, as a whole, recognizes marriage as anything other than the union of a minimum of two people, including at least one member of each sex.[1] The support of an established religious community, on which heterosexual unions may depend if they so choose, is rarely available to homosexual couples, regardless of whether their marriage is legally recognized. If we are to understand what our inherited institution of matrimony really is, we must examine the religious doctrines and insights that have so significantly influenced cultures around the world and tend to form a barrier to same-sex marriage.

## JUDAISM

Although Jews remain a small minority among the world's population and have never been a major political power, the Jewish spiritual and ethical ideals exert worldwide influence, mostly through Judaism's derivative faiths of Christianity and Islam. The Jewish contribution to human civilization is major, and Judaism remains influential in the Middle East and the United States.

From the beginnings of its recorded history, the Hebrew-Jewish tradition has not only honored marriage, but proclaimed it a religious obligation. According to Hebrew Scripture, God in the Garden of Eden declared that it is not good for man to be alone. Many familiar Jewish proverbs and adages praise matrimony:

"Any man who has no wife is not a complete human being."

"The sins of man are forgiven at marriage."

"Whoever spends his days without a wife has no joy, no blessing and no good in his life."

"A man is not even called a man until he is united with a woman."[2]

Among Orthodox Jews, a man who refrains from marriage through willful intent commits a sin and betrays the people of Israel. Women who remain single are incomplete, more to be pitied than censured. The begetting and rearing of children is also a positive duty for Jews, and the refusal to produce offspring has been likened to the shedding of blood, a veritable diminishing of the image of God in man.

Although the most revered of biblical patriarchs had several wives—especially if a first or primary wife produced young with difficulty or not at all—the general Jewish trend since late antiquity has been toward monogamy. It was finally made obligatory for the Ashkenazi (those who settled throughout northwestern Europe in the early Middle Ages) by Rabbi Gresham (960–1028). Monogamy also increasingly became the choice of other Jews, to be found largely in Spain, parts of Africa, and Turkey, and it continues among them in limited ways to the present day. Divorce in Judaism, while allowed according to the Law of Moses for offenses that have been clarified and specified by various rabbinical schools, has always been regarded as a failure and a tragedy.

The prophets, poets, and sages of the ancient Hebrews saw marriage as an analogy to God's bond with the descendants of Abraham, with whom he had established a covenant. The biblical prophet Hosea envisioned God Almighty as a frequently deceived, agonized husband who was nevertheless forgiving when his people rejected idols and returned to the covenant. The Song of Songs, a collection of ancient erotic poetry traditionally attributed to Solomon, found its way into the Sacred Canon as an allegory of God's union with Israel.

In Judaism, a man and a woman are wed in a ceremony that evokes the ancient Hebrew matriarchs: Sarah, Rebecca, Leah, and Rachel. When a ring is placed on the hand of a Jewish bride, it is with these words: "You are consecrated to me with this ring according to the Law of Moses and Israel." The ceremony is traditionally performed under a "huppah," a wedding canopy; benedictions are recited over wine, which the couple then shares; and the bridegroom dramatically crushes a glass with his foot. The symbolism of the broken glass is complex, but it serves to caution the assembled company that, even in moments of greatest gladness, they must never forget the destruction of the Jerusalem temple.

A persistent lament of Jews today, especially in the aftermath of the Holocaust, is the declining birth rate, which, along with marriage outside the faith, threatens the continuing existence of the community. The faith, in which the generation of offspring and the perpetuation of the covenant people looms so central, would seem to have no place for same-sex marriage. The *halakah,* traditional Jewish law, prohibits homosexual relationships. Although the biblical Book of Leviticus, the ultimate source of this law, does not explicitly condemn lesbian activity, as it clearly does male relationships, the decrees of the rabbis long ago extended the prohibition to lesbianism, although they never treated it as seriously as male sodomy. After all, it was to man rather than woman that God gave the commandment to be fruitful and multiply. Punishments for homosexuality have been lighter for women than for men throughout Jewish history. For men, the stated punishment for this "abomination" was the death penalty, although it is unclear how often it was actually carried out.

There was another reason that male homosexuality was prohibited. The Hebrews feared that they might lose the Promised Land if such conduct went unchecked, for in Scripture, the Lord had threatened to "spew them out of the land." In popular Jewish superstition, homosexuality caused earthquakes and solar eclipses. It was never forgotten that, according to the Bible, in the time of Abraham, the Lord had rained down fire and destruction on Sodom and Gomorrah because of homosexual behavior. There was, however, a certain ease in confronting these threats, because the Hebrews believed that homosexuality, so characteristic of pagans, was rarely a problem of their own.

Throughout the centuries of the Diaspora, Jews all over the world tried to maintain their laws and their memory of Zion. Some scholars have suggested, through a review of the Hebrew literature that was produced during the period when their culture was allowed to flourish in Muslim Spain, that homosexual love at that time became a familiar subject of their poets and that there was a respite from biblical authority. But it is easy to misinterpret lyric poetry, and the temptation to read it autobiographically should usually be resisted. Hebrew poetry in Spain certainly imitated the more explicit Arabic court poetry that celebrated erotic love in a generalized manner, without always being explicit as to gender. Rather than expressing an individual point of view, the poet might strive to speak of the erotic longings and spiritual aspirations of a community, often on an idealistic, even allegorical, plane. In following the familiar conventions of Arabic poetry, Jewish court poets frequently used the masculine pronoun, much as popular song writers do today, to suggest the yearnings of all humans for romantic love.[3]

There would appear to be little leniency toward gays and lesbians in Orthodox Judaism; on a popular level, Jews remind themselves that Adam and Eve rather than Adam and Steve were placed in the Garden of Eden. Still, there have been significant developments in contemporary reconstructions of the faith. The powerful film *Trembling Before G-d* sympathetically presents the plight of Orthodox Jews trying to maintain their faith yet unable to deny their homosexuality. Today liberal Jews, especially in the Reform and Reconstructionist movements, honor the high ethical teachings of Judaism but do not feel bound by ancient ceremonial laws and customs they feel have little relevance to their present lives. Even many conservative Jews, who still attempt to follow biblical teachings, generally affirm life in the modern world and in a pluralistic society. In this spirit, there have been attempts to reconstruct the religious prohibitions of male homosexuality. A newer reading by a few Jewish teachers concentrates on accepting the dignity of each human, making some room for committed same-sex relationships.

The traditional hostility of Judaism toward homosexuality continues to be singled out by some gay historians as the chief culprit in the widespread "homophobia" in the West. But Judaism, with over 14 million adherents worldwide, is far from monolithic. It is a way of life as well as a religion, and many liberal or secular individuals still consider themselves Jewish. Although Orthodox Judaism will only slowly, if ever, abandon its abhorrence of "gender bending," more liberal attitudes abound in secular and Reform Jewish circles. If they are concerned with biblical injunctions at all, these groups view them as applicable to the conditions of life among ancient Hebrews rather than to

Jews living in the twenty-first century. Although more conservative congregations are not yet ready for gay rabbis and commitment services, their general attitude has softened. By the end of the 1970s, the majority of Jews favored eliminating legal restrictions and civil disabilities on gay people.[4]

Gay and lesbian Jews began to appear openly and to organize in the 1970s. Gay outreach synagogues were formed, in part after the model of the Christian Metropolitan Community Churches. Beth Chayim Chadashim in Los Angeles, one such outreach synagogue, was in 1973 one of the first to be given formal membership in the Reform movement's Union of American Hebrew Congregations. More such outreach synagogues opened in the United States, Canada, and Europe throughout the 1970s. Even openly lesbian rabbis, a double abomination to the Orthodox, who still accord women secondary status in synagogues, have been employed in Reform temples in San Francisco and New York City. In 1979, against serious objection on the part of Orthodox rabbis and Muslim leaders, the International Conference of Gay and Lesbian Jews was held in Israel.

The modern scene is quite different from the traditional world of Ashkenazi or Sephardic Judaism. While Jewish religious law is separate from the Israeli Penal Code, the legalization of sexual relationships between men by the Israeli Knesset in 1988 does indicate a change of attitude in the environment of many Jews. Gay pride parades have taken place on the streets of Israel's leading cities, despite continuing protests of conservative rabbis and Muslim mullahs. In Europe and the United States, additional congregations of gay Jews have been recognized as members of the Union of American Hebrew Congregations of Reform Judaism, some of which have blessed commitment ceremonies and most of which look with favor on same-sex marriage.

## CHRISTIANITY

Accepting Jewish Scripture as the foundation and prophecy of its own gospel, Christianity agrees that marriage was instituted by God; it was no mere human solution to the problem of loneliness. But Christianity further applied to monogamous marriage the words of St. Paul, likening the love of husband and wife to that of Christ and the church. Stately Christian marriage liturgies further reminded all observers that Jesus honored marriage by his presence at the feast in Cana of Galilee, where he changed water into wine. Not only was this a foreshadowing, at the very beginning of his ministry, of the holy sacrament of his body and blood, but it was also an affirmation of the joys of marriage. At the very beginning of his earthly ministry, Jesus thus brought joy and festivity.

Classical Christianity stated three reasons for matrimony: the procreation of children and their nurture in the fear of God; the remedy for licentious behavior; and the provision for the mutual comfort and society of husband and wife. Some Christian churches venture further in designating marriage a sacrament, an outward sign of an inward grace. Roman Catholics speak of a mystical bond established between spouses that can never be broken, which not only bestows sanctifying grace on the husband and wife but blesses the Church itself and the broader community.

The sacramental doctrine of the Roman Catholic Church was fully formulated by the middle of the twelfth century, grounded in the teachings of the apostles, the Greek and Latin Church fathers, and the Councils of the Western Church. Before the Second Vatican Council (1962–1965), the Roman Catholic Church was highly legalistic and even stern in its regulation of marriage. Considering the two great ends of marriage, the Church taught that the primary one was the procreation of children, and the mutual well-being of spouses was secondary. Realistically, these aims frequently conflicted, but the church maintained that the duty toward children always took precedence. However, the Second Vatican Council lightened the load on Catholic marriages in several ways. In its *Pastoral Constitution on the Church in the Modern World,* the Council reasserted the doctrine that both marriage and the love of spouses "are ordained for the procreation and education of children, and find in them their ultimate crown."[5] Yet (and this is basic to any possible acceptance of same-sex marriage, however unlikely that acceptance may seem at the present time), the *Pastoral Constitution* declined to define primary and secondary ends of marriage. It taught instead that procreation "does not make the other ends of marriage of less account," further affirming that marriage "is not instituted solely for procreation." This was a notable shift of emphasis in Roman Catholic thinking.[6] The Council also was less hostile to religiously mixed marriages than the Church had been in the past, now allowing joint ceremonies with the clergy of other faiths and eliminating the "promises" that non-Catholic spouses were once required to sign, agreeing in advance that all children would receive a thorough Catholic indoctrination. Although children were still expected to be reared in the faith, the goodwill of spouses was now assumed. Consequently, Catholic marriage now permits more diversity.

Although Roman Catholics vastly outnumber other Christians in the West, since the eleventh century, the Christians of the East—including some of the historic churches of the Mediterranean area and the Middle East—have maintained their separation from the Roman See. Today they make up the second largest body of Christians, with churches throughout the Levant, Russia, the Greek Islands, and the rest of Eastern Europe. The marriage liturgies of the

Eastern Churches reveal their own emphases. Marriage is spoken of as the first blessing God ever bestowed upon humans, directly after their creation. Through procreation in marriage, humans become co-creators with God Almighty. Although this divine union was long ago corrupted by human sin, its sanctity was restored by Christ and sealed by his first miracle.

The marriage liturgy of the Eastern Orthodox Church is lengthy and rich in remembrance of the patriarchs, prophets, apostles, sages, martyrs, and saints who have gone before. The priest invokes the names of "blessed Abraham and Sarah, Isaac and Rebecca, Jacob and all the Patriarchs. . . . Joseph and Asenath, Moses and Sepphora, Joachim and Anna, Zacharias and Elizabeth . . . Noah in the Ark, Jonah within the whale, the three holy boys from the fire . . . St. Helena when she found the Holy Cross."[7]

While Judaism looked with disfavor on the unmarried state, Roman Catholicism and Eastern Orthodoxy gave celibacy a higher status than sacramental marriage. Jesus was unmarried—unusual for a Jewish teacher of his time or any other—and St. Paul, often referred to as the "second founder of Christianity," was not only unmarried but advocated celibacy as generally a more desirable state. Many church historians believe Paul's preference derived from his belief that he was indeed living in the last days, the end times, when the commandment to be fruitful, multiply, and replenish the earth seemed no longer applicable. It is also possible that early Christianity subconsciously incorporated from pagan mystical philosophies and cults a world-weariness that made the faithful less optimistic about bringing offspring into a failing world. Another explanation may have been a sexual aversion resulting from the hedonism of the pagan societies that surrounded the early Christians. A pragmatic explanation heard today is simply that people without family responsibilities may devote themselves more single-mindedly to great causes and noble deeds and therefore may serve the Church exclusively. Whatever the reason, classical Christianity has been in this respect more inclusive than most other religions, pronouncing both celibacy and matrimony respectable. Of course, it always assumed that marriage would be the joining of a man and a woman.

When the upheavals of the Protestant Reformation swept Europe, all the sacraments and rites of the Western Church were reexamined by the reformers. Although most of the reformers acknowledged only two biblically endorsed sacraments—baptism and holy communion—they took marriage no less seriously than had the Catholics and Eastern Orthodox. In some ways, they were even greater proponents, insisting that matrimony was appropriate for everyone and making little allowance for those who voluntarily chose celibacy as a religious vocation. Each Protestant tradition provided a different theological insight into marriage. According to John Witte, Jr., who has written a soundly researched and thoughtful book on Western Christian views of marriage, Lutherans emphasized the social dimensions of marriage, Calvinists the covenantal pact, and Anglicans saw marriage as a model of common-wealth.[8] Luther taught that marriage existed not only to convey Christian values, morals, and mores to children, but to be a witness in a sinful society of what a community of love, mutual help, and piety could be. Thus, marriage became a school for the teaching of restraint, self-discipline, and concern for the life and property of others. John Calvin believed that marriage is "a good and holy ordinance of God," although a matter of the earthly rather than heavenly kingdom. As Calvin further contemplated the meaning of marriage through study and his own brief but happy experience as the husband of a pious widow, his understanding deepened. Marriage for him assumed the quality of a divine covenant. He wrote:

God is the founder of marriage. When a marriage takes place between a man and a woman, God presides and requires a mutual pledge from both. Hence Solomon in Proverbs 2:17 calls marriage the covenant of God, for it is superior to all human con-tracts. So also Malachi [2:14] declares that God is as it were the stipulator [of marriage] who by his authority joins the man to the woman, and sanctions the alliance.[9]

After the Reformation, the eclectic Anglican communion assimilated many of the views of marriage already articulated by the Roman Catholics, Lutherans, and Calvinists, but added their own insights. English theologians spoke of marriage as a symbol of the divine love as well as a sacred covenant. But it was further emphasized as an institution that served the common good, with the church and state as active participants.

In fact all the reformers stressed the social uses of marriage, which they believed helped people cultivate the Christian virtues that also made them good citizens: love, patience, altruism, a cooperative spirit. For this reason, divorce was considered a tragedy for both individuals and society and was extremely rare in the early days of the Reformation.

One early reason the reformers made of marriage a near obligation was the horror they felt at the low moral conditions they believed characterized Catholic religious orders and geographical regions dominated by the Roman Church. Monasteries and nunneries were regarded by the reformers as places of sexual vice. As a young priest, Luther had made a pilgrimage to Rome and returned with reports of the moral decadence of the city. He claimed that nude women served at the papal table—although he would have had no way of knowing this directly and probably relied on questionable rumor. But the reformers were supplied with abundant witnesses to confirm their worst sus-picions of immorality among "the Romish clergy." Some of the Renaissance popes lived luxuriously with their concubines and occasionally, it was alleged, with their male lovers, placing their own children in lucrative ecclesiastical positions. Priests were said to have been among the most steady clients of prostitutes. The reformers believed this was only to be expected when priests were denied marriage.

With the lofty concept of marriage upheld by all Christians in theory, divorce remained uncommon in Christian societies until the modern era. Roman Catholics believed that a valid marriage was indissoluble, yet they were required, as were all others, to live out their days in the messy human world where failure occurs with regularity. Roman Catholic kings, like all other rulers, had the duty to produce heirs even when their marriages-of-state left them bound to barren wives. The Catholic solution was an annulment, upon the discovery of some impediment or flaw in the original marriage agreement. The ecclesiastical courts could then decree a union invalid, and, after appropriate penance, the parties were free to remarry. Many possible impediments were eventually enumerated, so that a skillful canon lawyer could usually find a way to annul almost any marriage. Grounds included consanguinity, affinities of various kinds such as adoption or god-parenthood, abduction, impotence, offenses against public propriety, prior bonds, and even disparity of worship. Marriages were declared invalid if either party had been below an age of consent or had taken earlier vows in a religious order.

Eastern Orthodox Christianity, which followed different canons that made more concessions to human fallibility, did permit divorce and remarriage, however reluctantly, if two people found themselves incompatible. The Orthodox Church limited the faithful to only three marriages in a lifetime, whether previous unions had been severed by death or divorce.

In theory, the Protestants may have been more lenient in the matter of divorce than the Roman Catholics, though in practice there was hardly any difference. Protestants sometimes referred to the Law of Moses in the Hebrew Bible, according to which a man was allowed to "put away" his wife for a variety of reasons (which later varied according to rabbinical schools) upon giving her "a bill of divorcement." However, in the Sermon on the Mount, Jesus, as reported in the Gospel of St. Luke, had reinterpreted the Law of Moses and taught that marriages were binding unless broken by adultery. St. Paul in his epistles had set forth another cause for divorce—later to be known as "the Pauline privilege"—by which a Christian was freed from the bonds of matrimony if a pagan spouse chose to leave bed and board.

Although the Anglican Church was born in the midst of a bitter divorce, with King Henry VIII's urgency to acquire a legal wife who could produce a vital male heir, that church was perhaps, until modern times at least, the most reluctant of all to endorse remarriage after divorce. In the seventeenth century, divorce had become so difficult in England that the poet John Milton, whose first wife for a time abandoned him, wrote three treatises in which he applied his great learning and powers of rhetoric to convince the English church and government that divorce for incompatibility was right and proper. His writings, despite their fervor, had little impact on England.

With its biblical heritage and these views on marriage between man and woman, it is not surprising that, at least until very recent times, Christianity has been unanimous in its rejection of homosexuality. Until the 1950s, homosexual marriage was not an idea to be contemplated. Christians added to the condemnations in Leviticus more explicit words of their own Scripture. St. Paul (in Romans 1:26–27; I Corinthians 6:9, and I Timothy l:10) denounced male homosexuality and lesbianism. Hebrew Scripture has been silent on the latter. Later chapters examine interpretations of these passages from the viewpoints of both traditional scholars and gay apologists, but serious revisionists did not appear until the last decades of the twentieth century. The attempts of John McNeill and John Boswell to demonstrate that homosexual unions were once sanctified in the Church have not proven generally convincing.[10]

The distaste of St. Paul and early Christianity for same-sex relations may be explained in some small part by their rejection of the licentious practices of the "heathen" peoples around them, who exploited children and slaves. In the Middle Ages, this abhorrence may have been confirmed by the alleged habits of Islamic courts, in violation of their own Koran. During the Reformation, the belief that homosexuality was rampant in Roman Catholic religious orders would have only intensified Protestant condemnation. But at least on this subject all Christendom, despite its other differences, was in official agreement. The churches did not waver throughout the centuries. The Greek and Latin fathers of the early Church regarded homosexual activities as a grave offense, as did St. Thomas Aquinas, possibly the most influential theologian of the Western Church. The Catholic Encyclopedia of 1967 maintained the same position as the church fathers:[11] the homosexual act by its essence excluded all possibility of transmission of life. Therefore such an act, according to the Catholic Church, could not fulfill the procreative purpose of the sexual faculty and was, therefore, an improper use of that faculty.

But the verities of the past are now frequently questioned. Today many people believe that a homosexual orientation is not a choice, though sexual behavior should still be under the control of the will. A note of compassion is ever-present in contemporary Catholic pronouncements on the subject. The current consensus affirms that a homosexual may be just as pleasing in the eyes of God as a heterosexual; it is the responsibility of both to conform their fallen will to God's law, always with the help of grace.[12]

The Roman Catholic Church has been forced to acknowledge that homosexuality is rampant in its priesthood. While Catholic historians acknowledge that certain saints and Christian leaders of the past have no doubt been homosexual in their desires, they are honored for temptations resisted rather than those never felt. But the contemporary situation is different. According to the estimates of some seminarians, as many as 40 percent of young priests are gay, though the actual number may be closer to 20 or 30 percent. Some Catholics have voiced their fears that the priesthood may become identified as a "gay profession." While closeted, some priests have found the required celibacy of their profession a respectable cover for gay orientation. As long as priests honored their vow of celibacy, no problem arose. Yet, as recent scandals have demonstrated, many vows have been broken.

Priestly celibacy is a major issue in the Catholic Church today, especially pressing considering the dearth of priests in North America and parts of Europe. Yet neither married men nor practicing homosexuals are presently acceptable in Western-rite Catholicism. While lay groups within the Roman Catholic Church, most notably the organization known as Dignity/USA, agitate for gay rights, and a few priests live openly with partners, the hierarchy of the church, from the popes through the bishops, remains unequivocal in its assertion that homosexual conduct is incompatible with ecclesiastical life. Very soon after his elevation to the papacy, Benedict XVI indicated his determination to cleanse the clergy of practicing homosexuals and all those who posed any threat to children.

Orthodox churches, which still dominate the religious landscape of Eastern Europe and are increasing in membership in the United States through immigration and conversion, have historically rejected homosexuality, perhaps more vehemently than their Western counterparts. Their abhorrence of the practice may stem in part from a perception that exploitative same-sex acts were widely practiced by Muslims in the Ottoman Empire, which often oppressed Eastern Christians. However, rumors have abounded of violations of the code of holy orders among the celibate wing of the Orthodox priesthood, and there were in the early 1960s scandals involving high-placed clerics in Greece. Most of the Orthodox parish priests are married. All officially reject homosexual practice as sinful and dangerous, although Orthodox communities historically have punished offenders less severely than has the West.

The vast majority of Protestants agree in their rejection of homosexuality. Martin Luther, not known for the mincing of words, called same-sex activity an "idolatrous distortion instilled by the devil," associating it with the Church of Rome. John Calvin, the other great reformer, pronounced homosexuality a sin against nature, deserving of excommunication and the severest civil penalties.

Protestant churches, however, which have no central figure with the authority of the Catholic Pope to promulgate dogmas or mediate disputes, have in the last two decades been ripped apart by this issue. It has become the defining line between liberals and conservatives in several faith communities. The Episcopal Church in the United States is presently in turmoil and schism, has lost a significant portion of its membership, and is in the courts daily as various factions that have formed over this and related issues battle for ownership of parish property. The Anglican communion has experienced the most agony over the gay issue, dividing an international fellowship of over 70 million members in more than 160 countries. The Archbishop of Canterbury, the titular head of the Anglican communion, said in 1995: "We reject homophobia in any form. Homosexuals must be treated as people made in the image and likeness of God."[13] While few of the faithful would disagree with the statement on its surface, definitions of "homophobia in any form" vary widely, and the use of the term is counterproductive. The consecration of Gene Robinson, an acknowledged homosexual who lives openly with a partner, as bishop of New Hampshire was the final outrage for conservative Episcopalians, who have for several decades battled over changes in liturgy, freedom of divorce and remarriage, and the ordination of women to all levels of the priesthood.

In the last half of the twentieth century, the population center of Anglicanism has shifted from Europe and North America to Africa, whose bishops, along with those from other Third World countries and Asia, have objected vociferously to the hedonism of wealthy Americans and Europeans, so "at ease in Zion," while the faith, courage, and fortitude of their own flocks are tested daily. The American and Canadian Episcopal hierarchies, including the current Presiding Bishop of the United States, Frank Griswold, have supported the ordination of women, the acceptance of practicing homosexuals, and the consecration of Gene Robinson as bishop. All this has not been without opposition from some bishops who have nevertheless chosen to remain, precariously, within the official church. But conservative parishes have sometimes made different choices.

Other Protestant denominations have, somewhat less dramatically, wrestled with the issue. Lutherans number more than 70 million worldwide, yet they are organized in several synods and differ widely in social attitudes and approaches to Scripture. Scandinavian Lutherans are more accepting of life-style diversity. The gay issue continues to be strongly debated among liberal American Evangelical Lutherans, while the conservative synods of Missouri, Wisconsin, and several others totally oppose the practice of homosexuality and the ordination of practicing gay clergy.

Presbyterians, the American descendants of Calvinism and the European Reformed tradition, are likewise divided on the gay issue. Some practicing homosexual clergy have been ordained in Presbyterian churches, but an outcry has usually followed from the congregations. Just as in other mainline denominations, the laity often tends to be more conservative than the seminary-trained clergy.

Liberal Christianity remains strongly influenced by the findings and theories of social scientists. High-profile clerics, among them the former Episcopal Bishop of New Jersey, John Shelby Spong, have defended homosexual rights and labeled the traditional Christian position as "bigotry"—not so different from the racism that was a problem in churches during the first half of the twentieth century. While the liberal voices have often been the loudest in the mainline denominations of Protestantism, their opinions have not always represented the flock. The current demand that same-sex marriages be consecrated in the churches intensifies the heated conflicts that have raged for years. How, it is asked, can homosexual marriages be viable if they do not correspond to the three functions of marriage as set forth in the historic marriage liturgies? Proponents of same-sex marriage respond that gay relationships often provide comfort, moral stability, mutual support, and an appropriate environment for the rearing of children.

American Protestantism is still dominated by fundamentalist and evangelical groups, which may show compassion but refuse to endorse gay conduct and strongly reject actively gay clergy or the call for same-sex marriage. Evangelical groups include the Southern Baptists (by far the largest Protestant denomination in the United States), the Churches of Christ, Missouri Synod Lutherans Seventh Day Adventists, various Holiness and Pentecostal Churches, numerous independent churches, as well as large contingents within the mainline denominations. Yet even in these churches, gay individuals are increasingly treated with compassion and understanding. Clergy who are "outed" are usually forgiven after a proper show of contrition and are reassigned to less demanding pastorates. Within the Seventh Day Adventist communion there is a gay activist group called Kinship, which, at this point, has not been disfellowshipped.

Other gay caucuses active in their various denominations include Integrity (Episcopal), Lutherans Concerned (Evangelical Lutheran Synod), Presbyterians for Lesbian and Gay Concerns, Affirmation (United Methodist), and Brethren/Mennonite Council on Gay Concerns. While the major denominations reject or waver in acceptance, there are other options for gay people in the vast North American marketplace of religious ideas. As early as 1963, the Society of Friends, which had already become the first American Christian group to establish agencies to serve the needs of gay people, delivered what many regarded as a shocking pronouncement affirming extramarital sex under certain circumstances and denouncing prejudice against homosexuals as stemming from fear, ignorance, and unprovoked hostility. In the 1960s, such statements were daring, inspiring newspaper cartoons in which colonially garbed graybeards exhorted the young to get on with sowing "those wild Quaker oats." The Church of the Brethren published an important position paper in 1983, clearly articulating a distinction that churches have increasingly made. The statement declared that sexual orientation is not a moral issue, but that sexual behavior does have moral significance. The paper further affirmed that sexual orientation should form no barrier to ordination in the church. Even among the Brethren, however, it was not clear how much distinction had been made between sexual orientation and sexual behavior. The United Church of Canada and the United Church of Christ in the United States (not to be confused with the Churches of Christ), despite some controversy, has affirmed the full status of homosexuals, including the right of ordination of qualified candidates. Although outside the creed of Christianity, the small but socially active Unitarian-Universalist Fellowship has provided full, unqualified support to sexually active gays and lesbians, accepting them as clergy and freely opening churches and halls to their organizations and commitment ceremonies.

Especially in the New World, Christianity long ago fragmented into a host of small and often curiously eclectic sects. Interestingly, it was one of these that first openly ministered to gays and lesbians. This happened in 1916, in Sydney, Australia, under the influence of Bishop Charles Webster Leadbeater, in what he called the Liberal Catholic Church. Although this sect spread to several continents, it never claimed more than a few thousand faithful. It blended theosophy (with ideas borrowed from Buddhism and other Asian philosophies) and high church Christian rituals and sacraments. Essentially a "believe as you choose" church, its members were united only by a common ritual. Although its clergy took all the titles that Anglican or Roman Catholic priests and bishops readily assume, they earned their livelihoods at other jobs and professions.

The spiritual pioneer in gay-friendly Christianity in the United States is the Reverend Troy Perry, who founded the Metropolitan Community Church (MCC) in the late 1960s. This fellowship, organized specifically to provide spiritual support for gays and lesbians, was one of the first assemblies to offer religious commitment services. Perry officiated at what is believed by many to have been the first public commitment ceremony at his church in Los Angeles in December 1968. In 1993, Perry performed a mass same-sex wedding ceremony, albeit without legal status, held outside the Internal Revenue Services buidingin Washington, DC. Joined that day were 1,500 gay and lesbian couples.[14]

Originally MCC sought to be a nondenominational church with evangelical beliefs, and its services did not strongly deviate from those that might be experienced in any conservative, Bible-based church. Perry had been an ordained minister in Pentecostal churches. He had fathered two sons and attempted to live for many years as a heterosexually married man. Finally, tired of the hypocrisy of his life, he openly acknowledged his gay orientation and vowed to provide spiritual comfort for others like himself. The first meetings of the fellowship he organized took place in his Los Angeles home, but the church quickly spread to other communities, flourishing especially in California. As its name suggests, its congregations were located in the metropolitan areas where gay people lived and felt most comfortable. This was not a church likely to be welcomed in small towns and rural areas. Still, by the end of the twentieth century, the MCC had over 40,000 regular members in more than 300 congregations in cities around the country. The denomination had also spread to 16 foreign countries. Not only was it welcoming to Christians from all denominations, but it further encouraged the gay movement in Judaism by offering its facilities for their initial gatherings. Because MCC did not regard sexual orientation as the primary mark of human identity, it extended its fellowship to straight members as well. After some work on the African mission field, congregations emerged there that were predominantly heterosexual. A primary doctrine of the church, however, remained that one could be simultaneously a dedicated Christian and a homosexual. While the early beliefs of the church leaned toward fundamentalism, the fellowship has remained inclusive and has recently seen the emergence of more theologically liberal congregations. Even though it affirms the major articles of the Christian creeds, MCC has been repeatedly denied admission to the National and World Councils of Churches, in part because the Eastern Orthodox Churches, which represent vast populations in Eastern Europe, have threatened to withdraw from the organization if a church is admitted that exists primarily to affirm homosexuality.

## ISLAM

Arriving in the seventh century after Christ, the Prophet Mohammed had much to say about the duties and responsibilities of marriage. In the Holy Koran, which Muslims believe is the word of God transmitted through the Prophet, the obligations of spouses are clearly outlined. While a Muslim man is allowed to have as many as four wives, the Koran demands that all be treated with absolute equality. Since it is impossible to love two people with the same intensity and bestow upon them equal favor, many Muslims have viewed this directive as an endorsement of monogamy.

While Muslim marriages are not celebrated with specific religious ceremonies, many Muslim societies make little distinction between the sacred and the secular. Thus, all family transactions are believed to be made in the presence of God. Muslims, like conservative Jews, consider marriage a serious obligation; to refrain from it is a social offense. Muslims generally reject celibacy as a valid choice, though small groups of mystics may occasionally provide a negligible exception.

The Koran teaches that marriage exists to uphold moral conduct, and the family is essential to human society. Muslims marry for the same reasons that Jews and Christians do: for companionship and mutual help, for stability, and to uphold the family as the foundation of social order. Marriage is a contract rather than a sacrament, and, while adultery is a serious offense, the *sharia* (Islamic law) views it more as a violation of property than as a personal betrayal. Nevertheless, the *sharia* calls for severe punishments, and adulterers have been publicly stoned in some Muslim countries, even in recent years.

Although Mohammed and subsequent Islamic law greatly improved the status of women in the lands they controlled, women have never been given, even in theory, a status equal to that of men. Although the practice of female infanticide was condemned in uncompromising terms by the Koran, and women were, under strict Islamic law, provided some inheritance rights, they still could be easily divorced by their husbands for a variety of reasons and often found it difficult to leave intolerable marriages. They were expected to live quietly chaste lives under the direction of their husbands. Today in some Muslim countries, women do not appear in public without covering their heads or, in extremely conservative lands, their entire bodies. In affluent Saudi Arabia, the Islamic Holy Land, women are not allowed to drive, and they do not attend the same schools as men. These restrictions, however, are not dictated by the Holy Koran but by local custom.

Islamic cultures have produced great love stories, and some cultural historians credit Moorish Spain with the invention of romantic courtly love. The world's most splendid monument to married love is certainly the Taj Mahal, the jewel-studded mausoleum in Agra, India, built by a Muslim ruler so that all the world would honor his devotion to his wife.

Perhaps the example of the Prophet Mohammed is central to any understanding of the duties and affections of an ideal Muslim husband. Mohammed was devoted to his first wife, Khadijah, who was also the first person to accept his prophethood, thus becoming the original convert to Islam. She was a wealthy widow 15 years Mohammed's senior when she first employed him as her camel caravan driver. So impressed was she with his character that she proposed marriage to him. Despite the difference in their ages and economic status, the marriage was loving and fruitful. She became the mother of Mohammed's only surviving children. After her death, when the Prophet consoled himself with multiple wives, as he had not done during her lifetime, he remained devoted to her memory. Among his later wives was the child bride, Ayisha, around whom many legends have grown. The Prophet is said to have played dolls with her and regarded her as something of a pet. Some of his later wives were the widows of associates, whom Mohammed took into his home more for their protection than because of any special attraction to them. Muslims cherish the accounts and legends of Mohammed, the "perfumed prophet of Allah," and his wives, and he has provided their model of family life.

The Koran is explicit in its condemnation of homosexuality. In most Muslim countries the issue is not up for discussion. The Koran contains three clear references to homosexuality, equating the destruction of Sodom and Gomorrah with this "abomination," and decisively pronouncing same-sex relationships a "great sin." In the Hadith (the legal traditions of Islam), punishment for the offense is 80 strokes of the lash or death by stoning, depending upon the gravity of the particular case.

Muslims do not engage in deconstructions of the Koran, in the manner of liberal Jews and Christians, when they approach their own Scriptures. Only in North America and to a limited extent in Turkey, does there exist a smallliberal Islamic movement openly questioning traditional beliefs. Although some Muslims in the West have asked for more tolerance, no established international movement or theological voice exists in Islam advocating a loosening of restraints at this time. Homosexuality is widely regarded as "a European vice," and Muslims tend to believe that its practice is rare in their own countries.

The Western perception, of course, has often been quite different. Europeans believed pederasty to have been common throughout the Ottoman Empire, and English speakers are familiar with the stories of T. E. Lawrence and his homophilic adventures in the desert. During the last part of the twentieth century, Tangier in Morocco became known in Europe and America as a haven for gay men, and in recent years a sex tourism for European women has emerged in Morocco. Fed by the poverty of the region, this sex trade is carried on despite its violation of both Muslim and Moroccan moral values. A number of well-known European and American novelists have written of their experiences in Tangier and other regions of Morocco; their writings suggest, and most Moroccans would concur, that, when Muslim men engage in homosexual acts with Westerners, they do so for money rather than their own pleasure. They may also be symbolically reenacting, in a masochistic way, the humiliations of Western colonialism.

Homosexuality is often severely punished in Islamic countries. Under the influence of the Ayatollah Khomeini in Iran, many people, possibly hundreds, are believed to have been executed for alleged homosexual acts. It is impossible to know how many of these deaths resulted from false accusations by political opponents. Still, it is not surprising that there is no organized gay movement in Muslim countries. It remains to be seen whether the more liberal views of some North American Muslims will ever have any impact.

In the United States, the Nation of Islam has received much attention in the media. This group strongly opposes same-sex relations, basing its opposition on Koranic prohibitions and the widespread distaste for homosexuality in the African American community. Furthermore, the black community, as a minority that feels persecuted, strongly opposes any practices that appear to weaken its strength. Some leaders have cited the promotion of both abortion and homosexuality as attempts to weaken them by decreasing their numbers. Louis Farrakhan, the most prominent leader in the Nation of Islam, has suggested that the practice of Islam can "cure" gays and lesbians. For those who remain incorrigible, some spokespersons have suggested the harshest punishments. In conclusion, Islam in the United States and elsewhere at the present time has no intention of condoning gay activity or same-sex marriage.

## HINDUISM

Although every major religion of the world is well represented in India, Hinduism dominates the culture. So deeply have Hindu ideas permeated the consciousness of Indians that many, despite their Christian, Muslim, or other confessions, find it difficult to set aside native beliefs in karma and reincarnation. While Hinduism has always maintained the allegiance of the majority of Indians, despite Buddhist, Christian, and Muslim missionary efforts, Hinduism has never been a religion that has traveled well. Vedanta and other associations may preach Hindu concepts abroad, but they have rarely gained more than cult following. Hinduism really cannot be separated from Indian society and its ancient civilization.

In Hindu communities, almost all marriages are arrangements between two families. Caste status is an essential consideration, while family history and economic resources are also scrutinized. Educational achievement, special talents, and personal attractiveness give the families of young people more bargaining power in the marriage market. Today in more liberal Indian families, sons and daughters are given veto powers in matrimonial negotiations. When all the requirements have been met, both families are satisfied, and the couple appear congenial, an astrologer is called in to cast horoscopes and determine auspicious dates for the wedding ceremonies. Seemingly brilliant matches have been canceled when horoscopes have been found to conflict. Love appropriately develops after marriage, and it is treasured. More motion pictures are released by Bollywood, the Bombay film industry, than by any other motion picture industry in the world, and the majority of these films celebrate romantic love. Indian literature contains great love stories, and recent fiction, no doubt reflecting a reality of Indian society, provides moving accounts of spousal devotion. The erotic classics of Hindu literature for centuries have testified to the valued place of sensuality in the lives of Indians.

Children also are treasured in Indian-Hindu society, especially boys. Many girls, however much they may be loved, are a financial drain on Indian families. Nevertheless, having a large family has been an expectation throughout Indian history, especially in rural areas. Attempts to deal with India's overpopulation have brought grave new social problems. With prenatal gender determination and the increasing frequency with which female fetuses are aborted, India, like China, faces the looming problem of a disproportionate number of men. Although present attitudes are mostly negative, both overpopulation and the preponderance of men in Indian society may have some bearing on the acceptance of same-sex marriage in the future.

Almost all Hindus believe that their families and marriage brokers are more successful in arranging lasting, happy unions than the singles clubs and dating Web sites popular in the West. The haphazard way most Americans meet and fall in love horrifies Indians. The seriousness with which Hindus regard the bond of matrimony is further attested by the fact that marriages are almost always regarded as indissoluble. The notorious practice of suttee, virtually eliminated by the British during the colonial period, required a widow, even a young one, to throw herself on the funeral pyre of her deceased husband. Otherwise, she was doomed to live in grieving widowhood, under the custody of her son, or else she was awkwardly returned to her original family. The Hindu Marriage Act of 1955 made divorce possible in India, but most Hindus still find it unacceptable and see it as a pathology of the West.

In the Hindu religion, even the happiest marriage is not an end in itself. It is believed that people are caught in an endless wheel of birth, death, and rebirth until the cycle is broken by a spiritual attainment that allows the soul to break the cycle and attain supreme consciousness. The serious striver views the period of family life as only a stage through which one must pass. For the person on an ultimate religious quest, there comes a time in life when he must leave his family and become a pilgrim, devoting himself to meditation and contemplation of the Ultimate.

Despite the ambiguity of certain Hindu myths, there is no established place for the homosexual within the marriage-family structure of Hindu-Indian society. Even though Hindu religious lore contains numerous tales of transsexual gods and goddesses, Hindus reject homosexuality, regarding it as a decadent import from Islam or the materialistic modern West. For many Indians it remains "the English vice," closely associated in their minds with the humiliation of a proud people of ancient culture by modern Europeans.

There is little evidence of homosexuality in classical Hindu writing. The celebrated erotic classic of world literature, the Kama Sutra, which is explicit about variations of heterosexual expression, almost ignores gay sexuality and certainly does not glorify it. The rigid structures of Hindu society, with the constant reminder of family obligations, would appear to leave little place for same-sex love. Superstitions have always surrounded suspect behavior, and it was widely believed in former times that men who "wasted their seed" would become incapable of begetting in a future incarnation, a terrible fate to befall a high-caste Hindu. An even worse punishment might await such a person in future incarnations when he might, because of his "animalistic behavior," return to earth as an unclean beast.

Both Hindu and Indian secular laws have in the past provided harsh punishments for homosexual behavior, which was considered rare.[15] The traditional languages of India do not have a useful vocabulary for any discussion of the subject. In one special respect, Hindus differed from Jews in their condemnation of homosexuality; they appear throughout most of history to have treated lesbianism more seriously than male sodomy. Hindus have generally been obsessed with the purity of women. An offending Brahman woman, as a member of the highest caste appropriately dedicated to education and religious observance, might have her head shaved if she violated propriety; a Kshatriya, who belonged to the caste best suited to governing, would be led through the streets on a donkey; women of lower castes might have two fingers cut off, the traditional lower-caste punishment for many sexual offenses. (It is instructive to note that European Gypsies, whose ancestral Indian origin is now acknowledged, sometimes punished women in their tribes in this way, well into the twentieth century.) Men caught in same-sex acts might be expelled from their caste and made pariahs, a situation more grim than death. At the beginning of the twenty-first century, there seems no respectable place for same-sex marriages in Hindu India.

India is, of course, the home of many religions, despite the cultural domination of Hinduism. Centered around Bombay is a small, prosperous, well-educated community representing the venerable faith of Zoroastrianism, older than Islam, Christianity, and modern Judaism. In India these people are known as Parsis—the Persians—despite their residence of many generations in India. Their faith is traced back to the prophet Zoroaster, who is believed to have lived in ancient Iran in the sixth century äÉÉ though most of the facts of his life and early ministry are shrouded in mystery. Today Parsis are strong, family-centered people. It is impossible for a person to convert to the faith; he or she must be born into it, with the family line being carried by the father. In such a faith, it would be hard to make room for same-sex marriage, and children of such a marriage, whether through adoption or artificial insemination, would have ambiguous status.

Sikhs, who maintain a colorful if small presence in Indian society, practice the youngest of the world's significant monotheistic religions. The founding prophet was Nanak (1469–1539 C.E.), and the Punjab region of India is the home base of this faith. Politically and geographically caught between Hindus and Muslims, Sikhism absorbed ideas from both faiths. Many Sikh ceremonies focus on the milestones of family life. Couples are solemnly married in a temple, in the presence of the *Adi Granth,* the holy book. When children are born, they soon are taken to the temple, where the holy book is consulted. It is opened at random, and the child is given a name derived from the opening letter of the hymn that appears on the page. Sikh men and women have clearly defined responsibilities. Women assume the care of the holy book, a copy of which is kept in a special room in comfortable Sikh homes. The holy book is prayerfully opened in the morning and lovingly put to rest at night. Sikh men are readily identified by the turbans that cover their uncut hair; they traditionally wear a bangle and carry a sword. This is a religious society highly dependent on sex-role differentiation, with distinct religious obligations demanded of each gender. It would require considerable reconfiguration before it could acknowledge homosexual practice or honor same-sex marriage.

## BUDDHISM

Buddhism originated in the sixth and fifth centuries B.C.E. as a reform of Hinduism, rejecting the inequities of caste and demanding a more austere path to enlightenment. Its founder was born to high estate in a province near the present border of Nepal. Like Christianity, the faith is built around the reverence for a historical figure. According to Buddhist lore, Prince Siddartha Gautama, known as the Buddha after his enlightenment, was born and reared in luxury. As a young man he won his beautiful wife in an archery contest; she produced a son, and they settled into a charmed life in the palaces provided by Siddartha's father. Yet the young prince could not ignore the ills inherent in the human condition. He became tormented by the sickness, old age, and death that he saw around him. He observed the Hindu holy men, denying their flesh in an effort to find some escape from the misery of life. Determined to find the true path to salvation, Prince Siddartha left his young family, never to return. Buddhist legend claims that many years later, when he had become a renowned holy man, he and his disciples were passing through the area where his family lived. His wife, now an old woman who had not seen him for decades, stood by the roadway and silently watched him pass.

Buddhist narratives record how Siddartha, after much perplexity, did achieve Enlightenment, outlining the Eight Fold Path and the Four Noble Truths.[16] Buddhism, following his teachings, understands all human longings as vanity. People have the responsibility to attempt to free themselves from the cravings that keep them chained to the wheel of birth and death and rebirth. Of course, not all people are able to achieve this state of renunciation in their present lives, but they may make some efforts toward eventual Enlightenment. In Thailand it is customary for young people, even royal princes, to spend time in a monastery, after which they must then return to the world and accept its responsibilities, including marriage. Others, whose circumstances permit, may commit themselves permanently to live as monks in the honored community of the Sangha; or, in old age, when necessary tasks have been completed, still others may retreat to a monastery to spend their last days in contemplation.

Marriage is not glorified in the Buddhist tradition, although marriages, when they exist, are respected, and husband and wife are expected to honor their obligations. The Buddha is said to have comforted a woman who had just lost a child by reminding her that bereavement is the fate of all humankind and that "He who has seven loved ones has seven sorrows, six loved ones, six sorrows" and so on. It is far better if human beings are able to renounce the affections and cares of the world and join the contemplatives seeking enlightenment. When this is not possible, marriage at best should be a stage in a spiritual path through which sensuality and worldly care eventually will be transcended, along with all human aspirations and longings.

Some gay scholars have interpreted the relative absence of denunciations of homosexuality in Buddhist literature as a reassuring neutrality. Others interpret the intense involvement of master and disciple that takes place in some Buddhist monasteries as instances of same-sex love. Japanese Buddhism, from most accounts, has been relatively tolerant of homosexuality and has even, from time to time, integrated a gay sensibility into Zen Buddhist monastic life. In North America, Japanese Zen teachings have proven very attractive to gay men. Among the first groups to open hospices for AIDS sufferers in San Francisco were Zen groups.

Another form of Buddhism that is sometimes labeled unorthodox is practiced in regions beyond China. This is Tantric Buddhism, most directly associated with Tibet. Tantrism advocates a very different way of transcending desire than the more traditional path of renunciation. In Tantrism, the disciple overcomes desire by exhausting it, to the point of utter tedium or inertia.

Tantric art luxuriates in wild sexual images of all varieties, but evidence of widespread homosexuality here is vague and contradictory.

Other Buddhist societies have rejected same-sex relationships or regarded them merely as isolated experiences or supplements to their more standard heterosexual practices. Because Buddhist tradition merely tolerates sexuality of any sort and regards all earthly cravings as further enslavement to the illusionary world of shadows, strong affirmations of homosexuality will not likely be found. Buddhist literature contains numerous unfavorable references to "unseemly conduct" on the part of monks, although all forms of sexual expression would be equally abhorrent here. Because the monastic order of the Sangha is so deeply respected in Southern Asian Buddhist societies, deviations from ideal behavior can be troubling for the faithful. There is a familiar story from Burma about a young man who, walking through a public park late one night, witnessed a monk making love to a nun. So horrified was the young man that he went home and blinded himself, shamed that his eyes had witnessed such violation. In view of the sexual reticence of Buddhism, it seems clear that, while the faith may be less judgmental of gay relationships than other religions, it is unlikely to promote or idealize them. In the near future, approval of same-sex marriage is not anticipated in Buddhist lands, even in Thailand, where a sex industry flourishes.

## CHINESE RELIGION

There may be no people in the world who honor family stability more than the Chinese, whose values are expressed within traditional Confucianism, the more mystical teachings of Taoism, as well as in contemporary Communist ideology.

Confucianism, the religious-philosophical system that dominated China for over two thousand years (until the Communist takeover of the twentieth century) was conservative, suspicious of innovation, and looked to the past, or to an imagined past, for its models. The greatest relationship was between father and son; the chief virtue, without which any degree of righteousness was believed to be impossible, was filial piety (*hsiao*). Throughout its long history, Confucianism promoted a classic austerity, a stronger concern for responsibility than for self-indulgence. Never as important as the prime bond between father and son, marriage, clearly recognized by the community, was still essential to maintaining the continuity of the family and the honor of its name through generations. The Chinese were the world's greatest keepers of genealogies, and in old China it was crucial to have descendants to maintain ancestral rites. Without children, the memory of a person would vanish; there would be no shadow remaining in the afterlife. Procreation was always vastly more important in marriage than love or companionship.

Confucian teachings, always specific and pragmatic, decreed that loving concern was the obligation of a husband, and obedience was decreed for the wife. When all people related properly, according to their clearly defined roles, peace and harmony would reign in the broader community. In old age, when the father and mother of a family acquired status, those without offspring were desolate. Chinese family patterns directed that an elderly couple live with and be cared for by the families of their sons. Children deferred aging parents and became the social security of the elderly.

The popular philosopher Lin Yu-tang observed that all Chinese are Confucianists in times of prosperity and Taoists in times of trouble. Taoism, the second most important religious influence in China, revels in the mysteries of life. Less inclined to promulgate rules than Confucianists, the Taoists nevertheless spoke of the necessity of equilibrium through the harmonious interaction of the great cosmic forces of Yang (associated with maleness) and Yin (associated with femaleness). Humans were exhorted to learn the lessons that nature teaches. Yin encompasses all that is yielding and receptive: the moon, water, clouds, and even numbers. Yang is a hard, active force, represented by the color red, the sun, and odd numbers. The proper intermingling of these two forces, the male and the female, brings into existence history, time, and all created forms. Two yang principles and two yin principles alone without the other would be powerless. Consequently, Taoism, as presently understood, would not be inclined to favor same-sex unions, though its distrust of definitive judgments would make it more tolerant than other religions.

Except under isolated Buddhist and other mystical influences, China, throughout its history, has shown little acceptance of the celibate life. Marriage was a social and family obligation, with personal rewards secondary. Marriages were long arranged by families or by special marriage brokers who clearly understood the rules. Even today in Communist China, where Mao's Little Red Book is presumed to have replaced the Analects of Confucius and where Taoist temples have fallen into ruin, marriage is still considered essential. Young people have many approved settings for meeting and choosing their life companions, with whom, if they follow the appropriate directives, they will have one child. For those who have inadequate social skills and who are unsuccessful in finding their own mates, committees have been formed to assist them.

Homosexuality as an accepted life-style, a permanent gender preference, or as anything other than a passing stage or an occasional fancy would have been unlikely in traditional China, which did, in certain times and among certain classes, tolerate temporary same-sex liaisons. Contemporary Communist China has not been so tolerant. Homosexuality is regarded as a serious derangement, and openly gay tourists have been, in recent years, summarily ejected. Maoists, no less than Confucianists, have insisted on a rigid moral code. Homosexuals who could not be "cured" and who have willfully persisted in their practices have sometimes done so at the peril of their lives. Although there is reported to be less invasion of privacy in China in recent years, the AIDS crisis has strengthened the resolve of many to resist any gay agenda.

Several possible historical explanations for the rejection of same-sex alliances among Chinese have been suggested. It is well known that the ancient Chinese invented government bureaucracy and civil service examinations in an attempt to provide fair employment. Perhaps, it has been postulated, the Chinese rejected same-sex relationships for fear that government functionaries would abuse their powers by favoring their male lovers with various government preferments. It seems more likely that the Confucian emphasis on family loyalty and responsibility, with the necessity of providing offspring, is the stronger reason.

## ZEN AND SHINTO

The Japanese—unlike Jews, Indians, and Chinese—are not generally considered to be deeply religious or creatively philosophical. To state that the Japanese genius arises from a unique skill in borrowing and adapting is to utter a cliché, but it is a meaningful observation nevertheless. From the Asian mainland, Japan adopted Buddhism and then gave it the distinct flavor of Zen, in which the devotee strives to penetrate the essence of being and achieve Buddha-nature. Family responsibilities and social obligations are secondary for such a devotee. Still, in Japan, even Buddhists priests generally married and demonstrated more enthusiasm for worldly pleasures than was deemed appropriate in older forms of Buddhism. Japanese marriage—like many activities and institutions—was influenced by China.

Japanese prefer to be married in the Shinto rite and buried with Buddhist ceremonies. Shinto is the quintessential religion of Japanese nationalism. Traditional Shinto supported the cult of the emperor and taught that all Japanese were descendants of the gods, the *kami*. The worship of a central deity in female form, Amaterasu, did little to raise the status of women in Japan. Although Shinto had little concern with doctrine and ethics, its household ceremonies reaffirmed family ties. Shinto marriage rites included the exchange of nuptial cups of sake, and vows were taken in the presence of ancestral gods.

Japanese literature, richly developed through hundreds of years, is rich in the poetry of love. The courtly pillow books from the past were filled with love notes, lyrics, and records of assignations. Emperors were unashamed to write love poetry. Belles-lettres of the golden age—the age of Lady Murasaki's *The Tale of Genji* (c. 1000 ʹ Ḁ Ḋ—were frequently written by men using female pseudonyms who narrated the amorous intrigues of courtly lovers.

Yet the ardor of the poetry was remote from the reality of family life in Japan, just as it was in Europe. Although women have been influential in Japanese history, their role as keepers of the hearth has long been clearly defined. Their lives have been largely confined to home and family, and they have been expected to be obedient to their husbands. Until the twentieth century, Japanese husbands and wives generally did not attend social functions together. Professional women entertainers, the acclaimed geisha, refined the art of pleasing men at male social functions. The wives stayed home.

In traditional Japanese society, marriages were usually arranged by a *nuked,* who was either a family friend or a professional marriage broker. Before the thirteenth and fourteenth centuries, a groom joined his bride's family and worked for them for a time. Later it became customary for the bride to join the groom's clan and perform appropriate services in their residence. This practice of working to earn a spouse lingers today in some regions of Japan. Nowadays there are two forms of courtship: some marriages are arranged and others are love matches. All official records have shown that the former are much less likely to end in divorce—perhaps in part because they are made by more conservative people, who, subject to family pressures, are less likely to seek divorce. Contemporary marriage ceremonies in Shinto temples are major family events, with elaborate receptions following. The marriage broker, usually a friend of the family, has an official, if only symbolic, role, much like the person who "gives the bride away" in Western ceremonies. The practice in both East and West is a remnant from the past that persists because it has been hardened into ritual. Another important symbolic feature of the Shinto ceremony is the drinking of sake by the couple and their families. Marriage in Japan today remains a commitment of families as well as individuals, and it is considered a union of those families. Same-sex marriage would require a major readjustment of all these customs based so strongly on sex-role differentiation and family expectations. Heading the list of these expectations is children to perpetuate the family line and attend to the ancestral rites.

Because Shinto and Japanese Buddhism have not enforced severe moral taboos, it is not surprising that Japan historically has shown some leniency toward homosexuality. Also, in Japan, same-sex relationships were long associated with the martial arts, in a manner somewhat reminiscent of classical Greece. A high incidence of homosexual activity appears to have occurred during the training of samurai warriors, a caste emerging in the twelfth century 'Éa Éand flourishing for 600 years. The warriors followed a code of honor known as *bushido,* which was a blend of Confucian, Zen Buddhist, and martial values. Although samurai were expected to eventually marry and beget children, numerous writings in Japanese literature clearly affirm a delight in same-sex love among these warriors and among Zen monks. Warriors did not regard such activity as unmanly, and Zen masters and their novices apparently did not consider it unspiritual.

As late as the twentieth century, one of Japan's most famous novelists, Yukio Mishima, although he was married and had fathered children, regarded his homosexual practice as a feature of his allegiance to Japanese nationalism and the military arts. According to Mishima: "Homosexuality forms part of the Japanese tradition. It was the American missionaries who upset this tradition in the nineteenth century."[17]

Another milieu in which homosexuality appears to have been prominent was the classic Japanese theatre, which also reflected the aesthetic values of Zen Buddhism and Shinto. The all-female and all-male Kabuki troupes were congenial settings for same-sex romance. Female impersonators were often successful on the stage and outside the theatre functioned as courtesans with well-placed, prosperous protectors.

From time to time, there were government crackdowns, because widespread homosexual practice has never been without its critics and its problems. The present legal code of Japan, notably, contains no restrictions on homosexuality, incest, or bestiality. However, contemporary Japan is not hospitable to gay lovers. People with gay inclinations, unless they are members of cliques in major cities, may experience a deep sense of shame, and most are still closeted. Many gay men have taken the way out so familiar to their tradition, suicide. The Japanese Society of Psychiatry, despite pressure from organized gay groups in major cities, continues to classify homosexuality as a deviation from the norm, a "serious diversion" according to some of the society's literature. Psychiatrists in the country still offer "cures" for what they regard as an affliction, although the evidence of their success remains thin.

## NEWER RELIGIONS

### Baha'i

Baha'i is a religion founded in the middle of the nineteenth century by Mirza Husayn Ali Nuri, a Persian who became known as Baha'Ullah, which means "Glory of God." It is a faith of noble intent, stressing the brotherhood and unity of all people and looking optimistically toward a time when there will be an international language and a peaceful world government. Historians of religion sometimes classify Baha'i as an offshoot of Islam, and the faith accepts the leading prophets of Judaism, Christianity, and Islam, while proclaiming a new revelation with its own highly distinctive features. Followers of Baha'i are found around the world, but the stately headquarters of the faith remains in Haifa, Israel.

Because Baha'is are good citizens, charitable, well-educated, and seemingly devoid of racism and many other prejudices, their faith has had considerable appeal to homosexuals, as it has to others who have felt themselves marginalized. Although members of the fellowship are ready to show concern for all people who approach them, they have never sanctioned same-sex relationships. In fact, they have been among those religious groups who have recommended reparative therapy for homosexuality. With the spiritual support of the community, Bahai'is believe that homosexuals can make the adjustments necessary for heterosexual marriage.

## Christian Science

Despite its name, its critics accuse Christian Science of being neither Christian nor scientific. Although in many ways inspired by the words of Jesus, and always honoring his name, this religious society has its own "key" to the Scripture, in the form of the writings of its founder. Christian Science appears to base its teachings more upon Platonic philosophy than Hebraic earthiness. Founded in the mid-nineteenth century by Mary Baker Eddy and centered in Boston, Christian Science has never been a sensual religion. Our bodily ailments, it teaches, are delusions. The church frequently quotes Eddy's views on "chastity" and has generally counseled gays and lesbians to "heal" their sexual "maladjustments" as they would other bodily afflictions. Christian Science has from its beginnings promoted equal rights for women. Older women from affluent families have found Eddy's teachings particularly appealing. But this acceptance of women in general has not extended to lesbians, and the church has not knowingly employed them. It continues to regard homosexuality as inconsistent with basic Christian teaching. Interestingly, it was the Christian Science Reading Rooms, which Eddy decreed should open in important cities, that furnished the models for early gay bookstores.

## Mormonism

The Church of Jesus Christ of Latter-day Saints, centered in Utah and by far the largest of a number of Latter-day Saints groups that stem from the nineteenth-century movement founded by Joseph Smith (1895–1844), is one of the fastest growing religions in the world. While Mormons revere Jesus Christ and refer to themselves as Christians, they have supplements to the Bible and uphold doctrines that are at odds with the beliefs of mainstream Christians. It would not be incorrect to say that Mormonism is as distinct from Christianity as Christianity and Islam are from Judaism.

Although the practice of polygamy by Mormons in Utah supplied titillating scandals in late-nineteenth-century America, the church today is one of the least tolerant of sexual deviations from what it now regards as the norm: monogamous heterosexual marriage. Even on the African mission field, where Christian groups have sometimes made what they believed to be necessary concessions to accommodate the family structure of converts, Mormons have insisted that marriage is a union—they add that it can be "for time and eternity"—between one man and one woman. Always an influence in conservative politics in the United States, Mormons have been leaders in opposing same-sex marriage and promoting the Defense of Marriage Constitutional Amendment. They also have been known to advocate, or even demand, their faithful who are assailed by homosexual inclinations submit themselves to "reparative therapy," which has occasionally included, according to several reports, such harsh measures as shock treatments.

## Neo-Pagan and Other Sects

We have seen that traditional religious societies rarely accept homosexuality and, therefore, generally refuse same-sex couples the rites of marriage. But ancient and traditional religions are not the only choices people have today. The United States, always at home with religious diversity, since the 1970s has seen a proliferation of sects and cults. In Europe, where attendance at Christian churches has declined, numerous sects, many with innovative and novel ideas, have appeared to attract the spiritually hungry. In cults, there is usually a dominant personality who bestows upon himself or herself the favors (sometimes of a sexual nature) of followers. For other members of the cult, rules may be very strict. Group marriages or polygamous arrangements are not uncommon. Some cults will tolerate same-sex unions while others emphatically will not. Sects, as contrasted with cults, are groups with distinctive beliefs and practices, less centered on a particular central personality, who yet see themselves as a people apart. While some sects maintain a stricter sexual code than mainstream society, others are more indulgent and more welcoming of sexual diversity. Some have even composed special ceremonies to celebrate this diversity.

Modern neo-pagan and witchcraft groups have sometimes honored same-sex unions and incorporated same-sex acts into their ceremonies. Consciousness raising has been an important part of these groups when they stress feminism or some other liberationist ideology. Women within the coven may be encouraged to explore their full sexuality, which may include lesbianism. Witchcraft cults can be especially attractive to lesbians because they are often dominated by women, sometimes women who have left husbands and families in a rejection of patriarchy. For some of these women, lesbianism may be more a political choice than an unambiguous sexual orientation. But it certainly appears that these nonjudgmental groups have allowed a substantial number of lesbian women to come to the forefront.[18] It may even be true, as some observers have suggested, that the women's spirituality movement has received its major strength and impetus from the lesbian element. Most members of neo-pagan groups, like the rest of society, are probably heterosexual, although bisexuality may flourish along with the other options.

In *Witchcraft and the Gay Counterculture,* Arthur Evans argues that gay men need to explore the harmonies between their unique spirituality and the old pagan nature religions. Since these ancient pagan religions no longer exist and records that remain are neither conclusive nor complete, it is possible to assume affirmations that they may not necessarily have made. Evans's book inspired a conference that met in Arizona, and a journal was published that covered what it called the faerie spirituality movement. Some spokespeople for the movement complained that gay culture had not served their spiritual and emotional needs. They found it an imitation of the worst features of straight society, with its bars and its casual, anonymous, shame-filled sex. Faerie gatherings, on the other hand, enabled them to celebrate their sexual natures and finest impulses. While the rest of society spoke of "empowerment," they preferred to describe their experiences as "enspiritment." They discovered that cross-dressing, role changing, and androgyny—all exercises in gender swapping— opened avenues of spirituality.[19]

The Church of Scientology is an organization that has attracted highly visible persons in the entertainment industry. Scientology was founded in 1955 by a science fiction writer, L. Ron Hubbard. He is supposed to have said: "Writing for a penny a word is ridiculous. If a man really wants to make a million dollars, the best way would be to start his own religion." After following his own advice, Hubbard earned many millions through the services sold by his Scientology-trained practitioners and his books outlining his teachings. Becoming a mysterious hermit, he spent the last decades of his life floating on a 300-foot ship, the *Apollo,* along with a flotilla called Sea Org. For years, people, including his own sons, wondered if he was still alive.

Scientology as Hubbard developed it, is a blend of Eastern thought, Freudian psychoanalysis, and science fiction ideas. Scientologists teach that the mind is divided into two parts, the analytical and the reactive. The former is the logical structure that perceives and remembers, while the latter records what the faithful call "engrams." Scientology claims basically to be a therapeutic system, which tackles painful experiences recorded on engrams during traumas that may have occurred prenatally. These memories, which cause the maladjustments of later years, exist only on the subconscious level, but they can be cleared through sessions with a Scientology practitioner known as an auditor. Auditors, for a considerable fee, employ a device they call an E-meter to measure physical and mental responses to engrams. When all engrams are removed, a person is pronounced clear and ready to lead a contented, productive life. Some followers of Scientology are reputed to have paid more than $80,000 in their search for ultimate clarity. Auditors must frequently contend with their clients' relationship problems, and it has been long reported—though with uncertain accuracy—that the therapy has been popular with homosexuals who wish to change their orientation. Actors who become involved with Scientology have frequently been suspected of this motivation, although, again, without any solid evidence.

The Unification Church, whose devotees are popularly known as Moonies, has made heterosexual marriage one of its chief preoccupations. This eclectic cult, which blends Christian symbols with Asian ideas, is centered around a Korean messiah, the Reverend Sun Myung Moon. Moonies have made their presence evident selling flowers and newspapers on American streets, and the church is reputed to have acquired a large fortune. The most spectacular event in its history took place in 1982 in Madison Square Garden: over two thousand couples were married simultaneously by the Reverend Moon. Many of these people had never met before the ceremony that united them; they had been chosen as partners by church officials, who had declared marriage essential for the fully realized life. These young people, for the most part, were from comfortably middle-class Jewish and Christian homes. While rebelling against their parents, they had unquestioningly accepted the authority of Moon over their most intimate affairs.

The Reverend Moon teaches that Jesus, who lived without sin, was crucified and resurrected spiritually rather than bodily. He was unable to complete his earthly ministry because he was executed before he could marry. Therefore, Jesus accomplished only spiritual redemption. Physical regeneration had to wait until a successor of Jesus could establish the "perfect marriage," which Adam and Eve had failed to achieve in the Garden of Eden. Thus, this successor to Jesus would be known as the Third Adam. Although Moon has been reluctant to openly declare himself this Third Adam, he has dropped many hints. Moon has been married several times, but his present wife, Hak Ja Kan, has apparently succeeded where the others failed and has been pronounced the "Perfect Mother." In the Unification Church, with its stress on the marriage of male and female as an ingredient of regeneration, if not salvation itself, there has obviously been no place for the same-sex union.

## CONCLUSION

Some general observations can be made on the present stance of world religions with regard to the legitimacy of homosexual activity and, consequently, same-sex marriage. While traditional religions and even most cults have given little affirmation to homosexual practice, vast numbers of gay and lesbian people are not ready to renounce the traditional faiths in which they were reared and to which they still give emotional and intellectual assent. The rites and ceremonies of religion are bound inextricably to pride of heritage and fond memories of youth. A person's identity has a strong religious component. For these reasons, gays and lesbians will often remain in the closet rather than risk rejection by their religious community. But increasing numbers are finding this status unacceptable. Even while recognizing the barriers they must overcome, they are unwilling to sever the strong ties with their inherited religious tradition, even when there are other faith communities ready to accept them. So the agitation for recognition of their unions by the world's established religions is likely to continue.

It is well to remember that the Roman Catholic Church, the largest and most powerful Christian body in the world, strongly and officially condemns homosexuality as incompatible with the Christian way of life. Conservative Protestant denominations today make common cause with Catholics in their opposition to same-sex marriage, abortion, and the secularizing of society. Mainline Protestant churches are divided on the same-sex marriage issue.

Most churches do not pry too deeply into the hidden desires or even the personal habits of their members. But same-sex marriage, by definition, is a public affirmation; its reality, if legally established, cannot be ignored. Certainly many people in all churches, liberal or conservative, just wish the issue would go away. It will not for several reasons. First, the homosexual lobby is highly articulate, especially prominent in the media and the arts. It is composed of gifted people who often make their case more persuasively than their opponents (who nevertheless significantly outnumber them). Second, gay people and their supporters believe that a principle is involved that is much more than a matter of making 2 or even 10 percent of the population comfortable. They think basic human rights, constitutional concerns, and ethical issues are at stake. Their opponents, they believe, are not filled with the spiritual virtue of charity.

To ignore homosexual complaints would be the moral equivalent of passively accepting racism, in their judgment.

On the other hand, the religious opponents of gay rights and same-sex marriage hold their views with equal intensity. They feel homosexuality is a violation of God's law, a law established at the very beginning of human life. They are convinced that they now totter on a slippery slope; once homosexual activity is regularized and accepted and same-sex marriage is sanctioned by the churches, there is no end to the forms marriage may take. The institution will lose definition and become meaningless.

## NOTES

1. Although her interpretations frequently differ from mine, I am especially indebted in this chapter to the work of Arlene Swidler and more particularly her edited collection *Homosexuality and World Religions* (Valley Forge, PA: Trinity Press International, 1993).

I am further indebted to Richard P. McBrien, ed. *Encyclopedia of Catholicism* (San Francisco: HarperCollins, 1995); Joseph Runzo and Nancy M. Martin, *Love, Sex and Gender in the World Religions* (Oxford, England: Oneworld, 2000); and John Witte, *From Sacrament to Contract: Marriage, Religion and Law in Western Tradition* (Louisville, KY: Westminster John Knox Press, 1998).

2. Widgoder, Geoffrey, ed. *The Encyclopedia of Judaism* (New York: Macmillan, 1989), 467.

3. There are fine discussions of Moshe Ibn Ezra and Judah Halevi, the most-important Jewish poets in the Arabic language, in Widgoder and in Rabbi Steven Greenberg's *Wrestling with God and Men* (Madison: University of Wisconsin Press, 2004). Greenberg provides a controversial prohomosexual interpretation of this poetry.

4. "Judaism," in Steve Hogan and Lee Hudson, *Completely Queer: The Gay and Lesbian Encyclopedia* (New York: Henry Holt, 1998), 318–319.

5. McBrien, 822.

6. Ibid., 821–828, 963–964.

7. For full discussion of Eastern Orthodox views and practices on matrimony, see Athenagoras Kokkinakis, *Parents and Priests as Servants of Redemption: An Interpretation of the Doctrines of the Eastern Orthodox Church on the Sacraments of Matrimony and Priesthood* (New York: Morehouse-Gorham, 1958).

8. Witte, 95.

9. Quoted by Witte, 95.

10. John Boswell, *Christianity, Social Tolerance, and Homosexuality* (Chicago: University of Chicago Press, 1980) and *Same-Sex Unions in Premodern Europe* (New York: Vintage Books, 1995).

11. Denise Carmody and John Carmody, "Homosexuality and Roman Catholicism," in Swidler, 142.

12. McBrien, 637–638; Swidler, 135–148.

13. Quoted in Hogan and Hudson, 34.

14. Ibid., 288.

15. Swidler, 53.

16. The Four Noble Truths are at the heart of the Buddhist analysis of the human condition. 1. Existence is suffering. 2. Suffering is caused by desire. 3. Suffering will cease when desire has been overcome. 4. To overcome desire it is essential to follow the Noble Eight Path, which includes right thinking, right aspiration, right will, right action, etc.

17. Quoted by Sandra A. Wawrytko, "Homosexuality and Chinese and Japanese Religions," in Swidler, 215.

18. Margot Adler, *Drawing Down the Moon* (Boston: Beacon Press, 1986), 341.

19. Ibid., 341 f.

# 2

# Homosexuality in History

When approaching such a seemingly novel proposal as legal recognition of same-sex marriage, there is a special urgency to seek some historical precedent on which to anchor the arguments, both pro and con. If world religions offer only one point of view, perhaps there are other traditions that have explored different paths. What lessons can be learned from the successes and mistakes of earlier generations? The argument from historical precedent is problematic. It is often difficult to separate what we value in our historical heritage from what we hope we have moved beyond. Just as our personal memories are selective, frequently intensifying happy experiences while forgetting others, we may idealize attractive features of the past, separating them from their darker social contexts. There are also obstacles to our understanding the witness of ancient texts. We read them from our twenty-first-century perspective, easily forgetting that ancient peoples did not share our language, values, expectations, or taboos. The vocabulary of personal relationships are especially susceptible to misinterpretation.[1]

Until the modern age, religion was rarely compartmentalized and separated from other basic institutions of society. There is, however, a history of homosexuality, if not same-sex marriage, that has unfolded despite the pronouncements of prophets, priests, and theologians.

## GREECE

It might be proposed that, if we can show that the ancient people who gave us democracy, logic, and our scientific outlook would have approved of same-sex marriage, then we might be on our way to accepting its reasonableness.

Proponents of same-sex marriage often point to classical Greece and observe that the great city-states—admired for their aesthetics, philosophy, and politics—not only accepted homosexuality without stigma but sometimes idealized and institutionalized it. Certainly the literature of ancient Greece would seem to provide a strong verification. However, upon closer examination, this classical precedent is not exactly what we might wish to follow today. The poets who were writing eloquent and passionate love songs to the boys they loved enjoyed the comforts of a society built on slave labor, and in which women were sequestered. If these great lovers from antiquity, who are frequently held up as models of homoerotic affection, were living in the United States today, most of them would be in jail. The objects of their affections, whether consenting or otherwise, were frequently underage boys. What we honor in ancient Greek poets and statesmen, we consider reprehensible in Roman Catholic priests today.

Before the classical age, c. 776–480 B.C., the record of same-sex love is less clear than it would later become. The epics of Homer, *The Iliad* and *The Odyssey,* became a sort of scripture for the classical Greeks, who interpreted them according to their contemporary perspectives, just as we do today. The Homeric epics praised conjugal love more than homophilia and provided several moving portraits of faithful wives. While Andromache—the gentle, tragic wife of the slain Hector—is unforgettable in *The Iliad,* it was Penelope—the loyal wife of Odysseus in the *Odyssey,* waiting longingly for many years for her husband's return from the Trojan war—who became the model wife of classical antiquity. The early Christians, trying to determine if it was proper for them to read pagan literature, found in Penelope a woman worthy of being placed beside the ideal Hebrew woman described in the Book of Proverbs.

*The Iliad* begins appropriately in medias res with the wrath of Achilles. Achilles, the mightiest warrior of the Greeks, has been deprived of his chosen concubine by his commander-in chief, Agamemnon, and is sulking in his tent, refusing to fight. Only when his beloved companion, Patrocles, the ultimate battle buddy, is slain by the Trojans, does Achilles, roused to anger, reenter the battle. It is clear that his concubine was merely a distraction for Achilles; his deepest affections are for the slain Patrocles. For later Greek civilization, these two warriors became models of devotion, even soul mates, but the rest is ambiguous. Before his death, Patrocles had been frolicking in his tent with his own concubine, just as Achilles had done. Furthermore, they were men of equal status as warriors. Love between equals was not the pattern of later Greek homoerotic relationships.

We know very little of the desires and expectations of women in ancient Greece. Women were, especially after the Homeric age, relegated to the domestic and private sphere, and, until recently, historians have shown little interest in detailing the private lives of ordinary people. History has been the record of battles, reigns, and public affairs. One notable exception to this general absence of information about women and domestic life is the legend of Sappho, whose incomparable lyric poetry survives only in dazzling fragments.

Sappho flourished on the island of Lesbos c. 640 B.C. If Homer is remembered as the father of Western literature, Sappho is the mother of lyric poetry—verse that records intimate experiences, impressions, aspirations, and longings. As a poet, she was always ranked by the Greeks just below Homer. In a later period, Plato called her "the tenth muse," even though he was not absolutely certain women had souls, and his regard for poets was so low that he planned to exclude almost all of them from his ideal state as outlined in *The Republic*. A poetic spirit himself, Plato loved Sappho's verse despite his better judgment, though it achieved precisely what he had feared in poets. It stirred the passions in its commemoration of obsessive love, which it pronounced a curse of Aphrodite.

Too many legends and too little fact surround the life of Sappho. She is believed to have conducted a sort of finishing school for young women of good families, preparing them for marriage. She presumably taught them to dance, play the lyre, and recite poetry to its accompaniment. Her own lyrics, unlike the panoramic sweep of the Homeric epics, sang almost solely of love and its sorrows. Her poems were love declarations to both women and men. According to tradition, Sappho was a wife and mother. Her daughter, Cleis, she tells us in one of her poems, was as lovely as a yellow flower. Legend also claims that Sappho loved, unwisely, a ferry boat operator. When he sailed away, she ran frantically along the shoreline, her dark hair streaming behind her. For centuries there was a cliff in Asia Minor known as Sappho's Leap, from which, according to the tale, she jumped after him, to her death.

Whether from her own experience or from the empathetic imagination that great poets possess, Sappho composed ardent declarations to both men and women. Because of the gently erotic poems addressed to young women, the name of her home island has become in modern usage attached to same-sex love of women. But it is sometimes forgotten that she was also a great poetess of heterosexual love. "As a windstorm punishing the oak trees," wrote Sappho, with some man or woman in mind, "love shakes my heart." But, regardless of its object, the love she expressed in her images and subtle lines was never happy for very long.

From 600 to 480 B.C., Greek civilization flourished. The Grecian urns, which so moved John Keats, told stories of tribal sacrifice and the love of men for one another. Lyric poets, including Alcaeus, Ibycus, Anacreon, Theognis, and the illustrious Pindar, glorified male love, and philosophical dialogues idealized it. The first sublime theatre in the West developed, with the tragic playwrights Aeschylus, Sophocles, and Euripides speaking of the fatal consequences of passionate relationships. The drama, which was produced during the flowering of the Athenian city-state, appealed to all classes. Sophocles, whom the British poet Matthew Arnold would later name as the one among the ancients who best understood the ebb and flow of human suffering, was said to have shared his countrymen's attraction to young men. According to Athenaeus, Sophocles was "as fond of young lads as Euripides was fond of women."[2] Most of Sophocles's work has perished, but the surviving plays contain abundant allusions to same-sex love, and there is evidence of lost plays that were built around central pederastic episodes.

The comic theatre, most notably the plays of Aristophanes, found same-sex love a fit target for its bawdy humor. In fact, sexuality of any sort was its appropriate subject. Aristophanes makes fun of all sexual obsessions, but finds effeminacy in men especially degrading. Strong men take dominant sex roles, it would appear, whatever the gender preferences in their lovemaking for the moment. Bisexuality appears to have been taken for granted in many of these comedies.

In Greek legend and literature, humans were often at their best when they did *not* imitate the gods. The gods and legendary heroes, according to the myths, ravished women and made love to men. Zeus, the king of the gods, in addition to the many encounters he had in his various disguises with mortal women, was a lover of men—as were Poseidon, Apollo, Hercules, Dionysus, Hermes, and Pan. In fact, Zeus's abduction of Ganymede was regarded as a prototype for such relationships.

In Athens and Sparta, important political leaders were lovers of boy, whom they regarded as apprentices. Socrates, thought to be among the wisest of the Greeks, spoke of the inspiration such love can bring, although he appears not to have been enthusiastic about its physical expression, at least as his words and conduct have been reported by his disciples Plato and Zenophon. Socrates found spiritual love superior to sensuality in any form and chose to de-eroticize the old legends and customs.[3] Plato's *Symposium* celebrates love and devotion between older and younger men but spiritualizes this love.

Even the Stoics—followers of the philosopher Zeno who were characterized by their preference for a calm life that avoided turmoil and passion—praised the love of boys. Zeno was reputed to have preferred boys to women as objects of desire. His philosophical school remained a minor influence among the Greeks but would later become the major serious philosophy of the imperial Romans. The later Roman Stoics, however, would not look with the same favor on same-sex relationships.

Almost everyone seemed to agree that from ardent, mentoring relationships between males, which the Greeks praised, would come the best soldiers and best rulers. While we know more about the practices of the upper classes, there is some evidence that these attitudes pervaded all levels of society. It is significant that the Greek language, which had so rich a vocabulary for discussing the various forms of love, had no word for homosexuality in general. Pederasty, or "boy love," seems to have been the closest. An older man, generally someone of status and attainments, would assume the mentoring role for a beloved youth, usually between 14 and 20 years of age. The older man thus became the boy's protector, teacher, and what we would call today his "role model," while the boy was cherished for his charm, budding wit, and the very potential of his youth.

Historians have sometimes theorized that ritualized homosexuality between an older man and a boy originated in Crete. One suggestion is that it arose as a check to population growth, but this seems an unlikely explanation, considering that ancient Cretans had few scruples about exposing unwanted babies to the elements.

In the Spartan city-state, institutionalized man-boy love, which may have developed under Cretan influence or independently, became an essential stage in the development of the much-admired strong body and disciplined character of the warrior. In militaristic circles, this relationship was regarded always as an incentive to valor. In Sparta as elsewhere, male love appears to have been a way military leaders initiated young warriors into the arts and ethos of warfare. Love and devotion between males became almost sacred in the heat of battle. It was said that no man could show himself a coward with his lover beside him on the battlefield.

In Sparta and other Greek lands, there were many incentives to man-boy love.[4] The passion for athletics brought men together in their prime of youth and beauty, and the custom of performing athletic feats unclothed increased the fascination with the male physique that is captured in Greek sculpture of the time. In fact, there is no record of another society, except traditional tribal ones, that so accepted male nudity. The gymnasia, the schools where physical training took place, were forums for discussing politics, philosophy, and art, They were also places where men could find the lads who became their lovers.

In Athens at its peak, male love gained another lofty association: freedom from tyranny. The "tyrannicides," Aristogiton and Harmodius, were revered Athenian martyrs. These young men had delivered Athens from the tyranny of the Pisistratidae in 510 B.C., and their statues, later carried away by the invading Xerxes and his Persian armies, were given immortal honors. In addition to sacrificing their lives for freedom, the tyrannicides were widely regarded as paragons of male love.

Philip II of Macedonia, who ruled from 359 to 336 B.C., was one of the unifying figures of the last period of Greek grandeur. He had several wives, but is said to have lavished special benefits on various boy favorites. He is believed to have died as the result of a homosexual crime of passion. Although the details are obscure, he was assassinated during the wedding celebrations of his daughter. His son, the even more illustrious Alexander the Great, is reported by Plutarch to have been much more restrained in his private life than his father. Not known as a womanizer, Alexander loved the epics of Homer and is said to have slept with a copy of *The Iliad* under his pillow, viewing Achilles as a model of the ideal warrior. The novels of Mary Renault tell of the Persian boy given to Alexander as a peace offering by a Persian general. Alexander's fondness for this boy, whatever the nature of the relationship may have been, has become proverbial. Certainly Alexander remains one of the giants of history; after his death, the importance of Greece as a political entity was over. The splendid culture would, however, survive in part through its absorption by the Romans. And the legacy of Greek love would be a part of this transmission.

Centuries later, during the Renaissance, the literature, art, and philosophy of ancient Greece would be rediscovered by Europeans; Greek culture would again be allowed to speak for itself, rather than be heard through the Roman filter. After the presumed darkness of the Middle Ages, Europe would come alive again to forgotten glories. Schoolmasters would speak eloquently of the wisdom of the Greeks, the strength of their literature, and the beauty of their visual art. But they would be reticent about "Greek love," which had inspired so many of these admired achievements. Later, in the Victorian period, the poems of Sappho would be modified, the gender of many of her lines changed in translation, as the idea spread that such a delicate spirit could not have been guilty of homosexuality.

## JUDEA

Some historians blame Judea—the ancient Hebrews and the continuing Jewish heritage—for the later widespread rejection of homosexuality in the West. This is, however, an oversimplification, especially in light of a pre-Christian Roman ambivalence toward same-sex relationships. The ancient Hebrews and their descendants, the Jews, might have exerted a slight influence on the powerful nations that surrounded them and in which, after the dispersion, they lived always with an alien taint. It was Christianity and Islam that spread throughout the world the ancient Semitic abhorrence of homosexuality. At this point, however, it is well to concentrate on the cultural influences rather than the specific biblical proscriptions.

Why did the ancient Hebrews find homosexuality so abhorrent? Several reasons have been advanced, quite apart from the Jews' own ready assurance that such conduct was a rejection of God's plan at creation. After their conquest of Canaan, and the gradual settlement of the land they believed God had promised them, the Hebrews found it necessary to separate themselves from the surrounding nations and assert their own identity. Many ancient Near Eastern peoples were regarded by Hebrews as impure and wicked, given to the worship of idols and other unspeakable practices. The Hebrews, a numerically threatened people, would also have been concerned with survival, which depended on their being fruitful and multiplying. Not only did they have the natural desire of all peoples to perpetuate their own kind, but after their prophets had spoken, they gained a stronger awareness that their survival was part of a divine plan by which eventually all nations would be blessed. They were to be "a light unto the Gentiles." Ancient peoples, the Hebrews especially, expressed anxiety over any "waste of seed." Sexual activity that could not be fruitful, they feared, would diminish their later ability to procreate. Their laws made it clear that procreation was the chief function of sexual activity.

Among the great Jewish thinkers of the time of Jesus and St. Paul, the most widely influential was Philo of Alexandria (c. 20 B.C.–50 A.D.), whose teaching had a profound impact on both Judaism and the early Greek fathers of the Christian Church. From an affluent and intellectual family, Philo took as his central project the reconciliation of Greek wisdom with the revealed truths of Hebrew Scripture. In doing this, he found it necessary to allegorize many of the narratives of the Bible. Because he allegorized much of the Hebrew Bible did not mean that he took its teachings any less seriously. He accepted the Levitical law against homosexuality in all its force, and he detested the effeminate men who officiated at the pagan religious rites he saw around him. He also advocated the harshest punishments against offenders of the Levitical law.

During the long years of their dispersion, Jews continued to disdain homosexual relationships. Both pragmatic and religious thinking supported this stance. Only in modern times have Jews taken a more compassionate approach to variations from the sexual norm.

## ROME

The Romans led the third great ancient civilization that has most influenced the Western world. Romans excelled in law, civic administration, and were the preeminent engineers of the ancient world. Some of their bridges, aqueducts, thermal baths, arenas, and roads are still in use. Although the Romans acknowledged Greek excellence in the arts, philosophy, and science, they adapted Greek ideas and customs selectively. They did not wholeheartedly acquiesce in the Greek glorification of same-sex love, and adult relationships with boys who were Roman citizens were scorned and eventually outlawed. There were, of course, other outlets. Records suggest that, during the period when Rome ruled the Mediterranean world and regions beyond, bisexuality was widely practiced among aristocratic and probably other classes as well.

Rome has a reputation for unrestrained sensual experimentation, conveyed in images and stories of gladiatorial combats, struggles between men and wild animals, and staged naval battles in a flooded coliseum. This image has been promoted by Hollywood, which from the early days of the film industry has thrived on epic spectacles with casts of thousands. Films that combined piety with violent, licentious panorama were especially popular, such as *Quo Vadis, Ben Hur,* and *King of Kings.* But ancient Rome is partially responsible for this imbalanced reputation. The one literary genre the Romans are credited with inventing is satire, and they made themselves its chief target. Their earnest satirists gleefully pointed out their own foibles, and too frequently the exaggerations of the satirists have been mistaken for balanced historical reality.

It must be remembered that our records of Rome cover a substantial period of time. Although events moved more slowly in the ancient world than they do today, attitudes did change during the long Roman period, fluctuating between social permissiveness and imperial attempts, through laws and courtly models, to improve the morals of the Romans. The great Augustus made one such attempt at reform, exiling his own daughter for her lewdness.

According to Louis Crompton, while Romans of the imperial period seduced young men, they "conquered rather than embraced."[5] They did not regard the occasional or even habitual adventure with one of their own sex as any threat to their manhood. Even some of the most avid womanizers enjoyed the caresses of boys from time to time, according to their biographers. Most historians concur with Crompton that homosexual relations among the Romans were primarily perceived as forms of dominance; only the passive partner in such arrangements was stigmatized. Rome had a large slave population at its disposal, available candidates for the role of passive partner. While the protégée system of the Greeks was not continued by the Romans, attractive slaves, some of them notable for their craftiness, often became the indulged favorites of their masters.

The literature of the Roman Empire can be revealing. The most important poet in the Latin language, and perhaps in any language, was Virgil (70–19 B.C.). His stated reason for writing *The Aenead* was to give Rome what Homer had given the Greeks, an epic poem celebrating national virtues. Virgil's work perpetuated the major conventions that had been established in the Greek epics. Because Homer had made Achilles and Patrocles devoted male companions in battle, Virgil introduced Nisus and Euryalus, two soldiers who die in each other's arms. Although theirs may be a Greek-style love, readers through the centuries have made little of it. What readers have never forgotten is Virgil's great and moving male-female love story of Dido and Aeneas, which inspired much music, painting, and later poetry. Virgil, thus, provides no strong witness to same-sex love.

Catullus (c. 84–54 B.C.), the most important lyric poet of the Romans, wrote verses in which he openly acknowledged the influence of Sappho. His poems, however, were erotic more than idealistic, and conveyed the disillusionment as well as fleeting happiness of a long love affair with a faithless woman. His most famous sequence of poems was inspired by a woman he called Lesbia, although her real name was probably Clodia. He details the separate stages of his liaison with this married woman, whom he fully recognizes is neither loyal nor virtuous. His attachment to her is obsessive rather than ennobling, and he dissects the relationship realistically, in powerful images. One of the Lesbia poems contains the oft-quoted line: "The words of lovers are written on water." According to Crompton, few Latin writers have dramatized "their anxieties about masculinity so vehemently" as Catullus. Savoring the range of sexual experiences, Catullus did not deny himself adventures with boys, although he could be unsparing in his verbal assaults on "faggots."[6]

Horace, a gentle poet less splendid than Virgil and less passionate than Catullus, wrote verses that are usually classified as satires, detailing infatuations with both women and men. Ovid, a more urbane satirist, was taken very seriously during the late Middle Ages—his writing regarded as a sort of Bible of courtly love. His *Art of Love* and *Remedy of Love* provide witty but workable instructions on how to conduct a heterosexual affair and how to recover when it crashes. Although Ovid was heterosexual, he dealt with the bisexuality of Greek myths without censure. In *Metamorphoses,* he treats the amorous pursuits of the pagan gods with the humor and tolerance that might be expected of an experienced man of the world who finds erotic fixation more amusing than offensive.

Any discussion of Roman conduct—or misconduct—must mention two writers of special relevance: Suetonius, a keyhole biographer of the Caesars and a lover of scandal; and Juvenal, who is called a satirist but was really a fierce moralist in the manner of the angrier Hebrew prophets. Suetonius's *Lives of the Twelve Caesars* is a salacious and uncritical report of every detail of gossip he heard, even when only whispered in the streets. It is not known how much of the story is exaggeration and how much is fact. Edward Gibbon in *The Decline and Fall of the Roman Empire* is following Suetonius when he observes, "of the first fifteen emperors, Claudius was the only one whose taste in love was entirely correct."[7] The rest, even the best of them, present a picture of treachery to loved ones, of incest, adultery, insanity, matricide, and general murder. Male-male relationships are also reported by Suetonius in a hostile context. His *Lives* appeared a few years after the more edifying *Plutarch's Lives* and has conditioned the way subsequent generations have viewed Rome's rulers.

Juvenal, the most severe Roman satirist of them all, has also influenced the popular view of Romans as obscene pleasure seekers. No lover of humankind, he detested effeminate men and masculine women. In his Sixth Satire, he attacks women as "shrews, spendthrifts, nymphomaniacs, murderers." These "painted harlots" reject the most basic feature of female life, motherhood. However, warns Juvenal, husbands must be content that their wives do not condescend to bear children, because any offspring born to such women would be of questionable paternity and "a Roman might find himself the parent of a blackamoor."[8]

The Second Satire, informally known as "The Fairy Queens," attacks effeminate males and may be the fiercest denunciation of homosexual activity to be found in classical Latin literature. Juvenal finds particularly repugnant the men who dress in women's clothing, paint their eyes, soot their eyebrows, and gather their hair in golden nets. They stage mock weddings, he tells readers, with the bride wearing a veil and presenting a dowry. Soon, Juvenal complains, they will even attempt to register these "marriages" with the authorities.[9]

Even though Juvenal loathed same-sex relationships, at least the sort that place Romans in passive roles, he does suggest, with fierce irony, that it would certainly be better to take to bed a young man, who would not wrangle and make constant demands, than to have relations with an untrustworthy Roman harridan.

The Romans, despite periods when all manner of behavior was tolerated, ultimately remained ambivalent about same-sex love. Both native traditions and Rome's more lofty philosophies often spoke with disfavor of such relationships. Cicero, the eloquent Roman legislator, attacked male liaisons and denounced what he referred to as "Greek love" in his *Disputations*. The surviving documents give the impression that the Romans especially despised lesbianism and did not, like the Hebrews, regard it as a lesser offense. Romans insulted their enemies or people they disliked by imputing various sexual practices to them, including adultery, incest, and passive homosexuality. When Julius Caesar, widely regarded as the greatest man of the ancient world, was called by Suetonius "every woman's man and every man's woman," it was not intended as a compliment. Such insults seem to have been taken rather casually, and accusations of misconduct, even when substantiated, do not appear to have ended careers as they have in Europe and the United States in modern times.

Mark Antony is remembered in story and song as the dashing lover of Cleopatra, a model of dangerous yet glamorous courtly love. His story would be rehearsed by medieval preachers as a cautionary tale of lawless passion, while the poets, embellishing upon his tale, would celebrate him as a noble figure ready to sacrifice the whole world for love. In Shakespeare, Antony is a heroic and tragic figure. Yet Mark Antony's contemporaries spoke of him more as a seducer of boys than as a man ready to throw family and career aside in order to savor the "infinite variety" of Cleopatra. However his story was interpreted, he remained an example of a great man too controlled by his impulses and brought low by poor judgment.

## ISLAMIC SPAIN

The Koran condemns same-sex relationships as much as the Hebrew book of Leviticus, and punishments in Muslim countries under the *sharia* have been, and continue to be, severe. However, prosperous, elegant societies that give lip service to stern religious codes sometimes honor them only as they see fit. The courts of medieval Spain encouraged intellectual exploration, relative tolerance, and gracious living; all branches of learning were allowed to flourish without much constraint. Not surprisingly, in this environment, the art of poetry flourished. And much of this poetry—written in both Arabic and Hebrew—because an educated Jewish elite also flourished in these courts—celebrated love. In Cordoba, Seville, and Granada, poetry was written that, if read literally and autobiographically, was homoerotic. Although the records are ambiguous, the popular attitude toward same-sex relationships, particularly if they were fleeting and only a part of a person's total network of associations, appear to have been tolerated. According to Crompton, "in sexual matters, Islam maintained a paradoxical ambivalence, not lest with respect to homosexuality."[10]

## THE EUROPEAN MIDDLE AGES

Throughout the European Middle Ages, under the influence of the Roman Catholic Church, there were harsh punishments for homosexual conduct when it was apprehended. It is likely that gay relationships were widespread within religious orders, but they were conducted in secret and are, consequently, poorly documented. Educational institutions in northern France, under the control of priests, were widely reported to be centers of same-sex activity, and some evidence suggests that homosexuality was practiced freely, if not openly, among the upper nobility of France and Norman England. From time to time, scandals erupted in the church and rumors circulated particularly among royalty. Although love poetry was widely written after the fourteenth century as an expression of the courtly love tradition, there was very little poetry of a homoerotic nature. The poets of the time, when they were not defying the church by celebrating the adulterous relationship between a grand lady and a humble knight, were competing with one another to demonstrate their affection for Christian ideals. In the French *Roman de Fauvel,* an allegorical poem of the fourteenth century, "Holy Church" condemns the Knights Templar as "heretics/And sinners against nature."[11]

One of the greatest philosophers of the Middle Ages, whose thought dominated Roman Catholic theology at least until Vatican Council II in the middle of the twentieth century, was St. Thomas Aquinas. Because Aquinas argued that Christian morality is a manifestation of natural law, his thinking had ramifications far beyond the medieval church. His *Summa theologiae* (1267–1273) was a magisterial compendium of Christian thought, anchored in Greek philosophy, the Scriptures, and human reason. Right-thinking people, he taught, even without the aid of divine revelation, would know through the exercise of reason that certain acts were wicked. Sexuality, like all other human activities, should be guided by reason. While embracing biblical prohibitions, Aquinas added a philosophical argument and believed that, even without the instruction of Scripture, homosexuality would be excluded from the conduct of rational people. He presented a hierarchy of "unnatural sex acts": first, there was "solitary sin"; then heterosexual relations in the "wrong vessel" or "wrong position" (though Aquinas's meaning here is not completely clear); third came relations with the "wrong sex"; and, finally, the most heinous of all, bestiality."[12]

While the Inquisition, established in 1233 by Pope Gregory IX, was commissioned primarily to stamp out heresy, it also attempted to enforce established moral rules. There were periods, perhaps when heresy seemed less threatening, in which more sodomites than heretics were sent to the stake. Both offenses were closely associated in the popular mind.

Just as the European Middle Ages had its giant theologian in Aquinas, it had its supreme poet in the Florentine, Dante Alighieri (1265–1321). What Homer had accomplished for the Greeks and Virgil for the Romans, Dante sought for his own people in his medieval epic *The Divine Comedy,* in which he succeeded in providing a poetic summa for the entire European Middle Ages. Some readers have suggested that from Dante's epic alone it would be possible to imaginatively reconstruct the entire century in which he lived.

Dante was an orthodox Christian who concurred with Aquinas's views of the seven deadly sins, including lechery. In the *Divine Comedy* he sends himself on a journey through Hell, Purgatory, and, finally, Heaven. In the first of the three parts of his epic, he is guided through Hell by the Roman poet Virgil, whom he regarded as the incomparable voice of poetry and as his own master. In Hell, Dante observes the sinners who are being punished for their deeds in life, and frequently stops to converse with them. He visits two groups of "sodomites" during this journey.

As Dante goes deeper into the circles of Hell, the offenses become more grave. He places the first group of sodomites below murderers, affirming that in his hierarchy "violence against nature" is the more horrendous offense. However, he is not without compassion, and he finds one of his beloved teachers in this circle of sodomites. Many readers have found this placement peculiar; perhaps Dante was merely confirming a popular belief of his contemporaries that homosexuality was widely practiced among intellectuals and teachers. Or perhaps he had other evidence. Before Dante's time, as early as 1271, Roger Bacon had already observed that "many theologians at Paris, and men who lectured in theology, were banished from that city and from the realm of France for the vile sins of sodomy."[13]

And perhaps this is also the reason that, when Dante, as he continues his imaginative journey through Hell, meets a second group of sodomites in Canto 16, he shows them the same pity he had earlier expressed for the illicit heterosexual lovers, Paolo and Francesco in a lighter region of Hell. This second group includes worthies of Dante's time—Guido Guerra, Tegghiaio Aldobrandi, and Jacopo Rusticucci—three Florentines who had won acclaim for their service as statesmen and soldiers. Dante expresses his desire to leap into the fiery pit to embrace them. As a poet and man of deep humanity, Dante respects the courage and character of these men, whose affections might have been considered honorable had they lived in classical Greece, yet he still feels obliged to uphold the Church's condemnation of homosexuality.

## INDIA AND IMPERIAL CHINA

In the East, different religions, traditions, and laws apply than in the West. The Chinese and Indians, with their stress on family, have generally rejected homosexuality as a permanent orientation, although it has been tolerated at some times and places—and in some social strata—as a supplement to sexuality with a wife or wives. In India, the Code of Manu, an influential legal code, required that the "twice-born man," a member of one of the two highest castes, perform ritual purification if he had sex with a female in an ox-cart, in water, in the daytime, or "with a male." Seemingly these offenses were regarded as about equal in gravity.[14]

In China, within cultivated circles, numerous records and early biographies mention same-sex love affairs. Poets, playwrights, and writers of fiction especially spoke freely of these relationships. Ancient emperors were said to have had many wives, concubines, and male consorts, "lovers of the torn sleeve," as these latter were called. The expression originated in a tale of an older man who was aroused from sleep, his arm around the young boy he loved. Rather than wake the sleeping youth, he cut out the sleeve of his kimono. In ancient China, as in medieval Europe, scholars were believed to be especially prone to such affairs with their protégées. But China, unlike Europe, exalted the scholar above the warrior. Such love affairs between men were sometimes regarded as elegant diversions, the subject of lyric poetry and mysterious love notes left in obscure places, rather than the alliances forged on the battlefield with oaths sworn on bloody swords. Some stories tell of Chinese scholars and their students who loved each other so much that they requested burial in the same grave. The old literature conveys the impression that, at times, among the upper classes, bisexuality was regarded as the norm.

Although Buddhist monasteries were suspected of being centers of same-sex love, just as Christian ones were, modern scholars have found few references to male homosexuality in Chinese Buddhist writings. Buddhist nuns, never as highly regarded as the monks, were frequently depicted, possibly inaccurately, as secret seductresses or lesbians.

From the middle of the eighteenth century to the middle of the nineteenth century, Chinese opera experienced a golden age. By the end of the eighteenth century, the Peking stage had become an important institution. Men, called *tan* actors, played women's roles. Although actors generally had low social standing in Asia, these actors acquired special status when scholars or important government functionaries took them as lovers. Records from the time suggest that numerous actors developed elegant aristocratic tastes and, if they were desirable, were able to live in the style of high-class courtesans in Western society. While there remained official disapproval of homosexuality, popular acceptance seems to have been widespread. According to Compton: "China indeed provides us with the longest documented period of tolerance in human history—two thousand years extending from 500 BCE to the fall of the Ming dynasty in 1644."[15]

Despite this long period of tolerance, the Chinese government today deals harshly with homosexuality. The Communist government believes that everyone has the duty to marry and produce precisely one child. Chinese communist theory has difficulty acknowledging that a homosexual preference exists in some people. When it cannot be ignored, this preference is treated as a social ill, much like prostitution, and the belief is that homosexuality, like other social problems, will disappear as the socialist state matures. Although Communist theory does not encourage ancestral rites, the strong traditions necessitating family continuity are very much alive. The government encourages later marriages, but there is great pressure in China for everyone to marry at what society considers the appropriate time. Bachelorhood and spinsterhood are not respectable, and the average Chinese finds it inconceivable that a person would choose not to marry someone of the opposite sex.

China is now being forced to confront the enormous social problem that has been created in the cities by the one-child-per-family policy. Because of Chinese family traditions, couples prefer that their one child be male. With prenatal gender determination and the ease with which abortions are available in urban China, an entire generation is coming of age in which males greatly outnumber females. How this problem will be addressed, especially in view of the official disapproval of same-sex unions, remains to be seen.

## THE EUROPEAN RENAISSANCE

We tend to think of the Renaissance, today increasingly referred to as the "early modern period," as the beginning of the age, when ancient superstitions and the benighted thinking of the Middle Ages were swept away, but, ironically, the scholars and artists of the Renaissance thought they were rediscovering the wisdom and eloquence of the past. They were inspired by the possibility of recovering the richness of ancient Greek culture and the stability and glory of the Roman Empire. The Renaissance also heightened European diversity, with the breakup of the near spiritual monopoly of the Roman Catholic Church. In parts of middle and northern Europe, the Renaissance was closely linked to the Reformation, which sought to rediscover the Christian Scriptures and the practices of the early church. The Reformation was not a plea for fewer religious restraints or for greater freedom of conduct. It was a revolt against the perceived laxness of the Roman Catholic Church and the moral waywardness of its popes, bishops, and priests.

The Renaissance, according to Crompton and other scholars, was also a period of "unprecedented" suppression of homosexuality. Protestants and Catholics seemed almost to be in competition to determine which could more thoroughly wipe out such "abominations." In Spain, the Inquisition organized by Ferdinand and Isabella, sought out sodomites as enthusiastically as it pursued heretics, Muslims, and Jews.[16]

### Venice

Many secular laws throughout the Italian city-states, notably in Florence and Venice, decreed horrible punishments against those convicted of sodomy. During this period Venice was in its glory, extending influence throughout the Adriatic as a model of noble grace, with an efficient government, great wealth, and power everywhere envied. Venetian records show that numerous people were burned alive in the Ducal Palace Courtyard, and a witch-hunt for offenders affected all levels of Renaissance Venetian society. Heterosexual prostitution was tolerated; on the authority of both Augustine and Aquinas, it was conceded to be a necessary evil. But such was not the case for homosexuality. As they heard their priests interpret Scripture, the Venetians believed that God had destroyed the cities of the plain because of this "vice" and had later sent Noah's flood (a reverse of biblical chronology) as the supreme cleansing agent when humans had not properly learned their lesson. Perched on the edge of the sea, Venetians had a special sensitivity to the threat of flooding. Sodomy was believed, superstitiously and on the basis of Scripture, to be a threat to the power and the very existence of any state that tolerated it. "I will spew you out of the land," was an Old Testament curse that even the most urbane Venetians, proud of their wealth, took very seriously.[17]

Nevertheless, despite punishments and threats, homosexuals were found at all levels of Venetian society. According to Patricia Labalme's research, they included "tailors, jewelers, fishermen, hatters, glass-makers, sellers of fruits and vegetables and wine, spice sellers, printers, censors, painters, cloth merchants, stone-cutters, a bombardier, a dancing master, a notary, and a government herald."[18] In other words, all the trades that made Venice the lively city it was were represented. Apothecary shops were especially known as likely meeting places for male homosexuals.

Throughout the Italian city states, awards were given for denunciations leading to homosexual convictions, convictions that were often secured through torture. Suspicion fell on the schools of music, singing, gymnastics, and fencing. Protégées and young male companions of older men were especially suspect. Boys between the ages of 10 and 14, if convicted of same-sex relations, were jailed for about three months, while adults received more severe and sometimes fatal punishments. Members of the clergy, particularly vulnerable to accusations because of their unmarried state and access to children, were turned over to the church courts. Many complained that these courts were too lenient and that the church often shielded its offenders. After the fifteenth century, exile from major cities or sentencing to labor in the Venetian galleys replaced the earlier executions that had taken place.

### Florence

Considerable homosexual activity must have been present in Florence, the center of the Renaissance, particularly among artistic and educated persons, possibly in imitation of "Greek love." Fiery preachers had earlier denounced Florence as "another Sodom." The celebrated preacher Bernardino of Sienna (1380–1444) had ranted against "the Tuscan vice," although there is some indication that he, unlike others in his time, recognized homosexuality as a permanent orientation rather than as a supplementary practice. He described the "sodomite" as a member of a unique species, set apart from others, recognizable by the fact that he scorned women and did not readily marry. Bernardino warned women not to marry sodomites because such husbands would only neglect their wives while they pursued young men. Rarely would their desires change, he cautioned. Bernardino looked with suspicion on any unmarried man over the age of 33 and thought that such a man should not be entrusted with important public offices.

By 1490, with the Renaissance in full flower, male love in Florence, under the rule of Lorenzo de'Medici, the Magnificent, came to be regarded as a peccadillo rather than the abomination that would incur God's wrath. Offenders were taxed rather than physically punished. Priests were heavily implicated then, as today, and were still treated lightly by their own ecclesiastical courts. There was, from time to time, widespread complaint that nothing was being done about the priestly molestation of young boys.

Art works, which often imitated Greek forms and demonstrated a fascination with the beauty of male and female bodies, provide an ambiguous witness to the inclinations and practices of the artists who produced them. The bronze David of Donatello, an esteemed work of art that may be seen today in the Bargello of Florence, is a prime example of the androgynous quality of much of the sculpture and painting of the period. David appears remarkably feminine, despite his boots and the glory of his youthful body. His shepherd's cap has been described as resembling "an Easter bonnet." He provides a vivid contrast to Michelangelo's virile David, one of the world's most celebrated statues, which may be seen today in the Academy in Florence.

Numerous artists did not marry, perhaps viewing their art as a type of priestly vocation demanding all their attention. Some had handsome young apprentices who worked intimately with them and to whom they served as mentors. It is not surprising that accusations of sodomy were made at the time and continue to be made by some biographers and historians. Botticelli has been the object of many speculations, but they are impossible to substantiate. Botticelli, Donatello, Leonardo, and Michelangelo were among the artists who never married. Michelangelo's students and associates, however, were unanimous in attesting to his almost-monastic behavior. According to Vasari, his student and biographer, Michelangelo's life was dedicated to his art and was totally chaste. A prototypical Renaissance genius, Michelangelo also was a skilled poet. His poems, admired even today for their perfection of form, are addressed to two individuals the artist loved deeply and, seemingly, chastely: a noble lady named Vittoria della Colonna and a handsome young man named Tomasso.

It seems likely that the other supreme genius of the Italian Renaissance, Leonardo da Vinci, was homosexual. He worked with an assortment of male protégées and was several times charged with sodomy. Attempts to gain insights into his sexual practices from his paintings are, however, futile. The work of these painters and sculptors contains an abundance of androgynous angels and blushing young men in their physical prime. These artists took their favorite subjects from the Bible and from Roman and Greek lore, and they frequently mingled biblical and pagan motifs freely. Several found artistic inspiration in the Greek myth of the rape of Ganymede by Zeus.

Of special interest is the Renaissance artist Giovanni Antonio Bazzi (1477–1549), who called himself Il Sodoma (the sodomite). Despite this public acknowledgement of his proclivities, he lived with his wife in Sienna. There he became known as a local eccentric, and his art was very popular. Despite his notoriety, he was successful in staying clear of the law and was even made a Cavalier of Christ by the Pope.

Benvenuto Cellini was not so fortunate. A flamboyant womanizer, he had numerous entanglements with the law. In addition to his many female conquests, he enjoyed seducing boys; the story of Zeus and Ganymede was a favorite artistic subject. Convicted of sodomy during the first Medici restoration (1512–1527), he was given light penalties. His punishment had little effect, because he confessed to later similar episodes. Not surprisingly, the story of Zeus and Ganymede was always a favorite artistic subject with him. In his autobiography, he bragged about his many amorous conquests with as much pride as he spoke of his artistic achievements. Both self-indulgent and mystically religious, he also claimed to have had a vision of Christ during an imprisonment in Castello San Angelo in Rome.

The Renaissance was the age of the notorious Borgia popes, who moved their mistresses into the Vatican, gave their children high clerical offices, and were more interested in advancing the fortunes of their families than in promoting the gospel. The record of the popes in Rome during this period of clerical self-indulgence is mixed. Pope Julius III (1550–1555) was rumored to have had same-sex liaisons, which infuriated the Protestant reformers, while other popes, notably Paul IV (1555–1559), lived ascetic lives.

### Spain in the New World

By the end of the sixteenth century, Spain ruled an empire that spanned five continents. Spain's official distaste for homosexuality spread to its colonies. While the early Spanish explorers in the New World had witnessed the horrendous *auto da fé* in their homeland, where torture and execution had become a public spectacle and religious rite, and should have been inured to violence, they were horrified by the frequency and ferocity of Aztec and Mayan human sacrifices. They also charged the native inhabitants of the New World with two additional sins, cannibalism and sodomy. Whether their observations were accurate or they were still in the grip of Spanish witch-hunt hysteria is not clear. They reported that sodomy was widespread and open among the natives. According to their witness, Aztec priests, with women forbidden to them, lived openly with the boys who assisted in their rites and served their domestic as well as sexual needs. The explorers claimed that homosexuality was also institutionalized in Mayan society. Responding to these reports, the Spanish found further justification for conquest. To subdue, civilize, and Christianize became the ready excuse for Spanish subjugation of native peoples. Histories, largely written by political enemies, have abundantly documented Spanish brutality. The "black legend," a defamation of Spain by English and Dutch historians, which thrived on these tales of atrocity, is perpetuated even today, although modern, democratic Spain is one of the most liberal countries in Europe.

## FRANCE

In France, Catholics and Protestants hurled accusations at each other throughout the sixteenth century, and they delighted in "outing" one another's officials. Pope Julius II was a special target of the Protestants, who were both intrigued and horrified by clerical abuses. It was widely reported by both Catholics and Protestants that the pope was enchanted by a 15-year-old boy, ironically named Innocenzo, whom he had already made a cardinal despite his lowly birth, inaptitude for priestly vocation, and questionable character. This child, said to have been picked off the streets of Parma, was referred to as "the new Ganymede." Whatever the relationship may have been, the pope was so taken by Innocenzo that he arranged for his brother to officially adopt him.

But the Catholic polemicists had their turn when Theodore de Beze, an autocratic personality often called "the Protestant Pope," became the successor to John Calvin in Geneva in 1564. Many stories circulated not only about his wild youth, but his adult behavior was also under attack. Calvinists, certainly more than Renaissance Catholics, stressed a stern sexual morality that they sometimes honored only in the breach. The Beze scandal, which included various accusations of sexual misconduct, was a painful blow for them.

## SWEDEN

Russia, Denmark, and Sweden eventually enacted anti-sodomy laws, but the controversy was not as heated in the lands of the North. A peculiar and ambiguous personality, Queen Christina became the ruler of Sweden in 1644.

Christina was actually an awkward woman of unkempt appearance, who preferred boyish attire to her royal gowns. Learned and pious, she showed little
interest in governing or presiding over her elegant court. Refusing marriage,
she maintained strong ties to several women. From the first, she was widely
suspected of lesbianism, although it was never conclusively established. After
several years on the throne, she abdicated, leaving Sweden for good, convert-
ing to Catholicism, and settling in Rome, where she cut her hair and permanently assumed male attire.[19]

## ENGLAND AFTER THE REFORMATION

Although homosexuality became known in Europe throughout the nineteenth century as "the English vice," the British saw themselves differently. They
believed homosexuality to be almost entirely "a foreign vice." Henry VIII passed
the first law against "buggery," with the penalty of hanging for anyone apprehended. For once, the clergy were not excluded, as one by one, the king dis-
mantled the network of laws and customs that had earlier protected them. Many
historians believe that these measures against "buggery" were part of Henry's
attack on the monasteries, in his successful project to appropriate their wealth
and destroy their influence. The laws targeting homosexuals seem not to have
been enthusiastically enforced outside clerical circles.

Elizabethan literature, especially poetry and drama, is replete with influences
from classical writing, and the poets of the period would have recognized the
characteristics of "Greek love." Christopher Marlowe, who, had he lived and
fulfilled his early promise, might have been a greater playwright and poet than
William Shakespeare, was almost certainly a homosexual. He delighted in de-
viating from the norms of his society, whether in religious heresy or personal
conduct. He was probably also involved in espionage, which in England has
long been associated with homosexuality. In 1593, Marlowe was killed in a
tavern brawl at the age of 29. The mystery surrounding his death has never
been solved, despite a shelf of books advancing the theories of one scholar or
historian after another. His biographers usually suggest either espionage, sexual
rivalry, or a combination of the two as the motives for his assassination.

Marlowe's death meant that William Shakespeare was able to establish himself as England's most revered poet and the greatest playwright in the language.
Although the basic events of Shakespeare's life are known, very little can be sur-
mised about his personal habits or character. His plays reveal virtually nothing
of a personal nature; rather, they reflect almost every philosophical and social
current of his time. Only one of his writings seems so personal, so intense, and
so strange that there has always been a temptation to read it autobiographically.
This is his sonnet sequence. Here Shakespeare addresses ardent poems to two

individuals: a woman who, though neither fair nor virtuous, is coveted by the poet, and an admirable young man, whom the poet idealizes. The woman, usually referred to as "the dark lady of the sonnets," has been the subject of much speculation. While Shakespeare employs the conventional imagery and language of courtly love poetry—which came to him from the Italian, French, and earlier English poets—many read the sonnets as intimate personal declarations of passionate love for both a woman and a man. Even if the man mentioned in the sonnets was a real person, Shakespeare still makes quite clear in Sonnet 20 of the sequence that his affection for that man is spiritual rather than sexual. Whatever amorous adventures he may have had in London, records clearly show that Shakespeare was married and the father of three children. At the end of his life he was laid to rest beside his wife in the parish church of Stratford-on-Avon.

While Shakespeare began his career during the reign of the Elizabeth I, her Scottish cousin and successor, King James I (James VI in Scotland), became the poet's second ruler and his patron. The son of the ill-fated Mary Queen of Scots, James had a lonely, neglected childhood. He grew up to be a scholar who would probably have preferred a career as a university man, and his most memorable achievement, as reckoned by today's standards, was his commissioning of the translation of the Bible known popularly as the King James Version. Although he married an attractive woman, Anne of Denmark, and had seven children by her, he seemed to prefer the company of the many attractive male favorites who hovered around his throne.

With kings and poets among those who have found their own gender physically seductive, the record of British treatment of homosexuals, though not without blemish, is less grim than that of Continental European countries. During the interregnum and Commonwealth periods in England, presided over by Oliver Cromwell, there were no recorded executions of sodomites. The Puritan government could have had little sympathy for same-sex love, but it had other more pressing concerns.

## JAPAN

Japan historically has been one of the more tolerant countries for homosexuals, approaching ancient Greece in its near-institutionalization of same-sex relationships in some periods of its history. Early European visitors, who may not always have understood what they observed of foreign customs, reported that same-sex relationships, at least among men, took place with frequency in Zen Buddhist monasteries, among samurai warriors, and in the No and Kabuki theatres.

The early Jesuits who visited Japan in the middle of the sixteenth century reported that male love was commonplace among warriors. St. Francis Xavier was horrified by the practice when he arrived in Japan. He and other Jesuits pronounced the Japanese guilty of three grievous sins: idolatry, abortion, and sodomy. That sodomy was an honored way of life among Japanese aristocrats and monks further convinced these Europeans that the Japanese were depraved heathen. However, while homosexuality might flourish among Japanese warriors and in the theatre, social and family expectations remained such that it was rarely a permanent or exclusive choice.

## THE EUROPEAN ENLIGHTENMENT

The Enlightenment, or the Age of Reason, brought to Europe a change in attitudes toward every institution and tradition, with religion and the taboos generated by religion placed under special scrutiny. Deism, the most characteristic religious-philosophical view espoused by Enlightenment intellectuals, was the belief that the creator had made the universe and everything in it, set its laws in motion, and now maintains a hands-off policy. The Eternal Watchmaker became the chief metaphor for the divine power. Tyrannical churches and governments were alike condemned. People were believed capable, with proper education, of governing themselves, and governments received their authority from the will of the people rather than by divine fiat. Neither people nor national groups needed tyrants or restrictive laws to restrain destructive behavior. They only needed education and the exercise of reason.

In France, where many issues were stirred by the Enlightenment, homosexuality was not a prime preoccupation. Montesquieu devoted a single page of his *The Spirit of Laws* to what he called "the crime against nature." He warned that tyrannical governments would make false accusations of sodomy, which would be severely punished, along with witchcraft and alleged heresy. He believed that social customs had frequently promoted homosexuality in the past. As an example, he cited the provocativeness of athletes in ancient times who had performed naked. In polygamous Asia, too few women had been left for the common folk. The segregation of boys and girls in European schools at a susceptible age was, in his judgment, responsible for the homosexuality of his own time. Changing these social conditions would, he thought, correct any problem. Montesquieu, like other thinkers of the Enlightenment, saw homosexuality not as a sin or a sickness, but as a social problem. Although it was not accepted as responsible conduct, homosexuality was no longer viewed as an offense against God or a perversion of God's creative intention.

Voltaire had many homosexual friends; even his patron, Frederick the Great, is generally assumed by his biographers to have had homosexual proclivities. But Voltaire was definitely uncomfortable with the idea of same-sex relationships. "I cannot bear," he wrote, "to hear anyone say that the Greeks authorized this license."[20] Voltaire often interpreted the writings of history according to his own values and taste. It was hard for him to understand how illustrious civilizations in the ancient world would have violated what he understood to be reasonable conduct that all right-thinking people could discern, even without any need of divine revelation. Temple prostitution was one practice he found abhorrent. Ancient writings, such as those of Herodotus, he concluded, could not therefore be authentic when they reported such facts. Likewise, Voltaire believed that the homoerotic verses of the ancient poets must surely have been written only in their youth and repudiated in later life. Yet, as distasteful and contrary to reason as Voltaire found homosexual conduct, he could not condone cruel and inhumane punishment of it. Execution he believed, was far too severe; surely reasonable Caesars and kings would reject such needless cruelty.

Voltaire reassured himself that while Mediterranean peoples might be so inclined, this "vice unworthy of mankind" was practically unknown in the lands where he chose to live.[21] Despite Voltaire's blindness to its reality, in eighteenth-century France homosexuality was well observed and even referred to as "the philosophical sin," because of Greek associations and perhaps more contemporary ones as well.

Another figure of the period who must be mentioned in any discussion of sexual practices is the Marquis de Sade, whose contribution to the Enlightenment was his defiance of society. He tackled the argument that homosexuality is contrary to nature and contended that no inclinations can exist in us except those that are based in nature. Still, he regarded homosexuality as "an innocent deformity" rather than a normal variation of human sexuality. In some of his opinions he anticipated later conclusions of psychiatrists. Certain children, he alleged, from an early age are attracted to their own sex and nothing ever changes them. De Sade asked that lawmakers deal with these individuals with prudence and wisdom. The person with homosexual inclinations, said the Marquis, is no more guilty than the one whom nature has created with physical deformities. Of course, because of his personal history, the arguments of de Sade, even when reasonable and compassionate, have carried little weight.

In 1791 the Code Pénal de la Révolution abolished sodomy as an offense. This does not mean, however, that the Age of Reason had accepted homosexuality as healthy or desirable. One major revolutionary leader, Jean-Paul Marat, expressed the legislative view shared by Montesquieu and Voltaire. "Male love," he said, is "an indecent love which nature rejects . . . a revolting crime which must inspire only horror." It was, nevertheless, prudent, he believed, that this practice be "left in the shadows" because bringing it to public justice and the attention of the masses risked corrupting the innocent. Marat further suggested that if it ever became necessary to punish same-sex lovers as threats to public order, it would be better to send them to insane asylums rather than prison.[22]

While the United States is the true political heir of the Enlightenment, religious attitudes remained strong in most regions of North America, and sodomy laws were widely enacted. Only in the twentieth century was there a gradual elimination of these laws. South Carolina kept its death penalty for sodomy on the books until after the Civil War, although enforcement was no longer attempted. Influenced by the publication of the first Kinsey Report in 1948, the American Bar Association recommended in 1961 that laws restricting private acts of consenting adults be repealed. Throughout the 1960s and 1970s such laws disappeared one by one in most states except in the South. As late as 1986, the Supreme Court upheld the constitutionality of sodomy statutes by a five-to-four vote, although Justice Lewis Powell later acknowledged he had made a mistake in his vote to uphold. Everything changed when, on June 26, 2003, the Supreme Court, ruling on a Texas case, overturned this decision. The United States now, along with 45 countries in Europe, has abolished all legal restrictions on homosexuality. This does not mean that Americans in general are ready to acknowledge homosexuality as right and healthy. In the twentieth century, Sigmund Freud's ideas were influential even though his specific theories seemed dated by the beginning of the third millennium. His *Three Essays on the Theory of Sexuality* postulate, even while rejecting theories of degeneracy, that homosexuality is an example of arrested development in the individual. This remained a dominant American view as the new millennium approached.

## TRADITIONAL SOCIETIES

Proponents of same-sex marriage have attempted to find precedents in the past, in response to those who oppose same-sex union on the grounds that it is a total revision of what matrimony has always been. While no conclusive examples of same-sex marriage have been presented, it is clear that some societies have, from time to time, made a respected place for homosexual or bisexual relationships, though usually not on an exclusive or permanent basis. Anthropological data are sometimes suspect, because it is difficult for outside observers to fully understand the practices of a community different from their own. Even famous anthropologists, notably Margaret Mead and Zora Neale Hurston, have been known to manufacture and falsify their facts. Still, examples of ritual homosexuality have been convincingly recorded in Melanesia and African tribal areas. European observers have reported that African tribes such as the Wolof and Lebou have at times fully accepted transvestite men functioning as women in sexual relationships.

The custom in certain North American Indian tribes of men keeping *berdache* (feminized men who dress as women and fulfill conventional roles) as supplements to their regular wives has been well documented. According to accounts of early explorers, the Aztec priests of South America who were forbidden to marry were permitted sexual relations with boys who dressed as women and attended the rites of the temples. These customs, followed in the most sacred precincts of the Aztecs, were especially repellent to Europeans.

The Alaskan Aleuts and the California Lacue are said to have in earlier times chosen boys with delicate features and reared them as girls, even securing for them positions in families as secondary wives to important men. These arrangements were sanctioned by the tribal chief and shaman. The famed Lakota warrior Crazy Horse is alleged to have had secondary wives of this sort, called *winkte*.[23]

Although situational homosexuality continues to be reported in African mining camps, in prisons all over the world, and in other places where sexes are segregated, those relationships have not been blessed by any religious functionaries. Citizens of modern nations in central and east Africa today are among the most adamant in their rejection of homosexuality.

## CONCLUSION

Louis Crompton, the leading historian of homosexuality, states emphatically that the Judeo-Christian tradition has provided the great divide; where the influence of the Abrahamic religions has been felt, same-sex lovers have been pariahs. Elsewhere these relationships have been more widely accepted. Unquestionably, the Bible has been the dominant witness against homosexuality in the Western world, and its indirect influence continues today in secularized lands. But this does not explain nor fully account for the status of same-sex relationships in ancient societies or modern ones influenced only peripherally, if at all, by the Bible. Even in pre-Christian Athens, the most illustrious Greek city-state, which celebrated male love in story and song, the comic playwrights made same-sex lovers objects of ridicule. Ancient Rome practiced tolerance but not idealization, and the appropriate same-sex love objects for Roman men were slaves. Even before Christianity influenced Roman law and homosexuals became criminals, the "faggot" was the subject of general contempt among the population. Indeed China and Japan in the past appear to have been more open to homosexual activity than the West. Thus it becomes more difficult to explain their hearty rejection of such conduct today. Despite centuries of missionary activity, these two countries remain largely unmoved by the Christian message. Also, it is well to remember that even the philosophers of the Enlightenment, most of whom proudly extricated their thinking from Christian dogma, still found homosexuality distasteful.

The fate of homoerotic lovers throughout much of history has been grim, with occasional respite in particular times and places. Only in our own time has the West taken the lead in extending rights of privacy to the sexual practices of all consenting adults. Now it is not merely such privacy that is being requested but a public affirmation of marriage between same-sex lovers. If same-sex marriage indeed becomes the norm in a significant part of the world, from a historical perspective, it will be a momentous innovation.

## NOTES

1. Although interpretations are my own, I owe a great debt for most of the information in this chapter to Eva Cantarella, *Bisexuality in the Ancient World,* Trans. Cormac O'Cuilleanain (New Haven, CT: Yale University Press, 1992); Mark Strasser Wardel, et al. *Marriage and Same-Sex Unions: A Debate* (Westport, CT: Praeger, 2003); and especially to Louis Crompton, *Homosexuality & Civilization* (Cambridge, MA: Belknap Press of Harvard University, 2003). Additional helpful information was found in Arlene Swidler, ed. *Homosexuality and World Religions* (Valley Forge, PA: Trinity Press, 1993).

2. Quoted in Crompton, 51.

3. Ibid., 6–10, 69–70.

4. Ibid., 80.

5. Ibid., 87–88.

6. Ibid., 101.

7. G. G. Ramsay (translator), *Juvenal and Persius* (revised edition) (Cambridge, MA: Harvard University Press, 1940), 19.

8. Juvenal's satires are also discussed by Crompton, 104–105.

9. Crompton, 170–172.

10. Ibid., 204.

11. Quoted in Crompton, 187.

12. Ibid., 209.

13. Quoted in Crompton, 213.

14. Crompton, 243.

15. Ibid., 295–299.

16. Ibid., 247–251.

17. Quoted in Crompton, 250.

18. Crompton, 254.

19. See Crompton, 355–360, and Virginia Buckley, *Queen Christina of Sweden: The Restless Life of a European Eccentric* (New York: HarperCollins, 2004).

20. Quoted in Crompton, 516.

21. Quoted in Crompton, 518.

22. Quoted in Crompton, 525.

23. See the excellent, thoroughly documented discussion by Robert M. Baum, "Homosexuality and the Traditional Religions of the Americas and Africa," in Swidler, 1–46.

# 3

# The Emergence of a Homosexual Subculture and Gay Liberation Movements

Until recently, homosexuality existed only on the periphery of the consciousness of most Americans. It was neither a problem nor an issue of concern. Suddenly it seems everywhere, celebrated on television and discussed in news magazines. How could Americans, in only a few decades, move from oblivion regarding homosexuality to a possible recognition of same-sex marriage?

Because same-sex marriage is such a startling idea for millions of people, it is helpful to review the steps that have led many to accept its inevitability. Before modern times, it is difficult to speak meaningfully of a gay subculture. People in the ancient world did not identify themselves as homosexual, even when they had same-sex lovers with some frequency. Apart from subcultures isolated from the dominant society—entertainers and performers in some countries, religious officiates in others—no group defined itself by a particular sexual style. In the modern period, this changes, and self-identified homosexual groups emerge, with their own styles and cultural markers. Opera, ballet, and figure skating have been specified as particularly expressive of homosexual aesthetics. Gays were among the most devoted fans of performers such as Judy Garland, Marilyn Monroe, and Edith Piaf. Self-identified gay choruses have made acclaimed recordings. Homosexuals have established their own charitable institutions, sporting events, newspapers, and social programs. Resorts and cruise lines seek their patronage, and a squad from Madison Avenue targets them as a lucrative market for products. Many advertisers and merchants have acknowledged a powerful potential same-sex marriage market.

We do well to avoid stereotyping any group of individuals, and in an era of political correctness there is always the risk of being labeled "homophobic" through any generalizations about homosexuals. In and out of the closet, homosexuals are farmers, police officers, truck drivers, plumbers, teachers, community leaders, and community followers all over the country. The majority live quietly and do not identify themselves with any movement or subculture.

Those who are vocal in affirming solidarity have been most responsible for the notable changes in social attitudes. The actively gay communities in cities have developed some recognizable features that give the subculture its character. While gays and lesbians teaching in public elementary and secondary schools typically keep a low profile, homosexual teachers flourish in the freer milieu of large universities, where the clients are usually young people, known to be more accepting and often in revolt against conventional attitudes of parents and society. Homosexuals are a large presence in the arts and make significant contributions in literature, theater, architecture, design, and fashion. Andrew Sullivan suggests that many gays are preoccupied with superficial appearances; hence their strong sense of form and style.[1] Again, it is probably because of their status as outsiders that homosexuals frequently express a different tone in their artistic expression—an archness and irony that becomes a way of examining reality. Decades ago, Susan Sontag analyzed "camp" in popular culture as a unique way of perceiving that results from the vision of the outsider, the homosexual, or member of an ethnic minority.[2]

Sociologically, a subculture is a group that shares certain values and habits and feels a sympathy that sets its members apart from the larger society in which they live and work. Some sociologists deny that gay people form a genuine subculture, but it seems that those who live in urban areas and consciously follow "the gay life-style" with some degree of openness do form a recognizable community. One young homosexual man moving to Minneapolis from a small town in Minnesota, where he was stigmatized by family and church, was amazed at how fast events moved within the big-city gay community. Acquaintances were made quickly and romantic adventures were immediately available. Networking was established, so that employment could be located expeditiously. There was even a sympathetic priest in whom he could confide. Within a few weeks, the new arrival had a wide circle of acquaintances and had found a steady partner. In the evenings and on weekends, the inner city of Minneapolis was a grid of gay bars and other entertainments; by day, gay bookstores and coffee houses were meeting places. Life in the city was definitely gay-welcoming. When this young man traveled to Europe, he discovered an international gay society flourishing in major cities.[3]

## GERMANY

Many historians of the movement believe that modern gay culture began in late-nineteenth-century Germany. Although the Levenstrecht organization in Holland in the 1930s may have been first to systematically advocate a distinct and open subculture, Germans were pioneers in developing a "homophile" rights movement, and German sexologists were first in attempts to document gay courtship patterns. Activists such as Karl Heinrich Ulrichs, Magnus Hirschfeld, and Adolf Brand worked to liberalize laws in Weimar Germany. Sigmund Freud (1856–1939) in neighboring Austria, and Richard von Krafft-Ebing (1840–1902) in Germany theorized about the causes of "inversion," and also used their influence to bring about more compassionate attitudes toward homosexuals.

The important Weimar German cities, most notably Berlin, became hubs of gay subculture, and the gay sensibility, still difficult to define but somehow unmistakable, permeated the arts and intellectual life. Transvestite balls, over three hundred "cruising" clubs, and bohemian cafes were familiar meeting places. Even the Kaiser was said to have been surrounded by homosexual retainers, much as the British royal family has been in recent years. It was in this environment that the term "homosexual," a very modern word, came into use. Gay men and lesbians came to Berlin from England and from all over the continent to experience the freedom and to enjoy the cabarets, along with a theater that specialized in plays with gay themes, performed by gay or gay-sympathetic actors. Magazines geared to the subculture's interests were sold all over the city. From this milieu came such celebrated performers as Lotte Lenya and Marlene Dietrich—who in the Hollywood of the 1930s and 40s wore a tuxedo and kissed a woman on the lips in one of her films. For a picture of gay life in the Weimar Republic, one can read Christopher Isherwood's *Berlin Diaries,* from which the play *I Am a Camera* and the film *Cabaret* were adapted.

This Golden Age of gay artistic revelry came to an abrupt end with the advent of Nazism in the early 1930s. The magazines were banned, the institutes of sexual research were closed, books were burned, and within a short time thousands of gay men would be carted off to concentration camps, where most of them died. Lesbianism had never been a crime in Germany, yet known lesbians, some of whom were Jewish and of liberal political persuasion, were arrested on other charges. Although homosexuals are believed to have remained active, even in the Nazi party itself, the subculture could no longer openly exist. Those who were able, including many artists and intellectuals, escaped Nazi-controlled lands. Others simply vanished. It was not until the 1970s that gay life could openly resume in both East and West Germany, and even then, it was with much public disapproval.

## FRANCE

In nineteenth-century France, the life of gay individuals was uncertain, their status ambiguous. Paris had a reputation for tolerance of the bohemian life, people from all over Europe and the New World flocked to Paris to escape repression in their own countries, and French writers—Honoré de Balzac, Charles Baudelaire, Paul Verlaine, among others—gave a certain glamour to gay relationships in their writing. Still there was much popular hostility in the land that gave a name to "the bourgeois sensibility." Life for a prosperous homosexual in Paris, however, could have been pleasant; there were lesbian restaurants and Turkish baths catering to gay men, where eager attendants spoke all languages.

Into the twentieth century, Paris remained the choice destination for bohemians of all sorts, whether gay, lesbian, bisexual, or heterosexual. Jean Cocteau, Colette, Andre Gide, Marcel Proust, and Simone de Beauvoir are some of the names associated with this liberated artistic and intellectual community, ready to experiment with all sexual styles. Gertrude Stein maintained her salon in Paris, where she entertained the major expatriate writers of the time, while her partner, Alice V. Toklas, distracted their wives. As elsewhere, this open society was strictly an urban phenomenon. Away from the cities, French attitudes toward homosexuality remained truly provincial.

After World War II, and still centered in the cities, a gay liberation movement developed that was closely associated in France with Marxism and Existentialism. In France, Marxism was an intellectual movement, and its leaders, who were free thinkers, would not have fared well in the more seriously Marxist countries of East Europe and China, which were repressive sexually as well as politically.

Closely associated with the arts and letters, gay cultural life has expanded in the major cities of France into the twenty-first century. The media have participated, and when the Internet arrived, the French became leaders in what has been designated queer cyberspace.

## ENGLAND

Throughout the nineteenth century and into the early twentieth century, homosexuality was identified throughout continental Europe as "the English vice." This reputation, possibly unearned, appears to have developed out of the many tales of British schoolboy life and through the notoriety of

Oscar Wilde (1854–1900). The very image of the urbane, flamboyant, ironic homosexual, Wilde was a talented writer whose *succès de scandale*, *Salome*, was written initially in French and has been called "an exercise in fleur de mal decadence." Although Wilde had married at the age of 29 and fathered two boys, he was predominantly homosexual. He enjoyed outraging society and had a bon mot for every situation. On his deathbed, he is said to have frowned at the garish walls in his sickroom and announced: "Either that wallpaper goes, or I go."

While the British savored Wilde's wit, he exhausted their tolerance in his affair with Lord Alfred Douglas, his adored "Bosie," an aristocrat almost twenty years younger than himself. Bosie and Wilde habituated houses of male prostitution without discretion. After altercations with the younger man's father, Wilde was brought to trial twice and, the second time, he was found guilty of violating Britain's morals laws and sentenced to two years of hard labor in Reading Gaol. Wilde was characteristically eloquent and quotable at his trial, speaking of the "love that dare not speak its name . . . beautiful, . . . fine, . . . the noblest form of affection. There is nothing unnatural about it."[4] The harsh conditions of his imprisonment, especially difficult for a dandy who enjoyed the good life, gave Wilde the status of martyr for the gay cause, a position he firmly holds today. His plays are still performed, his fairy tales are favorites with children, and *Salome* inspired a popular opera by Richard Strauss.

Although Wilde's plight was everywhere discussed, it was an English woman who represented the epitome of Edwardian revolt. Marguerite Antonia Radclyffe-Hall (1880–1943), born into a wealthy if neglectful family, devoted herself to writing poetry and novels, conducting affairs with prominent women, and living luxuriously in the lesbian enclaves of London and Paris. She was well versed in the sexual psychology of her day, having studied Krafft-Ebing and Havelock Ellis, and she labeled herself a "true invert." She regarded herself as a man captured in a woman's body. Today we might classify her more as a transsexual than as a lesbian, based on her self-analysis.

Radclyffe-Hall, who was striking in appearance, wore severely tailored suits under a black military cloak. She cropped her hair, affected a monocle, and carried an elegant cigarette holder. Her critics called her "a woman masquerading as a man," though she always wore skirts in public and never attempted to actually disguise herself as a man. It became her habit to attend first-nights at the theater with her companion Una Troubridge, whom she had wooed away from a distinguished husband. With her companions and properly attended by servants, she moved in literary and artistic circles, maintaining an artistic salon in her drawing room.

The book for which she became known, even infamous, was *The Well of Loneliness,* an autobiographical novel that, even today, ranks as the preeminent lesbian fiction despite its antiquated psychology, stereotypical butch-femme characterizations, and sentimentality. Not surprisingly, the book almost immediately upon publication faced censorship problems, both at home and abroad. Though never renouncing her lesbianism, Radclyffe-Hall in later years converted to Roman Catholicism and wrote sentimental religious ballads, including "The Blind Plowman," which, set to music, became a favorite concert encore for the great Russian basso, Fedor Chaliapin, and the American film baritone, Nelson Eddy.

While laws against "buggery" were passed in England, female homosexuality was presumed not to exist, even though there was a highly visible and vocal community of lesbians in London, where, despite the law, a network of bars catered to the large artistic and intellectual gay community of both genders. It is said that Queen Victoria was responsible for the freedom from legal oppression that lesbians enjoyed. Allegedly, the queen decreed women incapable of such actions; therefore, laws against lesbianism would be superfluous. Reformers started agitating for gay rights in the late nineteenth century, but laws against sodomy were enforced, sporadically, into the 1950s. Nevertheless, gay life continued to flourish in the theater and other arts. Even service in the royal household came to be viewed as a sort of gay profession. The contemporary gay rights movement in England was fully underway by the 1960s, greatly influenced by its rapidly developing American counterpart.

## THE UNITED STATES

In 1908, when Edward Prime Stevenson wrote *The Intersexes: A History of Similisexism as a Problem of Social Life,* he used a pseudonym, so delicate was his subject. He appears to have been the first to openly identify and describe a substantial gay male subculture in American cities. By the middle of the twentieth century, the center of international gay and lesbian subculture had shifted to the United States, as America became more and more the pacesetter and purveyor of popular culture for the Western world. American tastes and values came to dominate the worldwide media, first through motion pictures and later through American television programs, shown dubbed in other languages worldwide. At the same time, American cities—particularly New York and San Francisco—became cultural metropolises for gay and lesbian people. Here one could live shielded from the ire of families back in the provinces, while finding companionship and solidarity with hundreds of like-minded people. Here the bars, bath houses, bookstores, and publications were important in forging the sense of community.

Harry Hay, often called the father of the gay and lesbian movement, founded the Mattachine Society in the United States, which organized the first public protests against police harassment in the 1950s. The Daughters of Bilitis, brought together by Del Martin, Phyllis Lyon, and six other women, was the first lesbian organization in the United States.[5] These societies, which struggled for fair treatment in employment and housing and freedom from harassment, had to be cautious in the early years, and their activists frequently employed pseudonyms in their writing. Eventually the organizations adopted plans to educate the broader population, working to provide a more accurate public understanding of homosexuality. Initially they were not striving for radical change, merely tolerance.

The gay liberation movement of the United States generally dates from the Stonewall riots in Greenwich Village in 1969.[6] After the limited but decisive early successes of the movement, the more assertive slogan coined by Frank Kameny, "Gay is good," was widely used. In the later decades of the twentieth century, homosexual enclaves started appearing in many smaller North American cities, along with gay bookstores and numerous local publications. Agitation and changing social attitudes resulted in the gradual liberalization of state laws against sodomy.

Demonstrations—by the 1960s familiar spectacles as many marginal groups took to American city streets with their "nonnegotiable demands"— gave gays direction, focus and visibility. The gay pride parades that started in New York in 1969 became regular celebrations of gay life, spreading throughout North America and elsewhere. All manner of folk came out to view the spectacle. Aggressive segments of the gay population staged in-your-face demonstrations, sacrilegious displays, and confrontations on the steps of St. Patrick's Cathedral in New York, but most marchers simply enjoyed the festive occasions.

By the end of the 1960s many proposals were being advanced for the protection and betterment of gay Americans. One was Don Jackson's plan for a gay colony to be established in Alpine County in California. The media gave his idea ample coverage, and the notion of segregating gays and lesbians had a certain appeal for the general population. However, communes have rarely been successful for very long in the United States, and homosexuals were too deeply intertwined in mainstream life to make the plan viable.

In American cities, the question frequently posed by Andrew Sullivan has become meaningful: "What are homosexuals for?" Sullivan's view of gay life in the United States has been straightforward and honest. He has found values in the homosexual subculture, discovering insights from which the rest of society could well benefit. He has praised the sexual candor, "the lack of formal moral stricture" found among his associates. The awareness of being apart from the mainstream of society, he believes, has contributed a special clarity of vision. Most, though certainly not all, gay people are free of the responsibilities of childrearing. Their time and money is more nearly their own. Their parental instincts may productively be redirected toward the broader social good. Gays and lesbians, Sullivan believes, can become especially effective teachers, mentors, nurses, doctors, priests, rabbis, nuns, and social workers. Vocations that require an almost total dedication are good fits for gay people. Since antiquity, the military has provided a special milieu for male comradeship to flourish. Military life demands sacrifices that are often difficult for a person with family responsibilities. Likewise, university careers may be highly demanding and not conducive to family life, as high divorce rates in academia confirm. Substantial achievement in sports or any of the arts requires a single-minded concentration that may be difficult for one with family responsibilities.

Of course, Sullivan has put forth precisely the arguments often made for the selection of celibate individuals for these demanding roles. Ironically, considering the controversies of recent years over coaches and scout leaders, he suggests this "displacement of family affection" is appropriate for service in Little League and the Boy Scouts.[7] And Sullivan's argument, as he attempts to carve out a special role for homosexuals, would seem to undermine their demand for full marriage rights.

The reality of gay life in America near the end of the twentieth century was at odds with Sullivan's optimism. A tone of pessimism crept into some of his later writing. He conceded that gay life had become more somber, as he and his friends attended one funeral after another, while their heterosexual counterparts were celebrating weddings and baptisms. Writing in the midst of the AIDS crisis, he acknowledged: "Homosexuals in contemporary America tend to die young; they sometimes die estranged from their families; they die surrounded by young death, and by the arch symbols of cultural otherness."[8]

Many observers of the gay scene have noted the strength of friendships, in bonds that often exceed the more casual circles of friends that surround married couples. This supporting network that the community builds as its protection against the hostility of the outside is reassuring. Its ability to bridge the usual gaps that separate age, race, ethnic and class divisions is commendable. Yet observers are also quick to note that gay subculture is never smoothly monolithic; it sometimes has difficulty uniting its highly diverse segments to lobby for specific goals. Racial tensions and conflicts between men and women are evident in the gay as well as in the straight community. These are people who identify themselves as rebels, individualists, as people who make independent decisions and march to a different drummer.

By the 1990s a definite gay subculture had been so well identified in the United States that manufacturers and advertisers were targeting the market with distinctively designed products and ploys. Some advertisers have designated this demographic as "the last untapped minority market." It is widely assumed—though the data are contradictory—that gay people are better educated than average, earn more, and, because most of them lack family responsibilities, have more disposable income. To reach this lucrative market, it is necessary to determine the tastes and aspirations of gay people and then provide goods and services that most appeal to them. It is in good part the resulting market research that has provided the most detailed information about the current gay subculture in the United States. Alexandra Chasin has effectively summarized this information in her book *Selling Out, 2000.*[9]

Gays, no less than other Americans, are part of a consumer society. Like any community, this one identifies itself in part by the products it buys and the institutions it supports. Gay activists have quickly learned the power of the economic boycott. They can easily forgo orange juice when they find themselves attacked by a Florida orange juice spokeswoman. They can refuse to purchase a brand of tea when they do not like the employment policies of its makers. In the 1990s, boycotts were instituted against Bank of America for contributions to the Boy Scouts of America, which does not allow homosexuals to become scout leaders, and Marlboro cigarettes, because of contributions to the Jesse Helms Museum. Attempts, at least on a regional level, to boycott Cracker Barrel restaurants were not very successful, perhaps because the restaurant's clientele, Midwestern families, were not particularly sympathetic to gay concerns. Purchasing power and the influence that goes with it are evident in all the activities through which the gay community has found solidarity: the house parties, drag balls, bathhouses, bars, bookstores, reading material, movies, plays, operas, and ballets. Now the Internet further connects the vast anonymous gay population, alerting it to issues of concern.

Advertising, with its enticing appeals and attractive models, has done much to create the idea of a gay nation and to give it pizzazz. In slick advertisements, cruise lines show handsome young women walking hand in hand on tropical beaches and looking longingly into each other's eyes on moonlight deck walks. The gay man, so advertisers believe, is busy enjoying the good life, with his vacation home, private club membership, home theater system, notebook computer, and his 15 or more domestic flights each year. This prototypical gay man is an avid reader of quality, especially avant-garde books; he patronizes health clubs and hairdressing salons, and he dresses imaginatively in Armani suits. The lesbian, though generally less affluent, is inclined to be better educated than her straight counterpart, and she also chooses quality products.

With the arrival of same-sex marriage, the North American wedding industry has been quick to recognize a potentially lucrative, expanding market. Elaborate gay and lesbian wedding celebrations are growing in popularity. Jewelers provide specially designed wedding rings, some with the rainbow motif that symbolizes gay pride. Food, transportation, flowers, honeymoon retreats—all the commodities that are deemed essential for the nuptial extravaganza—are now proffered to same-sex couples.

Other gay products proliferate. The rainbow flag originated in 1978 to symbolize the movement. Jesse Jackson's rainbow political coalition, which was to include gays and other disadvantaged groups, used the rainbow image that continues to be associated with gay pride. It may be purchased on a variety of products, including jewelry, T-shirts, mugs, and clothing.

But the special clothes and commodities, or the more serious engagement with especially designed books, ballets, and opera, are not what give the gay community its identity. The most important function of gay subculture is activism. The first priority has been to achieve social tolerance for gays and lesbians and, after that, to demand absolute equality with straight society before the law and in polite company. The successes of gay rights movements in Northern Europe can be observed in the legal recognition of civil unions and same-sex marriage that has already been achieved in the Netherlands, Belgium, Spain, and Scandinavia. While the gay rights organizations in the United States have attracted much attention and have made progress, their ultimate goals are not yet achieved.

The AIDS pandemic of the 1980s brought many changes to the gay community. Gay activism became a more pressing concern than cultural expression. Although bathhouses closed in many cities and a note of caution crept into the gay cruising scene, the epidemic only made the subculture more determined to assert its rights. The social action program expanded to include equality and recognition in the military services, the passage of domestic partnership laws, and, finally, the demand for the full benefits and acknowledgment of same-sex marriage. This demand came earlier than most people expected, and the successes already achieved have been startling to many and encouraging to the movement.

## NOTES

1. Andrew Sullivan, *Virtually Normal: An Argument about Homosexuality* (New York: Vintage Books, 1995), 198–199. Sullivan attempts the difficult—and controversial—task of identifying a homosexual sensibility.

2. Susan Sontag's penetrating "Notes on Camp," originally appearing in the early 1960s, has been frequently republished. See "Notes on Camp," in Susan Sontag, *Against Interpretation* (New York: Picador, 200).

3. Based on a personal interview with a source who wishes to remain anonymous.

4. Quoted by Steve Hogan and Lee Hudson in *Completely Queer: The Gay and Lesbian Encyclopedia* (New York: Henry Holt, 1998), 577. See also Richard Ellman, *Oscar Wilde* (New York: Vintage, 1988).

5. Hogan and Hudson, 172–173. The name for this organization was inspired by a fictional work by Pierre Louys, *The Songs of Bilitis*, published in France in 1894.

6. For information on the Stonewall riots, see Hogan and Hudson, 526–527. For the complete record, see David Carter, *The Riots that Sparked the Gay Revolution* (New York: St. Martin's Press, 2004).

7. Sullivan, 201.

8. Ibid., 193.

9. Alexander Chasin, *Selling Out: The Gay and Lesbian Movement Goes to Market* (New York: Palgrave, 2000), 29–40; 113–118.

# 4

# The Argument for Same-Sex Marriage

## THE LEGAL, SOCIAL, AND PERSONAL CASE

The argument for same-sex marriage has been made by some of the most persuasive voices in society. This chapter presents their chief points, sometimes in their own words.

Legally married people in the United States derive, simply by virtue of their civil status, more than 1,049 benefits. The most important of these are a variety of fringe benefits that employers regularly make available to the spouses of their workers, including health care, educational stipends, insurance, and child or elder care assistance. Spouses are frequently granted leave to care for one another or their children during illness. The law also extends preferential treatment to married couples. They are allowed to make medical decisions for one another; they have automatic inheritance rights, social security benefits, and the opportunity to file joint tax returns. Respecting marital confidentiality, they are not required to testify against one another in courts of law. The foreign spouse of a U.S. citizen has immigration rights. Married couples may live anywhere they can afford, and they are legally protected from landlord discrimination. In the case of divorce, couples have child custody rights and numerous other protections that cushion the economic and, to a degree, the emotional consequences of ending a relationship.

Being married carries status. Married men and women gain identity, more social respectability, and more legitimacy in the eyes of the law and general public. Although marriage is widely believed to provide protection and security to women, many of whom have not achieved social and economic equality, men also benefit from the relationship. Men who live alone are more likely to commit crimes. They are more susceptible to mental and physical sickness, alcoholism, and many other personal and social pathologies. Employers have long regarded marital status as a sign of stability and trustworthiness in men. Even in the day when the few women who worked were expected to remain single, many of the same employers preferred or demanded men they hired to be married. Society has always been more comfortable with the submergence of sexuality into the integrated, regularized life that marriage represents.

Through marriage, two families are united, and young people become full participants in the concerns of their community. The major events in the lives of most people, after all, are birth, marriage, and death: "hatched, matched, and dispatched," as people used to say. A wedding is a very public commitment, supported not merely by law but by the expectations of a couple's entire circle of acquaintances. It is important that this occasion be sealed by ceremony, public vows, rites, and, for most people, prayers. Participating in the rite, the friends of a couple present carefully chosen gifts that frequently become mementos that are cherished throughout the marriage and lives of the pair.

The United States has strong principles of equal rights for all people. Thomas Jefferson's addition to John Locke's enumeration of God-given human rights has been accepted without much question. For many, the pursuit of happiness includes marriage. In the last half of the twentieth century, civil rights agitation touched almost every American minority and even a few disadvantaged majorities. Laws were passed to ensure the rights of African Americans, Native Americans, the elderly, the young, the handicapped, and women. Recent decades have seen much interest in the idea of diversity. The argument for same-sex marriage asserts that it is hypocritical to deny the full rights and opportunities of citizenship—which includes access to an institution as basic as matrimony—to a small but significant portion of the population that does not conform sexually to the majority.

Depriving homosexuals of the right to legally marry means more than simply withholding legal privilege. They are denied that seal on love, that recognition of equality and inclusion in the mainstream of community and history that heterosexuals automatically enjoy. Relationships are always difficult to maintain over long periods of time, and heterosexual marriages would be more fragile than they are if they were not buttressed by laws of church and state, demands of extended families, and community expectations.

Prohibiting same-sex marriage deprives a couple of the stability that is granted when their decision to live together and care for one another is acknowledged by everyone they know, when there is a public vow that responsibilities will be honored, even when they become onerous and difficult. To deprive same-sex couples of these seals of commitment not only discriminates against them but adversely affects all the people—children and aging parents alike—who may be dependent upon the couple. A third of same-sex couples rear children and many of them care for elderly parents but without the assistance that is frequently and generously provided officially married couples.

The failure to recognize same-sex marriage and promote its stability also imposes a burden on the state, and this may be the most serious argument in favor of legal recognition. Society needs to promote secure, permanent relationships, whatever the gender of the people involved. Married couples are more productive, and the general economy benefits. Marital partners provide for one another, putting less strain on social services. They eat better and have better general health, and this means that they make fewer demands on an already overburdened health care system. Regular partners are less likely to have sexually transmitted disease, engage in risky sexual behavior, or allow problems resulting from any lapses to go unchecked. These facts are supported by numerous sociological studies.[1]

Discrimination against gay couples who wish to be married is, first and foremost, a violation of their civil rights and a denial of their constitutional claim to equal treatment as U.S. citizens. Such discrimination is often likened to the prohibition on interracial marriage that was once widespread in the American South and is still on the law books in the state of Alabama—although it has been declared unconstitutional and has long been a dead letter.[2] In the late 1950s, on the eve of the Civil Rights movement, the governor of Tennessee, Frank Clement, stated on national radio that segregation was the will of a divinity who had placed the white man in Europe and the black man in Africa, segregated by a wide ocean. Some day, proponents believe, the arguments against homosexual marriage will seem as primitive.

The arguments in favor of same-sex marriage seem clear and reasonable to proponents. It is not only unfair, but illogical to define marriage by exclusion, as is currently done in 49 states. Valid marriage can exist between two people of different races, ages, religions, and ethnic groups, but it cannot serve the needs of two committed individuals simply because they are of the same sex. Marriage is legal when a man and woman decide—perhaps on the spur of the moment, even if under the influence of various legal or illegal substances—that they wish to be man and wife. Men and women may marry and divorce many times, in what has been designated by social scientists as serial monogamy. Criminals incarcerated in state prisons may marry. The courts have confirmed this right and even sometimes have allowed conjugal visitation. The marriage of James Earl Ray, one of the most notorious criminals in American history, in prison for life for the murder of Dr. Martin Luther King, Jr., was solemnized in Brushy Mountain State Prison in Tennessee. Murderers, rapists, child molesters, and registered sex offenders of all sorts are allowed to marry. Brittany Spears may have a twenty-four hour marriage. Elizabeth Taylor may go down the aisle eight times. While many ephemeral forms of marriage are tolerated, gay people, even those who have been committed to one another over decades and are thoroughly law-abiding, remain outside the institution. Only in Massachusetts, in the United States, may two people of the same sex affirm their union before the law, and even that hard-earned right is currently subject to the threat of public referendum.

The courts in Hawaii, Vermont, and Massachusetts, when called upon to examine same-sex marriage discrimination in light of their state constitutions, rejected this inequity. Canada, Belgium, the Netherlands, and Spain have concluded that civilized society can no longer defend this injustice. Agencies of the European Union and United nations are debating resolutions demanding equality of treatment for same-sex couples.[3]

In presenting their case for this basic human and civil right, advocates of same-sex marriage must respond to the many objections raised by their opponents. It is instructive to examine these objections and the responses to them. The first and most central objection, which must be confronted in every discussion of this issue, is that marriage will be redefined. By introducing into one of the oldest human institutions untried elements, all the accumulated wisdom of humankind would appear to be defied. It would make marriage, which has proven reasonably satisfactory to billions of people through the ages, an institution no longer recognizable. Yet these revolutionary changes would accommodate the perceived needs of a small minority of people.

In response to this admittedly powerful objection, defenders point to the research of anthropological and family historians who have documented their findings that marriage in history has never conformed neatly to any particular pattern. It is a culturally determined style of living that has been malleable to the needs of many different peoples and periods of history. Even the Hebrew patriarchs most revered by the Judeo-Christian tradition had multiple wives and concubines. Harvard history professor John Boswell has presented what he believes to be documentation of same-sex commitment ceremonies in Roman Catholic and Eastern Orthodox Christian monastic communities in premodern Europe. Any argument that the marital institution must be frozen into a particular mold—regardless of advances in knowledge, changes in social attitudes and circumstances, and the actual ways in which people choose to order their lives—is doomed by the verdict of the very history often cited to support only the heterosexual model.

Even within U.S. history, a diversity of forms of marriage has been countenanced. Common-law marriage was widely accepted on the frontier during much of American history because of the absence of ordained clergymen and justices of the peace in many isolated communities. The fact that African slavery became established in the United States and existed here longer than in other Western countries had further impact on the institution of legal marriage. Initially the insecurity of slave families, whose members might be quickly separated and never see one another again resulted in a less formal family structure. Later, many freed slaves chose not to marry legally because they were hesitant to leave a paper trail. Added to all this was the family instability caused by poverty, deprivation, and lack of education. It did cost something to get a marriage license, and one might have to endure the derision and arrogance of local functionaries.

Native American tribes had distinct marriage laws and customs. And one of the scandals of the nineteenth century was Mormon polygamy, which ended (only in practice and Church discipline rather than in theology) under pressure from the federal government, when the territory of Utah sought to join the United States. Although the Mormon Church centered in Salt Lake City is in the forefront of the movement to support traditional monogamous marriage today, polygamy is still practiced in some small fundamentalist Mormon communities of Utah and surrounding states. Such polygamy is illegal, and its practitioners are excommunicated from the main body of the Mormon Church, but it has proven impossible to outlaw entirely.

Some students of marriage sociology assert that same-sex unions are not the novelty in human history that their opponents claim. In addition to citing the findings of Boswell, they have sought other examples in historical and anthropological studies. In 1951, in a seminal anthropological study, Yale professors Clelland S. Ford and Frank A Beach asserted that in over half of the societies they examined, same-sex activities of some type had been acceptable and sometimes formalized.[4] Yale professor William Eskridge claimed to have found same-sex and transgender unions in Nigerian tribal society as late as the nineteenth century. Among the communities that were discovered to have approved such relationships, even if in a limited way, were pre-Columbians-South American, nineteenth-century Zuni, ancient Mesopotamian, ancient Egyptian, classical Greek, imperial Roman, and a wide variety of tribal groups in Asia, Africa, and the islands and continents of the Pacific.[5]

Admittedly, those who report the existence of sanctioned same-sex unions have not necessarily suggested that the societies where they existed should be considered appropriate models for our own. These researchers have usually been quick to concede that same-sex unions appear to have been tolerated only when clearly defined gender roles were not threatened. These societies made sure that women clearly understood what tasks were reserved for them, and it was almost always the men who were allowed to choose from a variety of family and sexual styles. Still, the findings present support for the normalcy of such unions in the communities where they existed.

Those who fear that any tampering with the institution of matrimony as we know it today—the union of one man and one woman—will lead to its demise speak apprehensively of "the slippery slope." If marriage is opened to same-sex partners, which pair or group of individuals will next demand admittance, and where will our innovations end? Perhaps polygamy won't be far behind. Perhaps groups of people will petition to be recognized as a matrimonial unit. Will young boys choose to marry their automobiles, young girls their horses?

The defenders of same-sex marriage state that these fears are based on fallacious thinking and are an example of the either-or fallacy and the fallacy of the excluded middle. If gays are allowed to marry, we will not suddenly be deluged with couples from the Man Boy Love Society besieging justices of the peace. Each change in marriage custom and law must first meet appropriate, even stringent tests. It is right that we are currently having this intense discussion of same-sex marriage, because established institutions must not be lightly changed upon the whims of the year or the decade. Society must answer a number of questions responsibly before it approves any innovation, especially in an area as basic as matrimony. Several questions must be answered positively. Will a change in custom and law promote state interests? Will it contribute to the health and happiness of the people involved? Is a contract such as marriage being made between two people who are legally capable of discernment, emotionally and intellectually able to commit to such a contract?

While conditions of life in the future may bring about any number of changes, it is safe to say that most of the old taboos will remain. Sexual relationships between adults and children, even if both parties appear to be consenting, are unlikely to reach any level of acceptance. Even if it can be proven that incest does not cause genetic defects, society is unlikely to tolerate incest because it would make the family lives of vulnerable youth intolerable. Although polygamy seems to have the sanction of Hebrew Scripture and much other authoritative literature and has been practiced in perhaps the majority of cultures, the very economic circumstances of people in the West today make it an unlikely option.

The third most important argument against same-sex marriage, after the historical and the "slippery slope," is the one most frequently made against homosexual practice of any sort: that it is contrary to nature and physically and psychologically destructive. Opponents of same-sex marriage find it difficult or impossible to dignify with the name of marriage a relationship that appears to them a violation of human physiology. Opponents believe that sexual acts between people of the same sex are contrived, often detrimental to health, and gross parodies of male-female unions. This improper use of the human body, critics further claim, is also inherently narcissistic. Same-sex partners choose mirror images of themselves rather than allowing themselves to experience the pleasure of joining with a compatible other, thus denying themselves a further exploration of human sexual potential. It is, therefore, not surprising that homosexuality or bisexuality is so prevalent in the performing professions, they add, because these occupations are by their very nature exhibitionistic. Critics are adamant that human bodies are simply not made for homosexual activity. Written laws cannot override the laws of nature.

The response to these objections comes quickly and decisively. The arguments against homosexuality oversimplify human anatomy, ignore the complexity of human beings, and reject the witness of history. A substantial number of individuals have always been sexually attracted to their own gender. Furthermore, same-sex conduct has been documented in several animal species. Though always a minority, there are some indications that homosexuals have remained a relatively constant percentage of the population throughout history, regardless of the society in which they have lived. To suggest that the human body is not designed for such activity is to deny the reality that it has always been so used. The argument that only heterosexual couples possess the physical equipment essential to complement one another in marriage has been eloquently answered by Carlos A. Ball, a professor of law at the University of Illinois and author of *The Morality of Gay Rights: An Exploration in Political Philosophy:*

The complementarily argument simultaneously diminishes marriage as an institution and spouses as individuals. The value of marriage arises . . . from the human needs and capabilities that it seeks to promote and protect, needs and capabilities that merit moral respect regardless and independently of gender.[6]

Ball goes on to assert that marriage encompasses the "full panoply of human complexity and diversity."[7] To reduce it to a simple matter of bodily organs, ignoring the range of emotional and spiritual aspirations that go into marriage, is to devalue it.

Closely aligned with this response is an increasing perception by the general public that homosexuality is an orientation rather than a choice. Liberated from the dubious psychological theories of the past, most homosexuals today do not find their inclinations and intimate expressions either "unnatural" or "immoral." Many insist that had they been given a choice, they would have chosen to be more like the general population. But the choice was not theirs; it was bestowed by Mother Nature or, for the more religiously inclined, by God. From early childhood these people have known that they were different. This difference, rather than an aberration of nature, is a central fact of their identity, possibly to be celebrated rather than hidden. While sexual conduct is under the control of the will (with the possible exception of compulsive individuals), homosexuality as an orientation is not a matter of choice.

It is not known what causes a person to be homosexual—or heterosexual, for that matter. Some have even speculated that God or nature has a special role for homosexuals. There have been several attempts to postulate an evolutionary explanation for homosexuality, though none of these theories has won general scientific acceptance. In ancient Crete, same-sex conduct increased when the island was threatened with overpopulation, suggesting the possibility that homosexuality is a natural corrective, essential for the survival of the race rather than a threat to it. Some pro-gay theorists have suggested that nature has designed certain individuals to be parents and others to assist parents as responsible guardians of others' children. These roles, it is alleged, have been observed in other primates, but it is unclear to what degree human behavior has mirrored it.

Some defenders of gay rights have stressed that sexuality does not neatly lend itself to bipolar division. While sexual orientation rarely appears to be a matter of choice, the inclinations of homosexual or bisexual people are not always constant. They may shift throughout a lifetime. There is vastly more complexity in the matter of choice of love object than is usually acknowledged. Although its results have been mixed and seem negative overall, some people claim that they have been changed by so-called reparative therapy, which may have limited success with those whose identities and orientations lack absolute and clear definition. Reparative therapy also claims greater success with women than with men, possibly because women's sexuality may be more fluid than that of men, or so the speculation runs. This would seem to indicate that we are wrong in our attempts to place people in a single category with an unqualified sexual label. With confirmed homosexuals, however, there appears to be little fluctuation throughout a lifetime, and reparative therapy has not met with much success. Counteracting the stereotypes many straight people have of homosexuals is a major struggle of the gay rights movement.

Opponents of same-sex marriage, including those who disapprove of homosexuals in general, sometimes viciously characterize them as degenerates and predators. At one time motion pictures fed these stereotypes, but a vast change has taken place in the last two decades and now more often than not motion pictures offer positive images of lesbians and gays and even sometimes present them in heroic contexts. But the stereotypes remain in the minds of many. Lesbians are stereotyped as man-hating, mannish, aggressive, unsightly shrews. A dominant image is that of the muscle-bound, cropped-haired physical education instructor lasciviously eyeing her young charges.

Paradoxically, many men find lesbians sexually enticing, as witnessed by pornography and the male erotic fantasies reported in the sexology literature.

Male homosexuals are stereotypically viewed as promiscuous, detached, sarcastic, and irresponsible. A common image is the gay man who has anonymous sex in a bathhouse or in the tough and menacing milieu of the leather bars. Another hostile stereotype that is still perpetuated by the media is that of the pervert who entices children, sometimes doing them bodily harm as well as destroying their innocence. An image recently reinforced by almost every newspaper is of the leering priest, in clerical collar, with dangling crucifix, looming over the bed of a terrified little boy. Although people exist who do embody these fears, the stereotypes are unfair to millions of homosexuals, the overwhelming majority of whom are law-abiding citizens, some of them conservatives, Republicans, and members of evangelical churches. These people lead honorable, productive lives, and most of them yearn for lasting relationships and social acceptance without the need to hide or dissemble. Excluding them from marriage causes great pain and pushes a few even farther into a life-style that is condemned. Loving relationships can best flourish and achieve fulfillment within marriage, a union recognized by family, community, and church.

Another argument, which opponents of same-sex marriage regard as conclusive, has to do with the rearing of children. Why does marriage exist in the first place, all over the world? Why do families encourage their members to marry, and often arrange marriages for them? Why do religions endorse marriage with special ceremonies? Why does the government grant so many rights to married people? The answer is quite simple, the argument goes, and it is difficult to refute. Marriages exist to bring children comfortably into the world, to nourish them, and to prepare them for useful and fulfilling lives in families of their own, in churches, and in nations. If children are not born into established families, who will perform the ancestral rites in religions that require them? Well-indoctrinated children will perpetuate whatever religion, system, or ideology is valued by the family and community into which they are born. Because married couples are expected to perform this crucial task of transmission of culture—training the next generation of productive citizens—governments and employers are willing to grant them many benefits.

Gay couples cannot conceive children, but they are indeed rearing children. In fact, in the last 15 years there has been a population boom in the gay community. Approximately one-third of households headed by a gay couple now have children in them, children born from previous heterosexual relationships or adopted (permitted gays in every state except Florida) or acquired through artificial insemination or surrogacy. These children are much desired, because parents have either fought in the courts for their custody or gone to extraordinary lengths to bring them into the world. And unlike so many American children who grow up in single-parent homes, these are attended by two loving parents. They are especially cherished, because gays do not generally give birth to children lightly and without forethought, as straight couples sometimes do. Gay parents often go to considerable expense and surmount legal hurdles to have these children and give them a loving home. And there is no clear evidence in the psychological or education literature that these children are disadvantaged by the alternative sexual orientation of their parents. There may, in fact, be some benefits in being reared by gay parents. Some studies have suggested that these children are less judgmental and more tolerant of differences among their playmates. Even if the community disapproves of the sexual practices of the parents, the children should not be denied the advantages society provides the offspring of heterosexual parents.

It might have made sense in the ancient world to stigmatize homosexual conduct, when infant mortality was high and human survival, so assaulted by disease and disaster, was at stake. Today the fate of humanity may still hang in the balance, but the overpopulation of the planet, with too many mouths to feed in some countries and global population doubling about every seven years, would appear to be the greater threat. Gays, even when they do have children, are not noted for irresponsibly contributing to this out-of-control population. Consequently, the argument that they cannot do their share in perpetuating the race has no merit. This argument might carry some weight in countries such as Italy and a few others in the European Union that lack native replacement populations and fear that their cultural identities may disappear, as immigrants from radically alien cultures must be imported merely to keep the industries functioning and the unpleasant tasks completed. Nevertheless, all the information leads to the conclusion that gays are doing their share in rearing the citizens of tomorrow, and often performing the task superbly; at the same time, they are not irresponsibly begetting children.

But this response still does not convince the skeptics. They believe that homosexuals, with their demand for legal marriage, are intensifying behavior that most people regard as offensive. Critics of same-sex marriage think that homosexuals have reduced human sexuality, designed to be procreative, to a mere hedonistic indulgence. The defense against these attacks comes quick and powerful; heterosexuals are the ones who have degraded sexual activity, creating a sexually obsessed culture in which recreational sex is the norm, with the added threat of bringing unwanted and neglected children into the world.

Acknowledging that since the middle of the twentieth century, sexual activity has been increasingly separated from procreation, gay advocates observe that as long as these changes worked for their benefit, heterosexuals did not object. Only the Roman Catholic hierarchy and a few ultra-conservative Protestants and Jews bucked the trend. The development of the contraceptive pill signaled the beginning of the sexual revolution for heterosexuals, who were apparently waiting for liberation from biological consequences before casting aside their own sexual taboos. With the development of in vitro fertilization, sperm banks, the legalization of abortion, and cloning, sexual conduct becomes less synonymous with begetting and conceiving. And even before all these developments, the Roman Catholic Church (still the West's greatest advocate of procreative sexual integrity) never sought to forbid sterile adults or postmenopausal women from matrimonial sexuality. Yet gays are singled out from all these nonprocreative groups and forbidden the same personal and social privileges?

Some of the most notable supporters of gay rights and same-sex marriage have been John Shelby Spong, retired Episcopal bishop of New Jersey; Jeffrey John, a London-based Anglican priest and lecturer in theology; Andres Kopppelman, professor of constitutional law at Northwestern University; Mark Strasser, professor of law at Capital University Law School in Columbus, Ohio; and Barbara J. Cox, professor of law at California Western School of Law and past chairperson of the Association of American Law Schools Section on Gay and Lesbian Issues. Quite often it is not argumentative logic that sways people as much as the sincerity and eloquence of persons who espouse the views presented. Same-sex marriage has some forceful spokespersons who know how to present the issues with clarity and persuasiveness. Of the advocates of same-sex marriages, perhaps none is more successful in reaching the undecided than Jonathan Rauch.

## THE ARGUMENT OF JONATHAN RAUCH

The widely published Rauch has been a correspondent for the *Atlantic Monthly,* a columnist for *National Journal,* and a writer-in-residence at the Brookings Institute. His work has appeared in *The New Republic, The Economist, Harpers, Reason,* and *Fortune,* and he has also written for a number of major newspapers, including the *New York Times,* the *Washington Post,* the *Wall Street Journal* and *Slate.* Washington-based, he is active in gay affairs, is in a committed relationship, and has written what is arguably the best book that exists on same-sex marriage, *Gay Marriage: Why It Is Good for Gays, Good for Straights, and Good for America.*

Rauch's approach is not to bemoan the mistreatment of homosexuals but to demonstrate what the regularizing of their unions could contribute to the welfare of the community and country. He knows how to speak to heterosexual audiences, constructing arguments that are so compelling that they must be seriously considered. Acknowledging what so many sociologists have observed, that marriage at the present time is a threatened institution Rauch further asserts that its demise would be a disaster. Equally unfortunate would be the acceptance of a wide range of proposed alternatives to marriage, such as cohabitation, domestic partnerships, and civil unions. He is a strong advocate of marriage as a permanent union of two people, and believes that same-sex marriage should not only be allowed but should be a social expectation of gay people who live together.

According to Rauch's calculation, gays and lesbians make up from three to five percent of the population. This would mean that between 9 million and 15 million Americans, a substantial minority, are gay in their primary orientation. They must be brought into the mainstream, he feels, so that their talents will be well used and they will be able to lead useful, respectable lives.

But Rauch, while advocating marriage for all, moves with caution into what he acknowledges is uncharted territory. He believes that only by proceeding slowly can major mistakes be avoided. Changes of such a momentous nature as the sanctioning of same-sex marriage cannot take effect in all places at once. People must be given an opportunity to know, see, and understand. Only then will they realize that extending marital recognition to homosexuals will strengthen rather than weaken the institution of marriage. Because of its federal system, its tradition of fairness, and its legacy of civil rights, the United States is the country best able to achieve this transition. Rauch suggests that same-sex marriage should first come state by state. Problems and legal issues we may not yet have anticipated can be spotted and confronted more easily in this limited setting. If the Supreme Court were to sweepingly declare same-sex marriage constitutional with all states immediately compelled to accept the decree, the effect would be catastrophic. The mores of a culture cannot be suddenly changed by law. If the courts require states to recognize same-sex marriage, while the community, with its churches and synagogues, does not, chaos and ill feeling will result.

Rauch believes that marriage, and the expectation of marriage among gay youth, would mitigate many of the problems the gay community now faces. Opponents of homosexuality complain of the transitory and promiscuous nature of many gay relationships. Yet without the bonds of marriage, the obligations publicly assumed, and the expectations of family and community, Rauch wonders how many heterosexual relationships would last. It is recognized marriage, he believes, that gives stability to intimate relationships, which need all the family, church, and community reassurance and support they can get.

Marriage, Rauch affirms, is the institution that best civilizes: "No other institution has the power to turn narcissism into partnership, lust into devotion, strangers into kin. What other force can bond across clans and countries and continents and even cultures?"[8] Marriage today is faced with many problems and must absorb revolutionary changes. The old sex role distinctions so basic to marriage law and public expectations are vanishing one by one. No-fault divorce means that marriages are often transitory, and many people are living together and even rearing children without giving their relationship official status. The courts have gradually narrowed the distinction between legal marriage and cohabitation, and marriage today is just about anything that a man and a woman agree that it is. Although most people still like the pomp and pageantry of a religious ceremony, some take their traditional vows with crossed fingers. Marriage in the United States in the twentieth century would be unrecognizable to people of most earlier periods of history.

But human needs have not changed. Robert Frost in one of his poems defined home as "the place where they have to take you in"; Rauch acknowledges Frost but redefines home as "the place where someone waits for you."[9] Marriage means that there is someone ready to drop everything and attend to you if a medical emergency occurs or if danger threatens. He believes marriage will become more cherished when it is opened to gays and lesbians.

Gay rights literature has stressed the deprivation of privileges that homosexuals suffer. Marriage now is underlined as the most serious of these deprivations. But Rauch stresses the obligations that marriage partners have always taken upon themselves. Married couples take care of one another in ways that impersonal charities, for all their good will, can never do. Rauch calls a spouse "the social worker of first resort, the psychiatrist of first resort, the cop and counselor and insurer and nurse and 911 operator of first resort."[10] Marriage is, more than anything else, today as always, a commitment that two people will assume responsibility for one another for a lifetime. To be married is to accept the problems of living intimately with another person, providing an anchor in a life filled with such changes that people can otherwise become disoriented and unstable. Society grants certain benefits and exemptions to married couples not simply because they may be parents, but because they have pledged to take care of one another, thus relieving the rest of the community of that responsibility.

Rauch believes that legally recognized and honored marriage will finally "close the book on gay liberation." All legitimate goals will have been achieved. There will be no more offensive floats in gay pride parades, no more obscene skits on the steps of St. Patrick's Cathedral, no more in-your-face tirades. The image of the homosexual as a sick member of society will gradually vanish when the respectability and civilizing influences of marriage are brought to bear. The focus will shift from achieving rights to accepting responsibilities. Marriage will be the last step toward maturity for the gay community, which will then cease to be "a separate and sometimes hostile sub-culture." While romantics might lament its demise, with its many artistic and intellectual achievements, Rauch believes that gay subculture, set apart from the mainstream, has become "marginalized and infantilized." Marriage will give gay relationships a clear direction, a calling. Full commitment and genuine affection in relationships will be supported and cultivated. The promiscuous life-style that straights find so offensive and many gays themselves shun will become as disreputable to them as heterosexual promiscuity is to the larger population. It is a recognized fact of gay life, even a matter for joking, Rauch observes, that when male partners settle down with permanent companions, they vanish from the swinging clubs, bathhouses, and riotous parties. Married gays will no longer drift in and out of the broader community but will gradually become a valued part of it. To be able to share "life's most sustaining institution" will make serious, committed citizens even of gays and lesbians who now feel alienated. This vision is, of course, idealistic, even utopian.

Rauch speaks in part from personal experience. He confides, as do the majority of homosexuals, that had he been given a choice at birth, he would have selected sexual conformity. He was not given that choice. Now, however, he works professionally in a receptive environment and, with social attitudes becoming more accepting, he finds his homosexuality only a minor inconvenience, much like left-handedness, he says.

But Rauch has the welfare of society at large on his mind. He is certain that when marriage is extended to homosexuals, the entire nation will reap benefits. When more people take responsibility for one another, in sickness and in health, for richer or poorer, social agencies are freed to more competently care for the remaining people who are truly alone and in need. Many straight people have been touched with the devotion that partners of AIDS patients have shown, often caring untiringly for their lovers during a last illness, though no social expectation or legal obligation was present. And this has frequently occurred when persons dying of AIDS have been rejected by their own kin. Rauch reminds readers that the gay world is "awash with many inspiring stories" of loving concern and sacrifice.

Rauch also examines that most powerful defense of traditional marriage—that it is the proper milieu for rearing children. But the question quickly arises: if society has such concern for the welfare of children, it must certainly acknowledge the substantial number of gay households that have them. Yet these children, no matter how devoted their gay parents may be to them, face discrimination in their peer groups, while their often-struggling parents lack many of the resources freely available to traditional parents. In the 2000 U.S. Census Bureau report, 594,000 same-sex households were recorded. From 28 to 30 percent included minor children. About a third of these families with children were parented by lesbian couples, and slightly over a fifth were headed by male couples.[11] While these parenting pairs will attempt to stay together and will continue to love their children even if they separate, only one parent in such a family is recognized as legal guardian. In the event of a breakup, the other "parent" has no rights at all. Should one of these partners die, the other may have great difficulty retaining custody of the children they both regarded as their own. While legal provisions can be made for this eventuality, such arrangements are often difficult to complete, time consuming, and expensive.

For these and many other reasons, marriage, Rauch believes, should not be a life-style choice among several equal options. It should be viewed as the norm, and responsible couples, both gay and straight, should be expected to move beyond cohabitation. Many gay couples, he concedes, will not hasten to the justice of the peace, because they have lived without marriage for so long. Marriage will come into acceptance gradually within the gay community. Some will never marry; others, like heterosexuals before them, will marry for the wrong reasons: money, security, social or professional advancement. One cannot expect more orderly conduct from a group that has so often faced disapproval of their relationships than one expects from heterosexuals, who have known none.

Rauch sees little merit in the "slippery slope" argument against same-sex marriage. He represents a conservative homosexual point of view that may, in fact, be more common than the in-your-face attitude of the more assertive activists in the homophile movement. There are many reasons, he contends, why both gays and straights will oppose polygamy and incest. People are not clamoring to marry "a sibling or a dog or a Volkswagon."[12] A liberal society that seeks the greatest good for the largest number of people will recognize that incest would make family life intolerable. Taboos against incest, though they have varied from society to society, are older than those against polygamy, and they will stand. Likewise, liberal society is almost certain to determine that the trend toward monogamy, which has been present in the West and, more slowly but certainly, in other regions of the world for two thousand years, is pragmatic. Not only will the economic circumstances of modern life and the strivings of Americans for equality and personal fulfillment continue to make polygamy unacceptable, but on a personal level, it is too great a task to make more than one spouse happy, and liberated women will never agree to share their husbands. Polygamy has never existed in lands where traditions of democracy and equality under the law flourish.

The argument from tradition, Rauch acknowledges, is a powerful one. Some lessons of history can be transmitted and do not have to be relearned by every generation. The hope of liberals and progressives is always that we may improve our institutions, correcting the mistakes of the past and transcending the ignorance of our ancestors. Here the acknowledgment that no society has totally or for very long given status to homosexual union confronts one bit of knowledge that appears to be unique to the twentieth century. We now generally recognize that homosexuality is not merely a behavior or a substitute when heterosexual partners are unavailable. Neither is it, at least for most individuals, an entertaining supplement to heterosexual relationships. We no longer consider homosexual experimentation merely a stage in sexual maturation. We now understand it to be a permanent condition for a constant percentage of people. This fact is not going to change; it has remained unchanged throughout history, as best as we can determine. While fashion may to a small degree dictate sexual behavior, the basic fact of orientation appears undeniable. Our present knowledge suggests that a modification in our past attitudes and customs is now reasonable, even essential.

Rauch knows that when we attempt to redesign society's bedrock institution we are placing ourselves in a precarious position. This proposed shift in the realm of marriage does not mean we think we are smarter than all the people who have gone before us or that we alone have the wisdom to rethink patterns of behavior established in prehistoric times. Marriage has already changed and had never been static. Today in the United States, marriages are no longer arranged by clans and families. People choose their own spouses. Dowries and bride prices are things of the past, at least in most of the western world. Even though someone still gives away the bride in formal church ceremonies, this is now simply a formality. The bride, who may have been living independently and earning her own living for years, essentially gives herself away. Marriage, for about half the population, is no longer a permanent state, despite the church-inspired vows most couples still take. No-fault divorce has changed the understanding of marriage, making it, for some, no more than a trial run. The changes in the laws regarding earnings and property remind us that the law no longer sees a married couple as one legal entity. Each party has his and her own rights and obligations, expects to control any inheritances that may be received, and is responsible for money earned. This makes marriage a union of equals rather than that of a provider and a dependant.

Throughout most of history people did not marry for love; they married because their families determined it was time for them to do so. When society moved from polygamy to monogamy, from arranged marriages to marriages for love, and from dowries and bride prices to financial independence of both spouses, it engaged in a more revolutionary action than the recognition of same-sex marriage could ever be.

Rauch's impressive book is witness to the fact that gay people often idealize marriage, a fairly common thought process when people are deprived of something they greatly desire. Certainly, many homosexuals wish to strengthen the institution even as they share in it, with legal recognition as the first step. However, many gays and lesbians feel that their marriages will never achieve par with heterosexual unions until religious as well as legal acceptance is achieved. Religious values have always been intertwined with matrimony all over the world, from primitive tribes to the most complex societies. Until priests, rabbis, ministers, and shamans can bless the union of same-sex couples, and parents and friends can smile and weep at their marriage ceremonies, many homosexuals will continue to regard themselves as second-class citizens.

## THE RELIGIOUS CASE

The United States today is widely recognized as the most religiously observant nation in the industrialized world. For this reason, it is essential to consider religious attitudes when issues as serious as marriage are examined. Interestingly, while the strongest arguments against same-sex marriage have come from religious sources, some of the most forceful proponents have also based their judgments on religious principles. Throughout history, marriage has been a religiously sanctioned contract and sometimes even a sacrament. Same-sex marriage will carry a taint until major religious organizations endorse it. Even in the secularized, post-Christian countries of Western Europe, couples still usually take their marriage vows in a church. And it is likely that the majority of homosexual individuals in Europe or the United States would choose to marry in the presence of the clergy.

With their general tendency to maintain continuity with the past and their vested interest in the children produced by heterosexual marriage, it may seem unlikely that major religions will soon accept same-sex marriage. Except for defiantly liberal sects, especially those that delight in confounding the fundamentalists, the orthodox, and the evangelicals, acceptance is at present unlikely. The Roman Catholic Church—the largest single religious body in the world and in the United States—is firmly on record as opposing homosexual practice. But a number of established branches of both the Jewish and Christian faiths have slowly but certainly moved in the direction of acceptance. And within a number of these faith communities that officially reject same-sex unions there are vocal groups advocating reform in the name of gay justice. Since the Abrahamic religions—Judaism, Christianity, and Islam—are the ones that touch the vast majority of North Americans, these are the ones to be first observed.

Within North American Islam today, Irshad Manji and her Canadian *Queer Television* cohorts often appear to be isolated voices.[13] Certainly, Islam, both in the United States and in the lands of its chief strength, has more pressing problems to contend with than same-sex marriage. Most Muslims dismiss the issue as another example of Western decadence, a distraction from the world's serious issues. But within Judaism and Christianity, there are several persuasive, pro-gay voices being heard.

### Judaism: The Argument of Rabbi Steven Greenberg

One of the most graceful religious spokespersons for gay respectability and a serious consideration of the viability of same-sex marriage is Rabbi Steven Greenberg. In his articles, speeches, and in a fine book he has shared his courageous and often poignant story of coming out as a deeply spiritual gay man with a religious calling. Although Rabbi Greenberg grew up in a secular, only nominally religious household in Ohio, he became in youth the protégé of a persuasive Orthodox rabbi. Enamored with the Torah, Greenberg enrolled in a philosophy program at Yeshiva University and eventually received his rabbinical ordination from the Rabbi Isaac Elchanon Theological Seminary. After serving an Orthodox congregation for several years and studying in Israel, he accepted a teaching fellowship at the National Jewish Center of Learning and Leadership, an independent organization dedicated to preparing Jewish leaders to relate ancient sacred tradition to the realities of modern life. Greenberg now associates himself with the movement known as "Modern Orthodoxy," which seeks to honor Jewish law and tradition while living in the modern world, accepting the benefits it has to offer, and contributing to it. Modern Orthodoxy does not eschew Gentile friendships, and Rabbi Greenberg genially approaches persons of all faiths. His personal struggle was supported by sympathetic Christian clergy, and he has in turn given comfort to Christians wrestling with the same problem. Identifying himself as the only openly gay rabbi in the history of Orthodox Judaism, he frequently speaks to university audiences, where he is noted for the clear, charitable presentation of his rather unique point of view.

In an affidavit submitted for use in Canadian law courts, when recognition of civil marriage for same-sex couples was being debated, Rabbi Greenberg presented his carefully reasoned position. His paper was in part a response to an earlier affidavit submitted by a more conservative Orthodox rabbi, David Novak, which presented the traditionalist Jewish position on homosexuality. Greenberg's response has become a classic gay religious defense. What he has to say about same-sex marriage from a Jewish perspective has much relevance to Christianity as well.[14]

Acknowledging that marriage as an institution has deep roots in every religious tradition, Greenberg explores the issues surrounding marriage from the perspective of Hebrew *halakah,* the law that Orthodox Jews attempt to honor. Although the Word of God is for eternity, Rabbi Greenberg reminds readers that the *halakah* has the task of reorganizing itself in response to the changing social realities of each generation of Jews. With its proper application constantly expanding, Jewish law must always be ready to interpret changing social situations without departing from its foundation principles.

At greater length in his book *Wrestling with God and Men,* Rabbi Greenberg makes a case for the acceptance of homosexuality within the traditional Jewish community. His argument is in most ways not unlike that advanced by Christians who want to make their own faith communities more inclusive. Rabbi Greenberg acknowledges his keen personal grief that Orthodox tradition has not yet advanced to the acceptance of gay and lesbian relationships in the same manner the larger society has. While some Reform Jewish temples have permitted same-sex commitment ceremonies, in Orthodox rites only a man and a woman may be properly married. Some compassionate individual rabbis have slowly achieved a measure of sympathy with the struggle of their gay and lesbian congregants, but the Orthodox rabbinate continue to regard homosexual practice as an abomination.

Rabbi Greenberg maintains the hope that eventually halakic strategies will evolve to better respond to the problems of gay Jews who want to be loyal to their faith. He believes that our new psychological understandings of homosexuality, along with the realization that gays are not willfully perverting divine intent, will hasten this time. At present, however, same-sex couples are among those prohibited from marrying in the Orthodox tradition. Others who likewise do not qualify include Gentiles who wish to marry Jews, divorcees or converts who wish to marry men within the Jewish priestly lineage, and children of an adulterous union. While these people still have recourse to the secular courts and may marry legally, same-sex couples in most places are denied this consolation.

Rabbi Greenberg reminds his congregants that, just as marriage is a product of civilization, Jewish law and traditions have adapted through the centuries. It is instructive to review the lives of the revered patriarchs of Israel, as recounted in Scripture. Abraham, the patriarch with whom God established an everlasting covenant, had sons by both his wife Sarah and his concubine Hagar. Jacob, the progenitor of the 12 tribes of Israel, had two wives—Rachel, whom he loved, and her less favored but more fecund sister Leah—in addition to two concubines. He had children by all of them, sons who gave their names to the 12 tribes of Israel. There are also instances in post-Biblical Jewish history, Rabbi Greenberg reminds readers, when even more questionable marital agreements were tolerated. A famed scholar of Talmud, named Rav, had the custom of requesting a wife for the day whenever he entered a new city.[15]

All these examples make clear that marriage, rather than being the same for all times and places in Jewish law and custom, has varied according to social context and the habits of peoples in the many parts of the world where Jews have lived.

Marriage in Judaism, as in other religions, has stressed the procreation and the rearing of children. After the European Holocaust in the twentieth century, which wiped out a third of the Jewish population of the world, the perpetuation of the people has appeared even more important. Yet, for the first time in their history, Jewish families are having fewer children than their Gentile neighbors. Even so, within Judaism, sterile and elderly couples unable to procreate have still been allowed to marry, and their unions are honored. It is, therefore, not the ability to procreate alone, important as it is, that creates and sustains a Jewish marriage.

Rabbi Greenberg is well aware of his precarious status within the Orthodox Jewish community. After his coming out, he was not surprised when an older scholar at Yesheva University declared "a gay Orthodox rabbi is an absurdity as inconceivable as an Orthodox rabbi who eats cheeseburgers on Yom Kippur. There is no such thing as a gay Orthodox rabbi."[16] Greenberg concedes that the usual Orthodox remedy for the homosexual who cannot be cured by "spiritual effort, moral will, or therapy" is a lifetime of celibacy. But he chooses rather to interpret the pertinent passages from Scripture that deal with homosexuality in light of his personal experience. In his book he carefully examines the Biblical passages pertinent to his plight. His reconstruction includes the Genesis narrative, with its explanation of gender and sexuality; the prohibitions of Leviticus, which label male homosexuality "an abomination;" and the account of the destruction of Sodom for wicked behavior. He then examines what is perhaps the greatest story of friendship in the Hebrew Bible: the bond between the shepherd from Bethlehem who became King David, and Jonathan, the son of his gravest enemy, King Saul. Greenberg approaches these Biblical texts with Talmudic knowledge and Hebrew linguistics tools.[17]

After examining the Genesis account of creation, where God gives Eve to Adam as a suitable mate, Rabbi Greenberg concludes that homosexuals "are either horrible corruptions of God's intention or variations of God's creative genius."[18] Jewish mystics have taught that all creation aspires to become like God, in whom the fullest procreative principle resides, where male and female components are not differentiated. One possible reading of the Genesis creation account of the first human parents, with ample rabbinical precedent, suggests that originally Adam was an androgynous being, a whole. Perhaps he was too much like God. Therefore, the splitting between male and female was essential, and Eve was created a separate being. This reading, whether literal or symbolic, leads to several speculations about gender and God's creative plan.

Another Biblical narrative frequently referred to in arguments against homosexuality recounts how Ham, the son of Noah, "uncovered the nakedness" of his drunken father (Gen. 9:22). Although Ham's actual offense is unclear, it was so heinous that he and his descendants were forever marked. Various interpretations by Jewish sages have suggested that Ham either castrated or sodomized his father. Therefore, "seeing the nakedness" is understood as an ancient Semitic euphemism for sexual violation of some sort. Possibly Ham degraded his father by making him the innocent passive partner in a homosexual encounter, an act understood as humiliating in most ancient societies. Whatever the meaning of this cryptic passage, it has frequently been used to attack homosexual behavior. A more modern reading of the passage, to which Greenberg appears to give credence, understands Ham's behavior as that of a son violating his proper place in the family hierarchy, usurping the rightful authority and status of his father.

The Biblical narrative of the destruction of Sodom is only slightly less ambiguous (Gen. 19 f). When Lot, a citizen of Sodom, entertains three angels, the men of his sinful city come and demand that he hand over his visitors "so that we may know them." This is usually understood as a demand for sexual access. Lot tries to pacify them by offering his virgin daughter in place of his guests. The word sodomy derives from this Biblical narrative, first used by English churchmen to describe male homosexual relationships.

But other interpretations of the Sodom story exist, some of them ancient, even Biblical. Ezekiel, a writing prophet of the Hebrew Bible, located Sodom's offense as inhospitality, just as Jesus later appears to have done when he tells his disciples that the cities that do not receive them will be treated more harshly than Sodom and Gomorrah in the Day of Judgment. (Although Greenberg does not allude to this New Testament reference, it would appear to support his position, at least for Christians.) Hospitality has long been a prime virtue among desert people, as one may observe even today with Bedouin tribes. Many rabbinic legends support the view of Sodom as a city of wealth and splendor, coveted by foreigners. To preserve and increase this wealth, the officials of Sodom may well have violated the desert law of hospitality to travelers, leaving wayfarers outside the city walls to perish of hunger rather than risk being despoiled of the city's great treasures.

But the passage in the Hebrew Bible that is most difficult to reconcile with same-sex relations is Leviticus (18:22), where male homosexuality is declared an "abomination" with the suitable punishment of death. Female same-sex relationships are not condemned, either because they were not believed to exist among the Hebrews or because they were not matters of concern. According to Jewish teaching, the Laws of Moses were given to Hebrews and their descendants, the covenant people. Therefore, certain expectations were placed upon them. They were to live as "a peculiar people," set apart, with a holiness code that they were commanded to follow.

Accordingly, people of non-covenant nations were not bound to keep the ceremonial law. The Creator of all, however, did expect righteous conduct of Gentiles. The rabbis taught that even before singling out Abraham for the special covenant, God had made a contract with the children of Noah, after saving them from the flood. Seven laws were given to Noah's descendants: these were prohibitions against idolatry, murder, sexual immorality ("uncovering the nakedness") theft, blasphemy, and cruelty to animals. The Seventh Law required the setting up of courts of law to administer justice. The prohibition against "uncovering nakedness" was generally understood as forbidding sexual violations of an adulterous or homosexual nature. This would mean that the prohibition against sodomy was not merely a part of the Hebrew holiness code, but was a Noahide law applying to all humankind.

Several principles should be kept in mind when examining these passages of Scripture, according to Rabbi Greenberg. One is that "all verses in the Torah are pregnant with multiple meanings, some on the surface, others more deeply hidden, and some yet unborn."[19] Also, Biblical admonishments must also always be observed within their proper contexts. (The popular Christian habit of reading random Biblical messages each day is not helpful for a deep understanding of Scripture and would be the antithesis of Rabbi Greenberg's method.)

Just as our contemporary experience may cast new light on ancient Biblical narratives, Rabbi Greenberg, always an earnest student of Scripture and rabbinical writings, provides the following example of how changing circumstances have led to a general reinterpretation of the eternal laws of God. His example is the prohibition of usury, once widespread in Judaism, Christianity, and Islam. With changing economic conditions, loyal Jews found ways of modifying ancient restrictions to become some of the most important bankers in the world. Christians eventually did the same and, somewhat more belatedly, some Muslims have joined them as moneylenders and financiers.

The laws of God, as Rabbi Greenberg and all other Orthodox Jews would acknowledge, do not have to be justified or rationally explained. Just because the Lord prohibits something is enough to make it an offense. However, the rabbis have long sought to articulate reasonable explanations for the laws that God has set forth for Jews and others. Greenberg identifies four traditional explanations for the Biblical law set forth in Leviticus: (1) Sexual conduct is sanctioned only when these actions are by their nature able to produce offspring. (2) Family solidarity requires that husbands be faithful to their wives and not neglect their spouses because of the temptation to sexual adventure with men. (3) Jewish law is much concerned with category confusion, and homosexuality blends the categories of male and female too awkwardly. (4) In the ancient world, as in the modern, sexual penetration was associated with humiliation and violence. Greenberg examines each of these reasons, relating them to the insights and concerns of modern people.[20]

If, as Greenberg is inclined to believe, the Leviticus prohibition was based on these considerations, he feels a modern reading is not out of order. This reading becomes more liberal while remaining faithful to the rationale behind the ancient law. First and probably most basic is the divine command to man to be fruitful and multiply. This law was especially important to the ancient Hebrews because they were a constantly threatened tribal confederation surrounded by powerful predatory nations. In the Middle Ages, Jews were scattered throughout all continents, always perceived as aliens. It was not until after World War II that they regained a nation of their own, diminished as they were by the Nazi Holocaust.

In the first century, the rabbis taught that it was the duty of men to produce at least one son and one daughter. Other rabbis decreed the limit of two insufficient to truly "settle the world," as Jews were commanded to do. Into modern times, Orthodox couples, like pre–Vatican II Catholics, were easily identified by their large families, typically with eight or more children. Many Jews felt that this commandment applied even in later life. If an older man remarried, a second family was not out of order.

Not only were children a joy and a treasure, but bestowing life was a way of affirming the goodness of God's creation and the assurance that God would bless the people of Israel. To reject this opportunity to become a helper of God in creation was, in a sense, to reject the Creator. In the first century, no rabbi was allowed to serve on the high court in Jerusalem, the Sanhedrin, who had not fathered children. (This thinking may have had a part in St. Paul's later judgment, in the Christian Scripture, that the qualifications for being an official in the early Church included parenthood.) Jewish mysticism, never precisely orthodox, presented other reasons for this command. Some mystics claimed that the messiah would come only when all souls created in the beginning of time and subsequently on reserve in heaven had been born and lived on earth. This would signal "the perfection of the end of days," when God would bring down the curtain, and all would enter the joys of the world to come.

Despite this stress on replenishing the earth, very few of the rabbinical sages believed that barren marriages should be terminated. Devoted couples not blessed with children were still respected, as were married couples who lived together long after their childbearing years were over. This would seem to demolish the argument that in Judaism only fertile sexual relations were regarded as worthy. Most Orthodox Jews would probably agree with David

Novak, who cites three legitimate purposes for human sexuality: pleasure, mutuality, and generativity.[21]

Hebrew Scriptures also voiced concern with the wasteful emission of semen, referred to as the "wasting of seed." Certainly this takes place in barren marriages as well as in male homosexual relations. Religious historians have sometimes attempted to trace the origin of this preoccupation to the experience of the Babylonian Captivity. During this period the Hebrews came into contact with the mighty Zoroastrian religion of ancient Persia, which had strong views on the wasting of seed. Liberated from the Captivity by the Persians, the Jews honored Persian rulers as "servants of God," and respected their traditions. Whatever the origin of this fear, early rabbis used it as another reason to condemn male homosexual acts. The prohibition against wasting seed appears to be more rabbinical than Biblical, despite the story of Onan (Genesis 38:4–10), who "spilled his seed on the ground," rather than fulfill his duty to beget a son with the wife of his deceased brother. Although his sin was more likely neglect of family obligation rather than the wanton waste of seed, he was nevertheless struck dead by the Lord, thus providing a further warning.

A devout Jewish homosexual is faced with a number of questions. Is he exempt from the obligation to beget children, even if he pledges himself to celibacy and devotes his life to a useful career and good works? Some rabbis, following the principle that God requires nothing of an individual that is impossible for him to fulfill, believe that he is. The entire people of Israel become the children of such a man. Most Orthodox rabbis would further counsel a life of celibacy for him. Fewer these days would, as in the past, advocate marriage as a possible cure for his same-sex attraction. Enlightened by a deeper awareness of psychology and the knowledge that such marriages are rarely successful, they would show greater concern for the disappointment and spiritual distress a wife might feel in such a marriage.

Another way of responding positively to divine concern for the next generation, suggested by some advocates of same-sex marriage, is to rear children acquired through surrogacy or adoption. (If these children are not the offspring of Jewish mothers, their status in the faith is ambiguous, and they would have to go through a process of conversion.) Aware of the current population explosion in the homosexual community, Rabbi Greenberg observes: "Gayness is no more an automatic intentional rejection of procreation than is straightness a sworn promise of it."[22]

Closely related to the obligation to procreate is the obvious fact that two men and two women are not designed by nature for procreative sexual relationships with one another; they replicate rather than complement each other physically. Still, Greenberg does not see this as a major concern. Human ingenuity has found amazing uses for the human body. He gives the example of the human mouth, which was designed for our nourishment. Yet we do many things with our mouths; we have developed complex systems of sound, so that all the languages of the world become intelligible to the communities that speak them. We laugh and sing. And when we kiss, our mouths express friendship and love. Few would argue that the mouth is being misused for these subsidiary functions.

Another argument against homosexuality is that it causes disruption in families. In ancient Greek and Roman societies, same-sex associations with boys and slaves did exist in addition to family relationships and may have sometimes been distractions from the obligations of family life. But husbands and wives in former times did not look necessarily to one another for their basic affection and companionship. The suggestion has also been made that irresponsible males might prefer homosexual relationships because they wish to be detached from obligations to wives and children. The argument that the prohibition against male relations is designed to prevent married men from straying from their homes and neglecting their family duties makes little sense to Rabbi Greenberg. When most men stray from their wives, the cause is other women. Heterosexual men have no desire for sexual relationships with other men.

Jewish law is concerned at several points with the mixing of categories and confusion of structures. The explanation of category confusion as a confounding of the orderly structure of creation is examined by Rabbi Greenberg. In clothing, mixtures of linen and wool are prohibited by Jewish law. The laws against cross-dressing in Leviticus are usually interpreted as discouragement of homosexuality. In nature, species do not fruitfully intermingle sexually. But it is easy to apply these rules beyond their reasonable applications. Not all humans conform neatly to the male-female dichotomy. Greenberg observes that God has produced unusual creatures from time to time, the hermaphrodite being the most notable human example. The ancient rabbis even composed a blessing to be recited upon seeing any strange, seemingly unnatural being: "Blessed art thou, O Lord our God, who maketh unusual creatures."

The question arises again, are homosexuals aberrations or further examples of God's creativity? Today we understand many categories somewhat loosely, and the process of categorization is recognized as an artificial (albeit sometimes useful) construct. Psychologists remind us that rather than being totally male or totally female, most people reside somewhere on a continuum.

Perhaps Rabbi Greenberg's most persuasive argument is that the prohibitions in Leviticus may stem from an abhorrence of humiliation and violence. Today it is recognized that an act of rape is motivated more by aggressive impulses than sexual desire. In the ancient world, where the status of women was generally very low, to be "penetrated like a woman" was to be subjected to a more powerful force, to be controlled. The Romans clearly recognized this when they passed the law prohibiting this abuse of even a slave who had once been a Roman citizen. Penetration was what you did to inferiors: women, children, and alien slaves. It was always an assertion of power. To say that a man commits an abomination when he lies with a man "as with a woman" is to say that he asserts his power aggressively over another who should be his equal. According to Rabbi Greenberg, "homophobia and misogyny" go hand in hand. In this reading, Leviticus 18:22 becomes a law against sexual domination, with relevance to both men and women, rather than a prohibition of gay relationships. Consequently, some Jewish thinkers argue that homosexual acts are more tolerable when penetration does not take place. If this is the case, it is clear why lesbian relationships have always been more tolerable.

Many people prefer to dispense with the logical arguments for or against homosexuality, simply concluding that the distaste that many people feel for the act has a rationale all its own. Accordingly, we should trust our instincts and impressions, which sometimes come from a subliminal wisdom. Rabbi Greenberg would reply to this argument by resorting to the race analogy. For decades many people in the American South and elsewhere found mixed race marriages repugnant. Today this view appears thoroughly benighted.

Greenberg presents still another analogy—imperfect but nevertheless instructive—pertaining to the Jewish Law. The U.S. Constitution originally declared the equality of all humans, yet it took years for this equality to be extended in popular thinking to African Americans and to women. Greenberg suggests that sacred texts, like the Constitution, can say to us only what we are ready to hear, at particular moments in our history:

The Torah is black fire on white fire, eternal and holy. It is also lovingly, brilliantly, divinely not clear. Its openness to successive interpretations is its assurance of eternity. The Torah is divine not because it finishes all discussion about right and wrong, but because it inaugurates and legitimates those very discussions, shapes their ongoing development, and empowers leaders in different times and places to make difficult decisions about its meaning.[23]

Because the Bible is so rich in messages for all occasions, one might well search for models of devoted same-sex relationships such as those found in ancient pagan literature. Greenberg believes the Bible and Talmudic writings contain a number of erotic, though not necessarily overtly sexual, relationships between men. Although most Bible readers have found the story of David and Jonathan, from the historical books of the Bible, an account of one of the world's great friendships, male lovers have sometimes interpreted it differently. The Bible relates that from their first meeting, the soul of Jonathan was bound to the soul of David, that Jonathan loved David as himself. So great was Jonathan's devotion to David that he bestowed upon him important tokens: his cloak, tunic, sword, bow, and belt. When Jonathan's father, King Saul, in his gathering madness, turned against David, it was Jonathan who protected him, defying his father. David and Jonathan wept for each other in separation and greeted one another with embraces when reunited. When Jonathan was killed in battle, David, the psalmist of Israel, lamented his friend: "I grieve for you, my brother Jonathan. You were most dear to me. Your love was wonderful to me, more than the love of women" (II Sam.1:25–27).

There are other expressions of deep devotion between Biblical personalities of the same sex. In the Book of Ruth, a Moabite widow leaves her land and people to cast her lot with her Jewish mother-in-law. Her famous words, "Entreat me not to leave thee" are often inscribed on friendship jewelry and incorporated into marriages ceremonies. They have in recent years also been used in lesbian commitment ceremonies.

Rabbi Greenberg is aware that not all goals of gay equality will be achieved immediately. The ultimate desire of most Orthodox Jewish people who are gay will be to share fully in the life of the synagogue with their partners and to have their relationships blessed in the ceremonies that heterosexual couples accept as their right. They will wish to bring their children to Jewish schools, instructing their young in the obligations and blessings of the Jewish law. Today in Reform Judaism, commitment services are offered, and practicing gay rabbis, both men and women, are tolerated in some communities. Conservative Judaism is also more understanding than in years past. But in the Orthodox community, as Greenberg admits: "The halakhic debate is just beginning."[24]

## Christianity

Although there are nuanced positions within Christianity on homosexual practice and same-sex marriage, the subject usually divides the faithful into two groups. Conservative Christians who place heavy reliance on the words of Scripture generally reject homosexual conduct, suggesting that those who have this "predilection" should either seek therapy or accept celibacy. There have been, however, a few attempts even in the Evangelical community to deconstruct or reinterpret passages in Scripture that present problems to gay people. Ancient documents written to address social conditions that have changed drastically almost three thousand years later can be ambiguous. While Christians do not have the benefit of centuries of rabbinical legal parsing to which Rabbi Greenberg can appeal, many still come up with arguments similar to his. The sin of Sodom, for example, is reinterpreted as a violation of the desert ethic of hospitality, and the words of Jesus seem to support this interpretation.[25] Leviticus and, later, St. Paul were concerned, Christian defenders of the responsible gay life-style believe, with heterosexuals who could not resist exploitative pederastic encounters. David and Jonathan can be seen as role models for devoted gay lovers, and the conduct of some of the more eccentric saints in Christian tradition bears looking into as well.

At the beginning of every conservative Christian defense of homosexuality is the fact that Jesus was silent on the subject, though he was not hesitant to denounce conduct that offended him: legalism, hypocrisy, exploitation of the poor, degradations of women. The fact that Jesus and St. Paul did not marry, though they were born into Jewish communities that considered matrimony a religious obligation, also appears significant. For the Reverend Troy Perry, Scripture is still authoritative, but open to reexamination. Perry, an ordained Pentecostal minister from Florida and gay activist, is firm in his conviction that one can be a practicing homosexual and a loyal Christian at the same time. The Metropolitan Community Church, which Perry founded, continues to grow and maintains its witness, performing commitment ceremonies and, where legal, same-sex marriages.

The liberal Christian position on homosexuality parallels that of Reform Judaism. Liberal Christians rely heavily on historical and critical Biblical scholarship in their understanding of Scripture. They read the Bible as a fine and frequently eloquent record of Hebrew faith as it evolved into the high ethics of Christianity. But liberals believe that Scripture must always be understood within the context of its own time. Context is perhaps the most important word. Patterns of conduct appropriate for a tribal nomadic people such as ancient Hebrews cannot be followed by urban Christians today. The New Testament, though addressed to a more cosmopolitan community than was the Old Testament, was never intended as a "contract" to guide Christians in every particular. Rather, the ethical teachings of Christianity present broad precepts against which all conduct must be measured. The highest ethical standard was set forth in Jesus' Sermon on the Mount, and its major principle, not unknown to first-century Judaism, is righteous conduct toward others. Loving concern and compassion should be the guiding principles in every relationship and situation. Liberal Christians agree very much with the great first-century rabbi Hillel: "There is one commandment. Love the Lord your God. All the rest is commentary." Or, as Jesus phrased the message: "Love the Lord your God with all your heart, soul, and mind, and your neighbor as yourself. On these two commandments hang all the law and the prophets" (Matthew 22:40).

In determining what patterns of behavior are ethical, it is necessary to consider choices in contexts. This ethical directive is sometimes referred to as "situation ethics." Behavior can never be reduced to any one set of rules applicable to all situations. For example, it is generally wrong to lie, and civilization could not exist if there were no standard of truthfulness. However, there are certain situations where a falsehood is necessary to avoid a greater evil. Suppose, for example, a Polish family hiding Jews during the Holocaust were asked by a Gestapo official the location of these people. Most would agree that the Polish family would be right to lie and conceal the Jews' hiding place.

Sexual conduct likewise must be judged in each relevant situation. Does a particular choice avoid harm to others and contribute to the happiness and well-being of the parties involved? Does a relationship enrich the lives of the people in it, and does it avoid betrayal of others? While not all progressive Christian ethicists give their approval to committed homosexual relationships, under circumstances that pass the "situations" test, a surprising number are ready to accept such unions as positive, especially when they take place between individuals who would qualify for matrimony were they of opposite gender. Committed, exclusive relationships, in which the partners intend to remain with one another until death, most commonly pass this test. Then, at least in the judgment of many situation ethicists, there is no reason why the church should not only accept but publicly celebrate these commitments, bestowing on them its full blessing.

This Christian view, based on an interpretive approach to Scripture and a situational understanding of ethics, holds that homosexual acts, like other sexual interactions, are neutral and become moral or immoral depending on the persons involved and their intentions toward one another. Instead of accepting as the supreme authority either Leviticus or the Epistles of St. Paul, this approach is based on reflection and experience.

While the Bible is still revered as a wise and informative ancient document containing the record of the Israelites, the Crucifixion of Christ, and accounts of early Christian struggles, all interpretations are acknowledged to be more or less subjective. Even modern documents present problems of interpretation; records from the distant past that have been translated several times would be expected to present more serious problems. The canon of Scripture, in the words of Professor Dan O. Via, "provides a rich and diverse—sometimes contradictory—context in which to try to understand individual texts."[26] This approach to Scripture provides much leeway for interpretations and developments.

In content criticism, as this approach to Scripture is sometimes called, Biblical students examine a particular text and place it within the larger framework of the Biblical book in which it is found. Then they attempt to relate the text to the entire Bible. This means that some texts will take on enormous value, while others will be largely disqualified by the overall message of Scripture.

One example might be the Mosaic penalty for adultery, which is stoning. Because two witnesses were required, the penalty was probably infrequently carried out. Both offense and penalty must now be considered in light of the words of Jesus to the woman taken in adultery (as recorded in some, but not all, ancient manuscripts of the Gospel according to St. John).[27] Here Jesus pardons the woman and tells her to go and sin no more.

It is also essential to consider attitudes within Christianity, precedents that have developed over two thousand years, not neglecting the insights and trends of the last decades. In this way it is possible to better discern the will of the Church and understand the directions that Christian thought has taken. Today, three fallacies about homosexuals are being refuted by some church spokespeople who are versed in the literature of modern psychology. In the first part of the twentieth century, almost all Christians viewed homosexuals as degenerates. A look at the high achievements of some gay people in history should have quickly dispelled this view, but biographies of distinguished people, particularly those written for young people, did not probe deeply into sexual matters. In the latter part of the century, a more charitable attitude prevailed among Christian people. Homosexuals came to be viewed as sick, their "derangement" perhaps the result of childhood trauma that left them damaged beyond their control. It was customary to blame parents for all such problems. The conclusion was that homosexuals should be given understanding, empathy, and treatment. After 1974, when the American Psychiatric Association dropped homosexuality from its list of mental diseases, a third view became dominant among Christian liberals. Homosexuals were indeed often troubled individuals, but the fault now was less with them than with the society that had either marginalized them or demanded they conform to conduct that violated their authentic nature.

The more contemporary liberal attitude is that it is society and its prejudices that need to change. Christians are now told that they must pray for forgiveness for their treatment of gays and lesbians, asking God for aid in overcoming prejudice and bigotry. Now it must be understood that gays are not disordered; they are differently ordered. In fact, their very difference may entail a major contribution to Christianity and to society. It may not yet be known what special gifts gay people may have to offer the Church, but their musical and other artistic contributions are already evident. The keen aesthetic sense that has come to characterize many has proven useful, especially in the ecclesiastical traditions that maintain a place for high drama. For all these reasons, it becomes especially important that Christians accept gays and lesbians into their ministries, into the leadership of their churches, and into their religious schools as teachers and students. As important positive role models, gays need to be seen in bishop's robes. They must be seen praying and performing charitable acts alongside their partners. The churches must develop rites to sanctify their unions and support laws giving them a marriage status equal to that of heterosexuals.

These goals of liberal, activist Christianity have been only partially achieved; in almost every mainstream denomination in which homosexuals have been ordained, a strong protest has arisen from the laity. This makes the task more difficult, say the activists, but no less worthy.

## Argument of Professor Dan O. Via

Among the most persuasive spokespersons for the rights of homosexuals within the Christian community has been Dan O. Via, Professor Emeritus of New Testament at Duke University Divinity School. Via shares an emerging perspective within the broader Christian community that much has changed in the gay dialogue during the last few years, and the burden of proof has shifted, among liberal Christians, to those who wish to deny recognition to gay persons. There is a growing acknowledgement that gay people are not perverse; neither are they sick, inverted, nor offensively effeminate in their mannerisms. Their only distinguishing feature is their choice of their own gender as primary love object. If they are Christian, they want to be able to live openly in peace with God and their neighbors, contributing their talents to the Church, asking only the same rights for themselves and their partners that heterosexual couples are routinely given.

In his reexamination of the Scripture usually cited in condemnation of homosexuality, Via concludes that homosexual acts were regarded as ritually contaminating among the ancient Hebrews primarily because of their associations with paganism. Leviticus, Via concludes, condemns such acts as a source of uncleanness rather than as sin. As in other primitive or ancient religions, uncleanness was understood by early Hebrew faith as an external contamination that is not the result of a sinful action of will. A person may become unclean simply by touching a taboo object. (Numerous examples of this type of uncleanness are found in the Hebrew Scripture; in one instance a man innocently touched the Ark of the Covenant and was struck dead. Women especially had to endure purification rites after giving birth, though the birth itself was a joyful event.)

The Scriptures state that homosexuality defiles or makes unclean (Leviticus 18:24–27). Unclean acts were "abominations" to the Hebrews, whether they entailed the eating of an unclean animal or the performing of a ritually impure sexual action. Via observes that the Christian New Testament in most ways "annuls, delegitimizes, and invalidates in principle the very category of impurity or uncleanness."[28] Sin, as the New Testament understands it, is a "deformation of the will and understanding," rather than a defilement by any "unclean" act or object. A mortal sin is a fully conscious defiance of the laws God has established for human justice and welfare.[29]

It is helpful to understand the precise nature of homosexual contamination according to the Hebrew Scripture. Via cites four familiar reasons for this defilement. His argument is not unlike that of Rabbi Greenberg, but there are differences of emphasis. First, homosexual practice, as outlined in the Old Testament, makes one ritually unclean. Second, in a threatened, tribal society it was particularly important to produce heirs, and homosexual acts by their very nature were not procreative. Third, homosexuality was one of the practices that clearly separated the Israelites from the licentious pagan nations against whom they constantly struggled for possession and preservation of the Promised Land. Fourth, in a patriarchal society, male homosexual practices, in which one party frequently "takes the female role," were viewed as an assault on male dignity.

Via points out that lesbian acts seemed of no consequence to the Hebrew writers of the Bible, perhaps because they were unaware of their existence. Centuries later, living in a largely pagan society, St. Paul would have known that they existed, and he condemned them equally with male same-sex acts. With Paul, the practice had ceased being a matter of ritual uncleanness and had become sin.

Even in the sophisticated Greco-Roman pagan environment in which St. Paul moved, there was disagreement about the moral status of homosexuals. Some moralists defended them since they provided apprenticeships for young men and a more humane, privileged environment for favored slaves. Others opposed homosexual conduct for many of the same reasons we hear today. For St. Paul, homosexuality was a violation of the natural order of creation laid down by God, a reason that had also occurred to a few pagan philosophers of his time.

Via and others think that St. Paul's argument collapses because of one fact that he could not have known, because it was unrecognized at the time he lived. Today it is generally conceded that sexual orientation is a predisposition not deliberately chosen or subject to individual will. The Mediterranean world of St. Paul did not speak of genes but had other ways of explaining human proclivities. A psychology, a science, and a prejudice held by people two thousand years ago no longer apply in the twenty-first century.

St. Paul believed that he was living at the end of time; consequently, he found the celibate life preferable for himself and other Christians to the married state, with its clear stake in an earthly future. Therefore, Paul had clearly reconsidered God's earlier command to be fruitful and multiply. He advised those who lacked the vocation for celibacy to marry respectably. This recommendation,

Via and other proponents of same-sex marriage suggest, should be applicable to homosexuals. Few people today, homosexual or heterosexual, feel called to the celibate life. Should not homosexuals, following Paul's reasoning, be free to choose a permanent commitment over a life of licentious indulgence?

To proscribe homosexuality is to assume knowledge we cannot possibly have. Despite a constant focus on psychology and many elaborate studies of sexual behavior, we still do not know what causes people to be sexually or romantically attracted to the persons they choose. These choices are often bewildering to family, friends, and even the persons involved. The motives for sexual choices seem to be deeply embedded in the psyche, whether innately, biologically, or genetically determined, or the result of prenatal influences or early conditioning. Even if it could be conclusively determined that homosexuality is inborn, this would not necessarily imply that it is good or desirable. Some traits that are a part of our nature, or a part of the inherited nature of some individuals, must be suppressed in order for that person to function harmoniously in family and community. Most people have to struggle against some of their urges. All that is conceded. But the question remains: How would society, family, or individuals be harmed by responsible, caring homosexual unions sustained by permanent commitment?

Via quotes with approval the gay Christian scholar Dale Martin:

Any interpretation of scripture that hurts people, oppresses people, or destroys people cannot be the right interpretation, no matter how traditional, historical, or exegetically respectable. There can be no debate about the fact that the Church's stand on homosexuality has caused oppression, loneliness, self-hatred, violence, sickness, and suicide for millions of people. If the church wishes to continue with its traditional interpretation it must demonstrate, not just claim, that it is more loving to condemn homosexuality than to affirm homosexuals.[30]

The wisdom literature of the Bible, like the literature of Confucianism, Taoism, and other wisdom traditions, speaks much about learning lessons from nature. The natural world, it is asserted, provides clues to the nature of God, and wise lessons may be derived from observing the most humble creatures. The Book of Proverbs tells us to learn industry from observing the ants. While we do not know what determines sexual orientation, we do know that the choice is not the result of a perverse nature. We might well regard the findings of modern science, even the social sciences which sometimes appear to have removed God entirely, as sources of information about nature, from which we may learn ethical lessons.

Via is not much moved by the argument, so basic to opponents of homosexual recognition, that only male and female natures complement one another. He believes that for homosexual people, homosexual acts are natural. The gay or lesbian is best understood as a member of a "different sexual order of creation," rather than an aberration of the more familiar one.[31]

Via, certainly one of the strongest spokespersons for the homosexual cause within Christianity, concludes that our present knowledge and experience with gay and lesbian Christians leads us to the realization that they must be respected. He believes that the great Biblical themes, in "the light of contemporary knowledge and experience" can justify an overriding of the seemingly absolute and unconditional Biblical condemnation of homosexual acts. The Bible shows that new insights into God's word, which initially may seem to conflict with the dictates of old, come as the result of expanding experience in the faith community. Christians have always held that the New Covenant of Christ supersedes the old Mosaic one. The Word of God, like creation itself, has never been static. God has always led the faithful on to new insights and revelations.

Via reminds readers that "no one has Scripture as it is 'in itself' but only from a point of view." It seems reasonable, indeed inescapable and even godly, to accept "whatever bodily-sexual orientation one has been given by creation."[32] The anti-gay argument of conservative Christians, Via feels, leads to an exclusionary and sad dead end. The Church cannot compel people to deny their very natures, their essential identities. In fact, attempts to do so may be challenging God's will.

### The Thesis of John Boswell

One of the most widely discussed Christian advocates of homosexual tolerance and same-sex marriage was a historian, John Boswell. He was born in Boston and was educated at the College of William and Mary and at Harvard. A distinguished student from the beginning, his academic credentials were impeccable. He joined the Yale history department in 1974, and from 1990 to 1992, served as chair of that department. His early work on Islamic Spain established him as a leading historian of the European Middle Ages. As an adult, he converted to Roman Catholicism and treasured this affiliation for the rest of his life. He said, rather paradoxically, "I believe probably as much of the Church's official teaching as the Pope does . . . but we interpret it very differently."[33] This quote illustrates his spirit of independence, as well as a possible bit of arrogance that is evident in his work.

In 1987, Boswell became a founding father of the Lesbian and Gay Studies Center at Yale, and the program became a model for gay studies departments throughout the country. His best known books have been widely regarded as historical vindications of gay liaisons, and his attempts to prove the homosexual life-style compatible with Christianity have received much media attention. *Christianity, Social Tolerance, and Homosexuality* was published in 1980, and *Same-Sex Unions in Premodern Europe* followed in 1994. These books have been used more than any others to buttress a view, still not widely accepted among historians, that homosexual marriage is no novelty to our own time but was even recognized by the Christian Church prior to the fourteenth century.

Boswell's controversial and original theories would have been more fully expounded had not his untimely death from AIDS in 1994 shortened his career. He died just before publication of his second book. In *Christianity, Social Tolerance, and Homosexuality,* which won the American Book Award for History, Boswell attempted to show that the Church has not been the chief enemy of gay tolerance. He believed that intolerance to homosexual practice arrived late to Christianity, well after the first millennium. His last book, published posthumously, was also an award winner initially reviewed prominently and favorably. In it, he tried to prove, through newly discovered documents and a rereading of previously published ones, that early Christianity had not only recognized same-sex unions but had developed ceremonies, essentially sacramental marriage rites, to bless them.

No one questioned that Boswell, working in 17 ancient and modern languages, possessed splendid tools of scholarship. Perhaps more than any other academician, he succeeded in achieving respectable academic standing for lesbian and gay scholarship. He scoured the Scriptures and Christian tradition for examples to support his theses, reinterpreting the lives of numerous paired figures in Biblical and early Christian history. After examining the Old Testament, Boswell, like others before him, paired Ruth and her mother-in-law, Naomi, as well as David and Jonathan. In the New Testament, Boswell was intrigued by Jesus' special affection for "the disciple whom He loved," St. John. The apostles Philip and Bartholomew appeared to form another pair. Although Boswell claimed no knowledge of the intimate relations of these heroes from Scripture, he presented them as models of same-sex devotion. From post-Biblical Christian lore, he included Perpetua and Felicitas, a noblewoman and her female slave, who were martyred together for their beliefs by Romans at Carthage in the early third century. Polyeuct and Nearchos, Roman soldiers of Greek ancestry, were described in the fourth century as "brothers, not by birth, but by affection,"[34] and Serge and Bacchus were devoted Roman soldiers of Christian faith.

Boswell also felt that he had uncovered clear evidence that at one time both the Western Catholic Church and the Eastern Orthodox churches had recognized same-sex unions through eloquent ceremonies that he discovered. From paintings in archeological ruins he found signals, which he believed had been used as "the principle gesture in same-sex unions." In early Christian art he discerned many icons of paired saints who had lived and died together, thus intertwined in the Church's hagiography.

Newspapers and popular journals reviewed Boswell's work with enthusiasm. The literary critic for the *Boston Globe* expressed a common early reaction from these reviewers:

By casting new light on a neglected and misunderstood past, he [Boswell] helps us see a premodern world much more diverse, complex and pluralistic than our simple-minded images of it, and a world that still has much to teach those of us who think we know so much and have come so far. To reflect accurately on the past may be the most revolutionary thing a historian can do. Boswell has done this splendidly, and even those who are bound to disagree with him stand with the rest of us in his debt. No discussion of the topic [same-sex marriage] will now be complete without reference to Boswell's work.[35]

Written in the shadow of the AIDS pandemic, dedicated to friends who had perished, Boswell's last book achieved a special poignancy through his own approaching death. He would be viewed as a martyr within the gay community. Numerous same-sex couples considered his work a vindication of their own choices and identities, and his books have been especially important to homosexuals who have longed for a Christian sacramental seal on their own relationships.

Boswell and his many admirers were not surprised by the immense controversy his works generated and the fervor with which other medieval scholars responded to his basic thesis, reported his errors, and accused him of rewriting history to support the gay agenda. The next chapter addresses these challenges to Boswell. It is sufficient here to observe that his critics did not dampen the excitement of Boswell's many readers who felt that he had provided them their strongest affirmation ever and had with his scholarship paved the way for an ultimate Christian acceptance of same-sex marriage.

## NOTES

1. While numerous studies provide support, detailed documentation is presented by Linda J. Waite and Maggie Gallagher, *The Case for Marriage: Why Married People Are Happier, Healthier, and Better Off Financially* (New York: Doubleday, 2000).

2. In *Loving vs. Virginia,* the U.S. Supreme Court struck down Virginia's anti-miscegenation law as a clear violation of the Fourteenth Amendment's Equal Protection Clause.

3. See Kathleen A. Lahey and Kevin Alderson, *Same-Sex Marriage: The Personal and the Political* (Toronto: Insomniac Press, 2004), 38, for a brief discussion of the

relevance of the European Convention on Human Rights and the International Covenant on Civil and Political Rights.

4. James D. Wilets, "The Inexorable Momentum Toward National and International Recognition of Same-Sex Relationships: An International, Comparative, Historical, and Cross-Cultural Perspective," in Lynn D. Wardel et al., eds., *Marriage and Same-Sex Unions: A Debate* (Westport, CT: Praeger, 2003).

5. Ibid.

6. Carlos A. Ball, "One Last Hope: A Response to Professor Teresa Stanton Collett," in Wardel, 164.

7. Ibid.

8. Jonathan Rauch, *Gay Marriage: Why It Is Good for Gays, Good for Straights, and Good for America* (New York: Henry Holt, 2004), 7.

9. Ibid., 19.

10. Ibid., 23.

11. Ibid., 109.

12. Ibid. 127.

13. For an unusual and interesting point of view, see Irshad Manji, *The Trouble with Islam Today: A Muslim's Call for Reform in Her Faith* (New York: St. Martin's Griffin, 2003).

14. Rabbi Steven Greenberg, "Same-Sex Civil Marriage," in Greg Wharton and Ian Philips, *I Do I Don't: Queers on Marriage* (San Francisco: Suspect Thoughts Press, 2004), 150–152.

15. Greenberg, *Wrestling with God & Men: Homosexuality in the Jewish Tradition* (Madison: University of Wisconsin Press, 2004), 92. Rabbi Rav was probably following an ancient Babylonion practice that some Jews in earlier times occasionally found convenient.

16. Ibid., 12.

17. The Talmud incorporates the Mishnah, a compendium of collected traditions, with the Germara, a commentary that further interprets the Mishna. The Talmud employs "precedent, logic, practical reason, literary content, formal legal principles, repetition, and common practice among other devices to get the active meaning of the Torah for the moment," according to Rabbi Greenberg, *Wrestling*, 33.

18. Greenberg, 43.

19. Ibid., 78.

20. Ibid., 147–214.

21. Ibid., 157.

22. Ibid., 158.

23. Ibid., 210.

24. Ibid., 264.

25. "Verily I say unto you, it shall be more tolerable for the land of Sodom and Gomorrha in the day of judgment, than for that city [that rejects your ministry]" (Matt. 10:15, King James Version of Holy Bible).

26. Dan O. Via and Robert A. J. Gagnon, *Homosexuality and the Bible: Two Views* (Minneapolis: Fortress Press, 2003), 3.

27. John 8:11.

28. Via and Gagnon, 9.

29. Ibid.

30. Quoted in Via and Gagnon, 37.

31. Ibid., 18.

32. Ibid., 35.

33. Quoted in Steve Hogan and Lee Hudson, *Completely Queer: The Gay and Lesbian Encyclopedia* (New York: Henry Holt, 1998), 97.

34. James Boswell, *Same-Sex Unions in Premodern Europe* (New York: Vintage Books, 1995), 141.

35. Review from *Boston Globe,* quoted on dust jacket of Boswell, *Same-Sex Unions in Premodern Europe.*

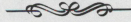

*Commitment Ceremony*

*Mr. Jimmy Dickerson McNeece*
*and*
*Mr. William Kelly Finley*

*request the honour of your presence*
*at their Commitment Ceremony*
*on Saturday, the twenty-ninth of January*
*two thousand and five*
*at two o'clock in the afternoon*

*Cafe 541*
*541 Franklin Street*
*Clarksville, TN*

*Reception immediately following*

*RSVP 931-645-9423*

Invitation to the commitment ceremony of Jimmy McNesse and Kelly Finley, Clarksville, Tennessee. Courtesy of Kelly Finley and Jimmy McNeese.

Commitment Ceremony. Photo of Life Partners, Kelly Finley, a Clarksville, Tennessee Merchant, and Jimmy McNeese, a Tennessee Civil Servant. Courtesy of Kelly Finley and Jimmy McNeese.

CHRISTINA,
*Queen of Sweden.*

*From the original picture painted in oil by Bourdon at Fontainebleau in 1653*

*London, published by Bull & Churton 26 Holles St, Cavendish Square.*

Queen Christina, a prime example of androgyny, who renounced the Swedish throne to live in Italy with a female partner. Music Division, The New York Public Library for the Performing Arts, Astor, Lenox and Tilden Foundations.

Professor Robert Gagnon, lead-
ing spokesman for traditional
Judeo-Christian family values.
Courtesy of Robert Gagnon.

Judge Robert Bork, renowned
jurist and law professor and
forceful spokesman for traditional morals. Courtesy of De-
clan McCullagh Photography.

Sarah Bernhardt, most celebrated actress of her day, in one
of her most famous male roles,
as ill-fated son of Napoleon.
Billy Rose Theatre Collection,
The New York Public Library
for the Performing Arts, Astor,
Lenox and Tilden Founda-
tions.

Marlene Dietrich in tuxedo, famous androgynous sex symbol,
who was permitted the first
same-sex kiss in an American
film. George Arents Collection,
The New York Public Library,
Lenox and Tilden Founda-
tions.

MARLENE DIETRICH

# 5

# The Argument against Same-Sex Marriage

## THE LEGAL, SOCIAL, AND PERSONAL CASE

Despite the advances that have been made in homosexual rights and general acceptance during the last three decades, the vast majority of the public remains unconvinced that same-sex marriage is either reasonable or beneficial. After all, opponents of same-sex marriage argue, marriage as we know it has served humanity, generally with success, since before recorded history. Why should billions of people be required to change their customs, habits, and mores to accommodate a slim minority of the population? Even in nations and states that have granted same-sex couples equal marital rights—the Netherlands, Belgium, Canada, Spain, Massachusetts—the laws have been passed over the heated objections of many people, sometimes the majority.

Some of the opposition to same-sex marriage comes from homosexuals themselves, who see no valid reason why they should be asked to partake of an institution they associate with oppression and patriarchy, which even heterosexuals abandon in great numbers.

Opponents of same-sex marriage observe that, although the forms of marriage may differ from one society to another, its basic character has been similar in every civilization. It is a public union between man and woman with rights and obligations publicly accepted and the understanding that children may be recognized by their families and clans and reared with the protection of both parents. Kinship, whether clan membership or share in a single family unit, is affirmed through marriage, along with clearly acknowledged paternity. Although religious status may be acquired through the maternal line, as with the

Jews, or thorough the father, as with Zoroastrians, family is crucial to a child's identity. Consider the number of nations that acknowledge legal fathers with the use of patronymics. The very form of most names and the ways people are addressed demonstrates how central a family or clan is considered. Property is transmitted through the relationships that marriage establishes. Erotic energies are further channeled into this institution, not always contained but certainly restrained. Everywhere, the family is the preferred milieu for the rearing of the next generation. Without the necessity or desire to rear children, marriage, which has perhaps more often than not originated in social obligations rather than affections, would probably never have come into existence. Family law everywhere is grounded in these kinship and conjugal relationships.

The first objection made to same-sex marriage by its opponents typically concerns children. Same-sex union does not generate offspring, though it can include the conscientious rearing of them. With the constant advances in reproductive science, it may some day be possible for two females or two males to merge their genes in a single child. But that seems more a scary science fiction scenario now than an impending reality.

Of course, not all marriages, even when blessed by the churches, produce children. Sterile couples and post-menopausal brides are not turned away from the altar. According to Richard Wilkins, Professor of Law at the Reuben Clark Law School and Managing Director of the World Family Policy Center at Brigham Young University in Provo Utah:

Procreation requires a coupling between the two sexes. Sexual relations between a man and a woman, therefore, even if they are infertile, fundamentally differ from homosexual couplings. Homosexual couplings do not have a biological potential for reproduction: children are possible only by means of legal intervention (e.g., adoption) or medical technology (e.g., artificial insemination). Accordingly, and by their very nature, sexual relationships between a man and a woman (even if they are infertile) differ in kind from couplings between individuals of the same sex: heterosexual couplings in general have the biological potential for reproduction; homosexual couplings always do not. This potential procreative power is the basis for society's compelling interest in preferring potentially procreative relationships over relationships founded primarily upon mutually agreeable genital stimulation.[1]

The expectation of children is central to most permanent heterosexual unions, yet many heterosexual couples choose not to have children. Contraceptives are advertised in television commercials by actors who may or may not wear wedding rings, and organizations have been formed to honor "the non-parents of the year." In India, transistor radios have been given as incentive gifts to men who submit to vasectomy. If it is acceptable for people to choose not to procreate, what is the objection to sexual activity by those who are unable to procreate?

While all these facts seem to provide a strong argument in favor of gay unions, social life is considerably more complex than population statistics alone suggest. People wish to perpetuate their own cultural and national traditions. In several European countries—most notably Italy, despite the presence of the Vatican in its midst—the birthrate is below replacement level. The very survival of Italian, French, German, and certain other European national cultures appears threatened, as more and more immigrants, most from Africa and the Middle East, are brought in to sustain the economies of these lands.

Many people who understand the gay community, including some of its own members, believe that a relatively small number of gay couples will ever seek legal marriage. Though estimates vary, a near consensus is that the gay community comprises no more than five percent of the total U.S. population. A generous estimate is that no more than a third of them would be likely to marry. Yet activists are demanding a total restructuring of society's most durable institution to accommodate that small minority.

Opponents of same-sex marriage strongly suspect that the present push is not the result of any urgent need of an oppressed minority but is the desire for a definitive symbolic statement. The demand is not really for health insurance or tax relief, or even inheritance rights. Practical benefits that may not be obtained in other legal ways are minimal. Last wills and testaments, powers of attorney, living wills, and adoption procedures take care of most concerns. Thus, the gay activists are suspected of demanding recognition of marriage as a powerful social statement, the supreme capitulation of a reluctant straight population.

Although homosexual relations have no doubt been practiced for as long as humans have existed, history provides little support for extending the legal definition of marriage to encompass this relationship. Marriage throughout time, with only a few possible and highly questionable exceptions, has been recognized as a sanctioned union of male and female only. John Witte, Jr., a professor of law and ethics at Emory University in Atlanta, suggests that, "If a thing has been practiced for 2,000 years by common consent, surely the case to change it needs to be very strong indeed."[2] Professor Witte goes on to state:

For nearly two thousand years, the Western legal tradition reserved the legal category of marriage to monogamous, heterosexual couples who had reached the age of consent, who had the physical capacity to join together in one flesh, and whose joining served the goods and goals of procreation, companionship, and stability at once. Marriage was a form of adhesion contract, to be accepted or rejected but not individually renegotiated. Marriage was the proper place for the enjoyment of sexual activities. Those who practiced sex elsewhere, with self or others, were subject to various moral and criminal sanctions. This was not just Christian doctrine. Hebrew jurists and prophets, Greek Platonists and Aristotelians, Roman moralists and jurists, church fathers and councils, high medieval Catholics, early modern Protestants, and eighteenth and nineteenth-century Enlightenment philosophers all accepted this core understanding of the form and function of sex and marriage and defended it with all manner of theological, philosophical, political, and social arguments.[3]

It has become customary for defenders of gay rights to quote eminent ancient Greeks and Romans who idealized same-sex relationships. Yet many of these sages reserved their highest praised for marriage as they knew it. A major theme of Homer's *Odyssey*, which comes from the heroic age of Greek civilization, is the longing for home and hearth. As early as 800 B.C., this father of Western literature shows his hero, Odysseus, bidding farewell to the young girl, Nausicaa, who had found him wrecked on the beach and had befriended him. When he leaves her to continue his journey homeward, it is with his supreme blessing, wishing her the best that the gods have to offer, a dear husband and a harmonious home. And for all those years after the Trojan War, Odysseus struggles through many adventures to return finally to his loyal wife, Penelope. It is worth remembering that the early Greek fathers of the Christian Church, despite their fear of the assumed depravities of pagan literature, placed the faithful Penelope beside the virtuous wife described in the Book of Proverbs as a model of spousal devotion.

Much later, Plutarch, the Greco-Roman moralist and biographer (46–120 A.D.) defined marriage as:

a union for life between a man and a woman for the delight of love and the getting of children. In the case of lawful wives, physical union is the beginning of friendship, a sharing as it were, in great mysteries. The pleasure [of physical union] is short, but the respect and kindness and mutual affection and loyalty that daily spring from it [render] such a union a "friendship". . . . No mutual pleasures are greater, no mutual services more constant, no form of affection is more enviable and estimable for its sheer beauty than when man and wife in harmony of mind keep house together.[4]

And Musonius Rufus (c.30A.D.), a significant moralist in a Rome not yet conquered by Christianity wrote of marriage:

The husband and wife . . . should come together for the purpose of making a life in common and of procreating children, and furthermore of regarding all things in common between them, and nothing peculiar or private to one or the other, not even their own bodies. The birth of a human being which results from such a union is to be sure something marvelous, but it is not yet enough for the relation of husband and wife, inasmuch as, quite apart from marriage, it could result from any other sexual union, just as in the case of animals. But in marriage there must be above all perfect companionship and mutual love of husband and wife, both in health and in sickness and under all conditions, since it was with desire for this as well as for having children that both entered upon marriage.[5]

These descriptions of marriage, idealized to be sure, can never apply to same-sex unions, no matter how self-sacrificing and supportive they may be. Marriage, its advocates remind us, was not invented by any human government. Nobody yet has found a satisfactory substitute for male-female marriage, which was formed by prehistoric humans to meet their needs, then sanctified by their developing religions, before being codified by their governments. Marriage has been called "nature's supreme masterpiece" so often that no one remembers who first said it.

Possibly the strongest argument against same-sex marriage is that it offends the sensibilities of most people. In the United States, in every state where a referendum on the issue has been held, it has been soundly defeated. Even in Canada and the few European countries that have legalized gay unions, substantial objection is still vocal. Although most people are opposed to granting marital status to homosexual unions, they are often a silent majority. They have been cowed by being labeled bigots and homophobes and are frequently intimidated by the media and university elite who have adopted the homosexual agenda. It is in the privacy of the voting booth that the will of the people has been decisively expressed. While the courts may continue to impose same-sex unions against the majority will, morality cannot be legislated, and the continuing social disapproval will be expressed in less vocal but still effective ways.

Traditional marriage has forceful and eloquent public defenders. Some of the most notable opponents of the same-sex marriage agenda have been Jay Alan Sekulow, a Christian convert from Judaism who has been called the "chief lawyer for the Religious Right"; Charles Krauthammer, syndicated columnist and television pundit; columnist William Safire, who supports domestic partnerships but stops short of marriage; Tammy Brice, conservative television commentator and lesbian; Maggie Gallagher, leading researcher and writer on marriage; John McKay, Canadian MP and Parliamentary Secretary for Finance; Stanley Kurtz, writer for *National Review;* Hadley Arkes, Amherst College political science professor; and even advice columnist Ann Landers, who, although pro-gay, stops short of advocating the legalization of homosexual marriage.

## The Argument of Judge Robert Bork

An important spokesman with a civic rather than religious argument against same-sex marriage is Judge Robert H. Bork. Bork has held a number of important government posts and is a former professor at Yale Law School. Most recently, he is professor at Ave Maria School of Law, a senior fellow at the American Enterprise Institute, and the Tad and Dianne Taube Distinguished

Visiting Fellow at the Hoover Institute. His books include *The Tempting of America* and *Slouching Toward Gomorrah*. Bork is recognized as one of the most brilliant legal minds in the country today. His nomination for the Supreme Court for which he was supremely qualified, was rejected by Congress because of his well-known conservative views. With eloquence and persuasiveness, he bases his opposition to the homosexual agenda on socially pragmatic grounds.

Judge Bork asserts that we are being asked to extend the full respect and sanction of marriage to a group of people identified by behavior that has adverse personal and social effects. Because homosexuals are still not generally accepted in American small towns and rural areas, most choose either a closeted existence or else move to an anonymous and impersonal city. There, if they are fortunate, they may become part of a homosexual subculture, which, while offering companionship and some protection, has unique problems. Gay people are often alienated from their families, and, even in understanding families, disappointment is usually expressed by parents who foresee a future without grandchildren and the other joys of an extended family. In the city, gay people are exposed to the very real physical and emotional dangers of the homosexual life-style.

Whatever the reasons, homosexuals, according to numerous studies, are less likely to be happy and satisfied with their lives than heterosexuals. Incidents of substance abuse and disease are much higher among homosexual men than in the general population. And this pathology cannot be explained simply by the social rejection that most homosexuals feel. Countries such as Holland and New Zealand, which are more accepting of homosexuals and therefore would seem to place fewer obstacles in their paths, report similar rates of suicide and emotional disorder as are found in countries that are less welcoming. Homosexuals are at a demonstrably higher risk for major depression, diseases of many kinds, and suicide.[6] The AIDS crisis has made the homosexual life-style even more threatening. Whatever it may be in Africa and elsewhere in the Third World, in the United States it cannot be denied that AIDS is a homosexual disease with a heavy toll. Although new drugs can prolong the lives of AIDS patients, the medical and drug regime required has grave personal and public economic consequences.

While the origins of homosexuality are unknown, one thing is certain: numerous individuals exist on the borderline, neither exclusively homosexual nor heterosexual. When homosexuality is widely promoted in the schools, the media, and even some churches, more people who could lead constructive and contented heterosexual lives may choose homosexuality, particularly when admired celebrities advocate this life-style. When such choices are made in youth, the full consequences of the decision will not always be clear.

The admittedly addictive promiscuity of many homosexual men is a further concern of society. When the AIDS epidemic started and epidemiologists interviewed the first men diagnosed with the malady, these men reported an average of 1,000 sex partners during their lives. Those who have further researched the HIV-AIDS epidemic have noted that some very active homosexual men typically have five to ten encounters in a single evening. Bell and Weinberg reported that their research revealed that 28 percent of white homosexual men claimed 1,000 or more partners, while 84 percent claimed 50 or more partners during their lives.[7] Five hundred and fifty different sexual partners was a lifetime average. Many of these encounters were anonymous, having taken place in bathhouses and other places of homosexual connection. With these facts widely acknowledged even by the gay community, it is not surprising that conservative straight society continues to be skeptical of demands for full rights and the recognition of marriage. Gay sex is associated with serious physical and psychological health problems. Yet the homosexual movement has done a brilliant job of presenting its case, labeling dissenters—even when the dissenters are primarily concerned with coping with the AIDS crisis—as "homophobic bigots." Homosexuals have demanded for themselves the benefits of a protected minority. They have hushed reasonable opposition, made it a social faux pas and in some countries a legal offense to suggest that homosexuality is not a desirable life-style.[8] They have further manipulated the language, claiming for their exclusive use the term "gay," a word that is sometimes the antithesis of the lives they lead.

Even lesbian women, the group in our society least in danger of contracting AIDS, show higher rates of hepatitis, gastrointestinal infections, cancer, and tuberculosis. Lesbians have higher rates of bacterial vaginosis, breast cancer (as do single women in general), and ovarian cancer. The incidence of violence is also reported to be higher in female same-sex relationships than in heterosexual relationships.[9]

Bork believes that giving homosexuals the sanction of legal marriage would be approaching too near the "slippery slope." Once the Supreme Court of the land puts its imprimatur on same-sex marriage, what arguments can then be made for refusing to recognize bigamous marriages? To insist that a man have only one wife might seem to contradict the record of the Hebrew Bible, violate the religious rights of American Muslims and Fundamentalist Mormons, and even resist human nature (as some anthropological and psychological research indicates that humans are not naturally monogamous). And after polygamy is accepted, what objection can be made to incest or relationships with animals? At present, the one clear sexual taboo that remains in our society is pedophilia. But that, too, may fall as agitation to lower the age of consent is already being made by organizations in Europe as well as in the United States.

Judge Bork laments the inroads that the homosexual agenda has made in our society. Not only is Hollywood glamorizing the life-style and schools are using books that present it as one family option among several, but even the institutions most trusted to perpetuate our values have capitulated. The Episcopal Church has consecrated a practicing homosexual bishop and given local congregations the option to celebrate same-sex unions. Unofficially, there are significant numbers of actively gay Roman Catholic priests and a growing pro-homosexual faction within the Church. Notably, a few years ago when Nigerian Cardinal Francis Arinze gave a commencement speech at Georgetown University, a commotion erupted. At Arinze's unfavorable reference to homosexuality among other forces in society he perceived as a threat to family and faith, a professor left the platform and a number of students walked out. Following the event, a protest letter was submitted to the dean of the College of Arts and Sciences, who had invited the cardinal as principal speaker. The letter was signed by 70 faculty members, ironically protesting a Roman Catholic cardinal who had uttered the Church's official teaching at one of the Church's primary educational institutions in the United States.[10]

Bork observes the success of the gay activist agenda throughout our society, making inroads into our most cherished conservative institutions. He feels this does not bode well for our future as a nation and as a civilization.

## The Argument of William J. Bennett

Another forceful defender of marriage as we now know it is William J. Bennett. Once widely referred to as "the morality czar," Bennett served two U.S. presidents, is co-director of Empower America, and is founder and chairman of K12, an Internet school. His publications include *The Book of Virtues* and *The Moral Compass,* in addition to his book that examined the contemporary American family in crisis, *The Broken Hearth.* A familiar television pundit, Bennett proudly informs audiences that his wife runs an abstinence program for teenagers. Although the recent revelation of his having lost $7 million at the Las Vegas gambling tables and the injudiciousness of some of his recent pronouncements may challenge his position as moral exemplat, the clarity of his arguments and the eloquence of his writing remain as persuasive as ever.[11]

Like other observers, Bennett finds the American family at a turning point. He quotes the late U.S. Democratic senator, Daniel Patrick Moynihan, a learned and outspoken academician before his service to several presidents, that the biggest change observed during his long life was "that the family structure has come apart all over the North Atlantic world." And this change, Moynihan further acknowledged, had taken place in "an historical instant. Something that was not imaginable forty years ago has happened."[12]

In the last half of the twentieth century, the family came under extraordinary challenges. Although we are all alert to the pace of modern life, this change transpired in such a short time that society has not had time to adjust to it in any comfortable way. People in middle or later years understandably exhibit the symptoms of "future shock," but younger people, too, feel these disruptions.

The institution of marriage, admittedly, has never been static throughout history and has had some features that Bennett admits we are better off without—such as the subjugation of women and the forcing of young people into marriages without their consent. Rather than being strengthened by modern advances, however, marriage seems now on the brink of collapse. Thousands of citizens of all political and religious persuasions have contributed to this breakdown; they have failed to honor the family commitments once made, in their search for some elusive good life and the pursuit of their notion of personal happiness. Although U.S. affluence plays a part in this attitude, marital instability is not merely an American problem. The family is also deeply eroded in some European countries, generally in the more prosperous ones. And Western society is feeling the consequences of this breakdown. Not only are divorce rates high, but increased social pathology is manifest in crime, imprisonment rates, welfare dependence, educational underachievement, alcohol and drug abuse, suicide, depression, and in sexually transmitted diseases.

Bennett is especially dismayed by the movement to legalize same-sex marriage. He is disturbed by the fact that many schools acknowledge the doctrines of gay activism; students in public schools are being taught that there is no essential moral distinction between gay partnership and heterosexual marriage. Bennett is further troubled by the political correctness movement that dominates the media and higher education and does not allow for a calm discussion of the pros and cons of issues related to homosexuality and other controversial subjects.

Bennett and others of like mind agree that the media, the entertainment industry, and the university have gone a long way toward validating homosexual practice. In the 1960s, the movie *Advise and Consent* attracted attention not by its artistic merit but as a novelty in its treatment of homosexuality. Based on a popular novel, it dealt with a novice congressman whose homosexuality was outed, resulting in the destruction of his career and his subsequent suicide. This was shocking subject matter but still comprehensible to a public that largely found homosexuality an unspeakable life-style. Today Congressman Barney Frank is open about his sexual orientation, and the governor of New Jersey defends himself against stronger allegations by announcing, "I am a gay

American." Comic Ellen De Generes outs herself on her television show, to great publicity, and her mother makes the media rounds pleading for same-sex marriage rights. *Queer as Folk* is a popular Showtime series, as is *The L Word.* In both shows, which not long ago would have been labeled as pornographic, several gay characters are involved in much homosexual experimentation. (Jennifer Beals, the star of *The L Word,* though heterosexual, acknowledges that her work has done much to prepare the country for same-sex marriage.) These shows, often dramatically engaging with attractive actors, soften many audiences to the demands of the gay movement.

Yet this bombardment comes to a still-reluctant American public. According to Bennett's calculation, which differs only slightly from others noted, no more than four percent of the U.S. population is gay. Although many gays live quiet, discreet lives, a number of highly vocal organizations promote the gay rights agenda, with methods ranging from moderate to in-your-face to coercive. Some of these organizations include the Human Rights Campaign, the Gay and Lesbian Alliance Against Defamation, the National Gay and Lesbian Task Force, and the AIDS Coalition to Unleash Power (ACTUP). At the far end of the spectrum is the North American Man/Boy Association, which most homosexuals themselves find repellent in its program "to end the extreme oppression of men and boys in mutually consensual relationships."

Today most state laws against sodomy have been repealed, the Supreme Court has affirmed privacy rights, and homosexuals who live without flaunting their sexual practices are able to exist in harmony with the rest of society. This is as it should be, even most opponents of same-sex marriage, including Bennett, agree. The Roman Catholic Church and many other religious bodies do not reject people because of homosexual orientation, even while upholding the Biblical prohibitions on homosexual conduct. As Bennett acknowledges, all people have trials to overcome and need to be met with understanding and forgiveness.

It is not when gays and lesbians ask for their rights as U.S. citizens that they encounter reasonable objections. It is when they demand extra privileges, preferential treatment, and legal and moral endorsement of their conduct that most Americans say they have gone too far. William Bennett, like others who value the American right to dialogue on contested issues, laments that voices of opposition are being hushed:

Moral criticism of homosexuality is today widely considered to be the equivalent of racism. Those who argue that marriage ought to be the exclusive preserve of a man and a woman, or who believe that homosexual adoption is not in the best interest of children, or who do not want their own children to be exposed to courses sympathetic to homosexuality, or who maintain moral objections to homosexual conduct are now routinely portrayed as bigoted, ignorant, and "homophobic." So much headway has this campaign made in the world of opinion that many middle-class Americans who oppose the homosexual agenda often hesitate to say so, and some even do not allow themselves to think so, lest they appear "intolerant." A kind of political correctness reigns, covering the issue of homosexuality with a protective veil of polite silence, if not yet full acquiescence.[13]

The homosexual movement looks upon AIDS victims as martyrs to love. Should we likewise make martyrs of those who die of lung cancer from excessive use of tobacco, Bennett asks? Instead of holding antisocial behavior responsible for AIDS, anger has been directed at the general public for its refusal to pour more funds into AIDS research, although it is already the recipient of extensive funding, with money and effort that might otherwise be used to develop treatments for other diseases. Bennett could well have added to his examples the widely repeated comment of Dr. Jocelyn Elders, former Surgeon General of the United States, who said: "They [older people] will probably die of somethin' anyhow."

Bennett's criticism of the homosexual agenda and his advocacy of traditional marriage is powerful and informed. Yet he has not blamed all society's ills on any one segment of the population; he has, in fact, identified other current social trends as more destructive of family life than homosexuality. He has singled out many public figures as particular offenders of public morality. And he is especially hard on celebrities who have children out of wedlock, believing that their doing so further weakens matrimony. These wealthy media personalities become role models for their fans and admirers, who often lack resources for bringing up children, with or without a partner. Because he did not hesitate to name names in setting forth his pro-family agenda, Bennett's own brief fall from grace was especially noted by the press and gleefully documented by his enemies. But his argument remains no less powerful.

Bennett observes that the scale of marital breakup in the West has no real historical precedent, and its future consequences are still unclear. Out-of-wedlock births, single-parent families, cohabitation in place of marriage among all social classes and religious groups, no-fault divorces, and the increasing separation of sexual conduct from procreation all point toward what may be the ultimate assault on family—the same-sex marriage movement.

While Bennett laments the loosening of standards of family values among Protestant groups and cites the example of a well-known Southern Baptist preacher who divorced his wife of over forty years and still maintained his pulpit and influence, he might also have cited, as many of his co-religionists have done, troubling facts within his own Roman Catholic Church. These include the ease with which couples in some dioceses have been able to obtain annulments since Vatican II, despite the expressed concern of Pope John Paul II. This practice further adds hypocrisy to the abrogation of marriage vows for Catholic couples who seek annulment even after the birth of several children.

## THE HOMOSEXUAL PROTEST AGAINST SAME-SEX MARRIAGE

It may be easy to anticipate the objections of known conservatives, but many homosexuals themselves feel that same-sex marriage would be detrimental. The initial rush to Canada, Massachusetts, and San Francisco (when the mayor was briefly issuing marriage licenses that turned out to be invalid) gave the impression that gays and lesbians all yearned for matrimony. Most homosexuals, even those in committed relationships, are not so eager. If they choose to make their lives together, they ask, in relationships that are meaningful to them, why not fashion an institution that meets their specific needs, that avoids the matrimonial injustices of the past and the baggage of history? Why not make of this uniquely gay union precisely what they want it to be? In a unique position to fashion a new institution to their liking that meets their needs, homosexual couples might wonder why they should adapt to one that has served, occasionally well but often badly, a heterosexual population for thousands of years. Some like to quote Mae West: "Marriage is a great institution, but I'm not ready for an institution."

Because they exist in a fringe culture, often ridiculed by the majority, many gay writers have adopted a "camp" sensibility, a protective stridency. An amusing and lively writer who exemplifies this attitude and point of view goes by the designation of "Gay Shame of San Francisco." The writer (whose gender is not clear) defines himself/herself as "a Virus in the System." While much of Gay Shame's rhetoric is over the top, it does occasionally strike home. He/she defines same-sex marriage as "a meaningless symbol of normalcy."

In an essay published in *I Do I Don't: Queers on Marriage,* Gay Shame deplored the actions of Gavin Newsom, mayor of San Francisco, in distributing same-sex marriage licenses, regarding the mayor's actions as a political stunt by an elected official who had long evaded the real problems of his city. Likewise, Gay Shame excoriated the people who rushed to City Hall to be married, the same people who "only ten years ago would have proclaimed that marriage is violent, racist, and homophobic—serving as one of the central instruments of society necessary for organizing a misogynist, sexist, and oppression-ridden world that has no intention of building anything resembling supportive communities."[14] Whatever happened, Gay Shame asked, to those who once saw being gay as a challenge to "misogyny, gender hegemony, and the imperialist, bloodthirsty status quo?"

Examine the rhetoric behind the same-sex marriage movement, suggests Gay Shame, to find out what its true intentions are. With marriage proponents hoping to transform gay identity into something acceptable to heterosexuals and gain all the advantages that conventional approval brings, they are, Gay Shame protests, sacrificing the force that has driven their movement to its own empowerment, while renouncing its productive challenge to the ills of the broader society. Furthermore, Gay Same believes this "gay-marriage media circus" in his city helped people forget for a time the genuine concerns of welfare, education, health care, housing, homelessness, and all the other problems for which the San Francisco city government has no solutions.

Homosexuals who reject the same-sex marriage initiative have revived some of the old anti-marriage arguments presented earlier in the century by dissenting social architects, and they have added a few points of their own. First they ask what marriage entailed in the past, and they acknowledge that it has always been, in addition to its patriarchal possessiveness, the chief setting in which children are born and nurtured. How much of this, they ask, really applies to gay couples living today in American cities? These couples want social and economic equality, but are usually far removed from the problems of family dynasty. Between themselves they cannot have natural children. So, what does anything resembling marriage have to offer a gay couple? The general outlook on marriage is bleak, so all sociologists and moralists seem to agree. Despite some legal benefits, the financial burdens of marriage can be enormous and inequitable. And divorce, especially in community property states such as California, can be an economic disaster.

Homosexual couples may well ask what Americans are really looking for in marriage today. How many of the expectations of the 1950s and early 1960s, periods that many look back on as the golden age of the family, remain with young people today? Are there not more intelligent and realizable options available? Is marriage still essential for the healthy, adjusted life—as many psychologists and therapists once believed?

It may come as a surprise to many people that there are conservative homosexuals, but, in addition to the highly publicized Log Cabin Republican caucus, they do exist, possibly in the same proportion as straight conservatives. Gays of this social or political persuasion usually resist attempts to tamper with any established institution, including marriage. One of the most visible lesbian conservatives is Tammy Bruce, the author of several popular books, commentator on the Fox news channel, and hostess of a nationally syndicated radio talk show. Bruce objects vociferously to what she regards as the tactics of gay politics, while holding what she identifies as the "classically liberal American point of view of allowing people to live their lives while expecting the same tolerance, respect, and dignity that you live by, in return."[15] She questions numerous dogmas of what she calls "the Gay Gestapo," including the assertion that people have no choice as to their sexual behavior. She challenges the constant reference to homosexuality as an orientation, the tendency of the movement to label the slightest criticism as homophobia, and the implication that there is consensus in the gay community on all important facts and issues. Affirming that her strongest defenders have been American Christians who, while disagreeing with her sexual preferences, have extended tolerance and affection, Bruce states her position:

I am not alone in the gay community in my respect and understanding for the growing concern about the disintegration of our traditions and values. Consequently, I respect the majority of Americans and their opinion that marriage should be defined as between one man and one woman. . . .

Frankly, I believe the cultural trouble and moral vapidity in our society today has sprung from the "liberation" movements of the sixties and seventies. It was then that the Left began to attack tradition in the name of liberation and equality.[16]

Gays and lesbians have asked several questions in response to the push for same-sex marriage. They question the contemporary credence of sociological treatises about unmarried men, who were once believed to be more lonely, sick, and prone to crime and dependency than married men.[17] After everything that has happened in the last three decades, it is not clear whether the married state should be regarded as the norm, the determinant of social and psychological health. And why have gays bought into the American bourgeois family ideal? One participant in the same-sex marriage debate, Jonathan Rauch, has suggested, only half facetiously, that marriage should not only be allowed; it should be made compulsory. Several have observed that were this to come about, we would see the largest gay protest march ever and finally learn how many people really want to marry.

In recent decades a considerable academic establishment has developed of sociologists, psychologists, and people in the arts, known as "queer theorists." Almost all of them, at least until recently, have been suspicious, if not hostile to the idea of same-sex marriage. At the least, they consider the agitation for marriage as an inappropriate emphasis at this time within the gay rights movement. Paula Ettelbrick, in an essay titled "Since When Is Marriage a Path to Liberation?" observes with some irony:

It [same-sex marriage] would make it easier to get health insurance for our spouses, family memberships to the local museum, and a right to inherit our spouse's cherished collection of lesbian mystery novels even if she failed to draft a will. Never again would we have to go to a family reunion and debate the correct term for introducing our lover/ partner/significant other to Aunt Flora. Everything would be quite easy and very nice.[18]

Ettelbrick continues, frankly and realistically acknowledging that marriage will never truly liberate lesbians and gay men. She feels that instead it will absorb them into the mainstream and "undermine the goals of gay liberation." A major goal of the organized gay movement has been the affirmation of gay existence and the culture it has developed, including the acknowledgement that many different types of relationship can be rewardingly experienced. Marriage is only one. Ettelbrick feels liberation will come not when gays are able to imitate the sexual and marital habits of straight society but when this society is compelled to recognize that gay life is an identity in its own right and has produced a culture with many unique variations. "Being queer," she concludes "means pushing the parameters of sexuality, and family, and in the process transforming the very fabric of society."[19]

Ettelbrick further rejects marriage because she does not want to submerge her identity into that of another person, becoming known primarily as someone's spouse, someone's "Mrs." She does not choose to submit her most intimate relationship to the dictates and whims of the state. Accepting legal marriage would greatly limit the range of choice that presently exists within the gay community and only within this community. Suddenly, with marriage, gay life would take on all the judgmental features that have afflicted straight life. She concludes her discussion by affirming:

We must keep our eyes on the goals of providing true alternatives to marriage and of radically reordering society's view of family. . . . We must not fool ourselves into believing that marriage will make it acceptable to be gay or lesbian. We will be liberated only when we are respected and accepted for our differences and the diversity we provide to this society. Marriage is not a path to that liberation.[20]

Frank Browning wrote an opinion piece for the *New York Times* (April 17, 1996) as the marriage debate was heating up. He found many problems with marriage as it exists today. The gay and lesbian movement might more usefully devote its energies to seeking acceptance of different kinds of families rather than agitating for some counterfeit marriage, he feels. "By rushing to embrace the standard marriage contract, we could still one of the richest and most creative laboratories of family experience."[21]

## THE RELIGIOUS CASE

Western countries are secular. The European Union recently rejected an attempt to acknowledge the continent's Christian heritage in its founding documents. It also rejected as one of its chief officers a distinguished Italian diplomat because of his avowed disapproval, on religious grounds, of homosexuality. A few years ago, Spain was dominated by conservative Roman Catholic sentiment; today it is one of the most liberal countries in the world, on the brink of giving full marriage rights to homosexual couples. Despite very low church attendance, England still maintains a state church. In the last few years the Scandinavian countries, among the last to maintain state churches, have been divesting themselves of these remnants of an earlier age. Italy has a culture saturated with the images of Roman Catholicism, yet is one of the most welcoming countries in the world with regard to gay concerns, despite the constant condemnation of homosexuality by the popes. Even Ireland and the Canadian province of Quebec, once called "priest ridden," have revolted against ecclesiastical domination. The United States from its founding erected that Jeffersonian doctrine of separation of ecclesiastical and political powers, yet remains one of the most religious countries in the world. Religion continues to be an influence in U.S. politics, even as the courts protect American laws from religious inroads and as organizations such as the American Civil Liberties Union and Protestants and Other Americans United for Separation of Church and State work to keep Bible study, prayers, and Christmas carols out of the public schools.

Yet even in these modern, secular Western democracies, it is impossible to deny that attitudes toward family, marriage, and sexuality have been historically determined and continue to be influenced by traditional religions. In the United States, religion is a choice, truly what one professes. In most of Europe, as elsewhere in the world, religion is an historical ingredient of ethnicity. In either case, it would be unwise to deny religion's continuing influence, even when it is experienced only indirectly. The idea of heterosexual marriage is deeply rooted in the Judeo-Christian tradition, which has undergirded the laws of these states. In parts of Africa, Asia, and throughout the Middle East, religious law, often based on Islam, remains the foundation of law. The wisdom—and sometimes the folly—of religious traditions should be considered in any attempt to change the mores and institutions of these communities.

In Europe and North America, the overwhelming religious influence continues to be the Judeo-Christian tradition. Judaism and Christianity, while not in total agreement on the precise meaning of matrimony or the conditions for divorce, have historically concurred on the issue of homosexuality. Traditionalists within each faith are opposed to the idea of same-sex marriage. The liberal wings of both traditions—influenced by the social sciences and more open to the secular life—have been moving toward acceptance of the gay movement agenda. The orthodox and conservative wings of both faiths, with a few notable exceptions, retain their belief that homosexuality and same-sex marriage are repugnant to human sensitivities and "an abomination" to God. Holding marriage in high regard, they see the homosexual demand for it as a sacrilege.

The key passages in Scripture, to which both faiths adhere, have been well rehearsed.[22] Added to the authority of Jewish Scripture is the vast body of Talmudic commentary. Christians appeal to the wisdom of the Greek and Latin fathers of the church, the determinations of acknowledged theologians, papal decrees, or the writings of Protestant Reformers. In these sources, a consensus is found that homosexual activity is sinful and detrimental to civilized society.

## The Jewish Perspective

The Jewish religious argument against same-sex marriage is basically as follows. First, there is the witness of Holy Scripture. Genesis, the first book of the Bible, provides an account of God's creation of the world, his determination that it is not good for man to be alone, and his forming of woman from man's rib. Pregnant with symbolic meaning, this passage of holy writ has been scrutinized by some of the best theological minds for over two thousand years. The immediate conclusion would be that God designed man and woman to complement one another.

The Genesis narrative has lent itself to varying interpretations of whether man or woman is inferior and which should dominate. An observation of some ultra-traditionalists is that the naming of animals gave Adam dominion over them. Likewise, the naming of woman indicated her position as inferior to his. This interpretation is not widely favored today. Some Jewish feminists have theorized (perhaps somewhat facetiously) that the Bible presents a progression of creation—from inanimate things, to animals, to man, and, finally, as the crown of creation, woman.

A rabbinical tradition more compatible with contemporary sentiment long ago observed that woman, significantly, was taken from man's rib, suggesting an equality with him. She was not taken from his head to rule over him nor from his foot, to serve him. She was intended as his companion. John Milton, an English poet of thorough Christian persuasion, relying on both his imagination and non-Biblical Jewish traditions, suggested that Adam's participation in the first disobedience—when he ate from the fruit of the tree of life given him by his spouse—occurred because he chose to share her fallen lot rather than live in Paradise without her.

Some commentators have observed that there are no parallels in the other literatures of the ancient Near East to a woman created from the rib of man. The name Eve appears to be a form of the Hebrew word for life, perhaps in recognition of the unique role of woman in giving birth. Adam, although at peace with the beasts, appears to recognize when Eve is given to him that at last a suitable companion has been found. The Jewish rabbis made much of this point. The language does not suggest female subservience but rather a common nature shared with the man and a role as his "helper." The implications of the story are that man and woman are sexually drawn to one another and through their ability to produce offspring together they become co-creators with God. According to the most familiar English rendering of the Bible, a man leaves his father and mother and cleaves unto his wife. The terms translated into English as "leave" and "cleave" are covenant terms, suggesting that when man and woman depart from their parents' home and commit themselves to one another they are accepting a covenant relationship stronger than a legal contract. The words of Genesis, among other levels of meaning, present a poetic, symbolic interpretation of a profound action of God and a great sense of awe in the presence of creative mystery and the divine ability to solve problems as they arise in the new Creation.

The second passage of the Bible referred to in the argument over the legitimacy of homosexual relations is the narrative of the ill-fated cities of Sodom and Gomorrah (Genesis 18–19). Most interpreters have found in the destruction of these two cities a strong statement of divine disapproval of homosexuality. According to Scripture, because of the wickedness of these cities, God wiped them from the face of the Earth. Abraham, who had already established some credentials with the Lord, tried hard to bargain, in the best techniques of the Bedouin marketplace, for the salvation of Sodom, but to no avail. Only a few of his close relatives were spared as sulfur and fire rained down on the two cities.[23] According to the Biblical narrative, Lot, Abraham's nephew, survives and goes on to some additional unsavory adventures, including incest with his daughters. The besetting sin of Sodom has generally been considered homosexuality, and other interpretations are felt to carry less weight.

Even if the destruction of Sodom and Gomorrah is subject to more than one reading, the unequivocal condemnation of homosexuality in the Hebrew Bible appears in Leviticus 20:7–16; 22–27. According to Leviticus, any two men who "lie" with one another as is fitting to lie with a woman have committed an "abomination," with the suitable punishment of death. The prohibition against homosexuality did not exist merely to separate Hebrews from surrounding pagans, argue the opponents of homosexual activity, or to mark them apart through a holiness code. Incest, adultery, defilement with animals, and homosexuality were all prohibited to Gentiles as well as Hebrews, as the rabbis have always taught.

## The Argument of Dr. Nathaniel S. Lehman

Nathaniel S. Lehman, a prominent physician, has expressed an impassioned traditional Jewish response to the demand for gay rights and, consequently, presents a strong argument that encompasses same-sex marriage as well. Lehman is the former clinical director of Kingsboro Psychiatric Center in Brooklyn. He also has served as chairman of the Task Force on Religion and Mental Health and was active with the Commission on Synagogue Relations and the New York Federation of Jewish Philanthropies. He states categorically that the prohibition of homosexuality remains a reasonable Jewish response to irresponsible sexual conduct that continues to exist in the modern world, just as it existed among ancient pagans. The Bible's enlightenment on sexual matters is a major Jewish contribution to civilization, part of an ethical revolution that has touched all humankind.[24] Judaism's teaching that all sexual activity should be channeled into marriage has been world changing, Lehman believes.

Lehman associates modern attitudes toward homosexuality with Germany, the major antagonist of the Jewish people in the twentieth century. He points out that about 150 years ago the Germans coined the term "homosexual," asserting that this was an inborn identity rather than a questionable practice— a novel idea at the time. Lehman reminds readers that before World War I, in parts of Europe, homosexuality was known as "the German vice."[25]

In the United States, Lehman observes, the gay rights movement has been active since about 1970. Two gay activists, Marshall Kirk and Erastes Pill, have been open in outlining their plans for the movement, and Lehman is alert to their tactics. First, the public is to be desensitized to homosexuality so that its repugnance will be replaced with indifference, if not immediately with full acceptance. Another plan is to equate homosexuals with disadvantaged groups in society, particularly African Americans. This appeal is especially strong for Jewish people who have in modern times tended to identify with oppressed minorities. Homosexuals will be presented as victims who need the protection of all right-thinking people. Another tactic will be to speak about homosexuality so often that it begins to seem a norm. The impression will be given that the entire world has turned gay. Opponents will be vilified, called "homophobes," and associated with racists, sexists, and other bigots. The AIDS epidemic will also be used to generate sympathy, playing down the chief ways it is spread and showing the many talented and admired people who have fallen victim to the disease. Since some of these people are world famous as highly accomplished artists, the task will not be difficult. The fact that the spread of AIDS is caused by "the unimaginable level of promiscuity" that exists in the gay community will be downplayed.

The plan continues, as Lehman observes. Opponents will be roughly dealt with. Those who suggest religious or other objections will be accused of hate speech; if possible, laws will be passed to limit such speech. Coming-out days will be scheduled on college campuses and in other places where susceptible youth are to be found. Any organizations, whether religious or otherwise, that reject homosexual activism will be accused of discrimination and, if feasible, ejected from campuses.

The media also will be widely used to legitimize homosexuality—not a difficult task since so many gay and lesbian people work in the media and have sympathetic friends throughout. This legitimization will begin with the Broadway theater, which already addresses an audience that is urbane, liberal, and receptive. Motion pictures, reaching a more general audience, will next be mobilized. Finally, the message will reach into North American living rooms via television. The ultimate focus of the campaign to "normalize" homosexuality will be the same-sex marriage issue. Lehman concludes his discussion by declaring: "The time is long overdue to recognize, combat, and reverse the fierce effort to legitimize homosexuality in America. Societal stability rests on the faithful marriages and enduring families whose basic structure Judaism was the first to define."[26]

## The Argument of Dennis Prager

The revolution in ethics started by the Jewish Torah is one of the most far-reaching changes in history, agrees Dennis Prager, noted author and influential talk show host on KABC radio in Los Angeles.[27] His newsletter, *The Prager Perspective,* provides a detailed explanation of Judaism's rejection of homosexuality. Societies that have not placed boundaries around sexual activity have been stymied in their development, he asserts. He shares Lehman's belief that without the Torah's prohibition on non-marital sex, Western civilization would not have been possible. The subsequent dominance of the Western world can be largely attributed, therefore, to the sexual revolution initiated by Judaism and later carried forward by Christianity.

It was all part of "the arduous task of elevating the status of women," continues Prager. The first thing Judaism did was to de-sexualize God, further separating him from pagan deities. In achieving this, it was necessary for the Bible to take an "unambiguous" attitude toward homosexuality, which was never, under any circumstances, declared right and proper conduct for either Jews or Gentiles. God commanded the entire human race to propagate and replenish the Earth. Prager believes that in the ancient world, and in the modern world as well, there is a direct correlation between the prevalence of male homosexuality and the degradation of women. Ancient Athens, so greatly admired for its artistic and philosophical contributions, glorified male love while wives and daughters were sequestered and regarded as hardly human:

While traditional Judaism is not as egalitarian as many later twentieth century Jews would like, it was Judaism—very much through its insistence on marriage and family and its rejection of infidelity and homosexuality—that initiated the process of elevating the status of women. While other cultures were writing homoerotic poetry, the Jews wrote the *Song of Songs,* one of the most beautiful poems depicting male-female sensual love ever written.[28]

Prager goes on to explain why he feels the homosexual life-style, which does not promote loyalty and fidelity, is not conducive to spirituality. He speaks first of the acknowledged promiscuity of gays; even lesbians today, he asserts, although he does not identify his sources, are likely to have had as many as 10 lovers. In an era when heroes are scarce and much-needed, homosexuals serve as inadequate Jewish role models.

Prager also believes that if the door is opened to gay sex, it will be only a short time before other questionable forms of sexual behavior (such as adultery and incest) will be brought into the social mainstream. Pointing out that honest Jews have always been defined by their responsible sexual conduct, Prager quotes from the *Syballine Oracles* written by an Egyptian Jew in the first century B.C. comparing Jews to the people of other nations. Jews were mindful of "holy wedlock" and did not have relations with boys as did the pagans who lived around them, according to the Egyptian document. In the twentieth century, sex historian Amo Karien quoted sex researcher Alfred Kinsey, to the effect that homosexuality was "phenomenally rare" among Orthodox Jews.

Prager rejects the theory that homosexuality is biologically programmed and says there is no solid evidence for this belief that has now been almost thoroughly sold to the public. He is somewhat more accepting of the view that many people are naturally bisexual. If this is true, then the argument that homosexuality is a chosen life-style is strengthened, not weakened. If people who have a bisexual nature suppress through acculturation the homosexual part of it, then heterosexual identity becomes a choice that society should foster. Prager notes that many, perhaps most, homosexuals have had hetero-sexual experience. Numerous homosexuals first lived, with whatever degree of happiness or misery, as heterosexuals and produced children in these relation-ships. Social expectations may be stronger determining factors in patterns of sexual conduct than is currently acknowledged.

While Prager bases his objections to homosexuality ultimately on the Torah, which he believes to be the Word of God, he also gives pragmatic reasons why he believes it is not sound public policy to encourage homosexual conduct. He concludes his discussion with these words:

The acceptance of homosexuality as the equal of heterosexual marital love signifies the decline of Western civilization as surely as the rejection of homosexuality and other non-marital sex made the creation of this civilization possible.[29]

## The Christian Perspective

The Christian Scripture, the New Testament, also condemns homosexuality, without exception. This condemnation is even more pervasive than that of the Hebrew Bible, because St. Paul specifically designates female as well as male same-sex relationships, eliminating any distinction the earlier Scripture may have made between male and female conduct. Christianity affirms, at least in the words of St. Paul, that "in Jesus Christ there is neither male nor female, Jew nor Greek, bond nor free."

It is sometimes pointed out that the gospels record no words of Jesus about homosexuality, either pro or con. Liberal Christians have concluded that this implies that the matter was of no concern to him, that he would have approved committed same-sex relationships. Conservatives respond otherwise. Jesus lived in a Jewish community that totally rejected homosexuality; there was no reason for him to waste words on an issue that was not in contention. But St. Paul addressed newly converted Christians, who lived in pagan societies that did not always find homosexual relations so offensive. It was, therefore, necessary for him to speak forthrightly on the subject. Paul broaches homosexual conduct in writings to both Roman and Corinthian churches. He sees such conduct as no less an abomination than did his Hebrew ancestors.

Like traditional Judaism, conservative Christianity rejects the validity of homosexual experience and is deeply opposed to calling such unions marriage. Even though the liberal wings of several Christian denominations, with their gay ordinations and their tolerant pronouncements on homosexuality, have received much publicity, the vast majority of Christians around the world do not support the homosexual agenda. They believe common sense, historical experience, and the directives of Scripture are united in opposition. In denying the legitimacy of Christian homosexual experience and rejecting the gay demand for marriage, opponents begin with one strong advantage. The Bible thoroughly and without equivocation supports this position. Christians who disagree have the difficult task of deconstructing or disregarding the Scripture they revere. The Bible condemns male homosexual practice and, at least as far as the Hebrew Bible is concerned, attaches severe punishment to it. In the New Testament, St. Paul labels as sinners both men and women who engage in same-sex behavior, suggesting that they will have an uncomfortable time in the world to come.

Throughout its history, the Christian Church has been rocked and sometimes rent by major controversies. In the early centuries of Christianity, the decisive conflicts were over the nature of Christ, the operations of the Holy Spirit, and the use of visual images as aids to worship. In the West, with the Protestant Reformation, the major issues became the nature of church government, the abuses of religious office, and the organization of the Church itself. In modern times, issues of personal conduct have come to the front, with matters of theology and church structure of less concern. In the United States today, the major issue of heated discussion in the churches is homosexuality. (This is not a central issue in most churches in Third World countries, where homosexuality is universally condemned.) Denominational publications are filled with news and debates relating to gay demands. The authority of the popes, who have spoken with consistent voices against homosexual practice, is challenged in some liberal Catholic publications. The American branch of the Anglican communion is now in full schism over the issue. More than any other problem or question—whether of faith, church organization, or conduct—this issue draws the line between liberals and conservatives in Christian churches.

Church members—and they remain by far the majority, though not always the most vocal—who oppose homosexual conduct and abhor the idea of homosexual marriage even more strongly, do so on three basic principles. First, there is the intense, consistent voice of Scripture. Second, Christian tradition for two thousand years has remained unwavering on the issue. Third, there are practical reasons; homosexuality is not conducive to mental or physical health and the abundant life to which Christians are called. While many Christians, though disapproving, may be ready to leave private sexual conduct to individual discretion and conscience, they are usually horrified by the suggestion that churches should develop holy commitment or marriage ceremonies to accommodate two men or two women who wish to pledge their troth to one another. Homosexual behavior may be found objectionable yet tolerable; same-sex marriage remains unconscionable.

## The Argument of Professor Robert A. J. Gagnon

Giving a rational, balanced, and charitable voice to the Christian opposition to the homosexual agenda is Robert A. J. Gagnon, an associate professor of New Testament at Pittsburgh Theological Seminary. He is the author of two major books and several articles on the subject. Few people have expressed the traditionalist position so effectively and buttressed it with such a command of scholarly tools and sources.

For the Church to suddenly declare homosexuality acceptable and same-sex marriage worthy of celebration, Gagnon warns, would mean not only "a radical devaluation of the place of Scripture in the life of the church," but it would be a total disregarding of the practical moral advice of Scripture. It would mean accepting the accusations hurled at sincere Christians by the opposition that brands them "homophobes," suggesting that they, in following Scripture, have become the moral equivalent of racists. It would soon mean the acceptance in public schools of the indoctrination of children into the idea that homosexuality or bisexuality is a life-style equal in value to heterosexual marriage. Soon, as has already taken place in a few European countries, our laws might even deprive us of the ability to criticize the gay life-style in churches, declaring any criticism of the homosexual persuasion as libel or hate speech.

For religious fundamentalists, whether Jewish or Christian, the clear Biblical prohibition is sufficient. God has spoken, and it is not for men and women to question his word. Gagnon, however, identifies his approach to the Bible as "historical-critical." Unlike rigid fundamentalists, he is ready to see development and tension within Holy Scripture. He realizes that many passages of Scripture apply universal principles to special historical circumstances that may no longer exist. There was, for example, in the church in Corinth a question about eating meat that had first been offered at a pagan shrine. That problem hardly concerns Christians today, though Paul's advice—to refrain from actions that could offend others—still applies. Gagnon's approach to Scripture readily acknowledges that parts of the Bible are poetry, with a variety of metaphoric meanings. An example would be the Semitic hyperbole of Jesus when he observed that it is easier for a camel to go through a needle's eye than for a rich man to enter heaven. He was surely not excluding father Abraham or King Solomon or even Bill Gates from the opportunity for salvation. The belief of a faithful Christian, even using the historical-critical approach is that Scripture, when studied intelligently, provides principles for living today and remains the central authority for faith and conduct in the life of the believer.

Gagnon's scholarly interpretation of Scripture still allows no place for homosexuality in the Christian life. Point by point, he answers each argument raised by gay activists. The Bible, he observes, is consistently, strongly, and without exception opposed to homosexuality.[30] While Gagnon would not argue that today we are required, as Leviticus decrees, to put to death those who "lie with a man as with a woman," he finds the basic moral principle still applicable, however controversial. He explains that even when this law was first enunciated in Scripture, it was already countercultural. Pagan peoples who surrounded the emerging Hebrew nation practiced homosexuality under certain clearly defined circumstances. Some appear to have made it a part of their cultic life. When St. Paul renewed the Old Testament prohibition, he was speaking to a Greek and Roman pagan world that tolerated homosexual conduct, while not always glorifying it. The Christian community, in every branch, maintained the Biblical prohibition for over two millennia, even when it meant defying the norms of the societies in which they lived. The witness of Christian people over time and space confirms this consensus.

Gagnon examines the argument frequently voiced that the prohibition against homosexuality appears in the Mosaic Law in the midst of a multitude of commandments and taboos that have little or no relevance to the life of Christians today. Most of these taboos have been long ago rejected. Even fundamentalists do not follow the Hebrew kosher rules; their Biblical justification is an allegorical dream of St. Peter on a rooftop releasing him from Jewish dietary restrictions along with further words of St. Paul on the subject.[31] Christians today do not keep the Sabbath, substituting the first day of the week, in honor of Christ's resurrection, as a day of worship and relaxation but without the restrictions on movement of a traditional Jewish Sabbath. Few Christians worry about wearing garments that may mingle cotton or wool with a synthetic. Why should they, then, pounce on one ancient prohibition and uphold this one Biblical taboo when they reject others?

Before the Christian era, Gagnon reminds readers, the rabbis had already decreed that honorable sexual conduct was required of all human beings. That this prohibition against homosexuality was not merely a Jewish eccentricity should be clear to Christians from the teachings of St. Paul. Even though Paul believed he was living in the last days when the divine command to "be fruitful and multiply" no longer applied, he still found homosexuality abhorrent.

If one accepts the argument that sexual conduct that affirms the bonds of affection, appears to damage no one, and does not detract from the performance of one's religious obligations is faultless, then many forms of sexual conduct may be condoned on the same grounds. As Gagnon points out, prostitution, plural marriage, incest, general promiscuity, commercial sex of various kinds, pederasty, and even bestiality might not have any immediately observable ill effects. In each case, a friendly, if not loving, bond might be affirmed, and these activities would not necessarily cause a person to neglect religious duties. Yet we instinctively are repulsed by most of these suggestions. Perhaps there is a wisdom in our revulsions.

But not all people, not even all Christians, find homosexuality repugnant. Attitudes sometimes change across the centuries. We use the Bible in relation to our own modern experiences, since we cannot, even if we chose, live in the manner of ancient peoples. Slavery was tolerated in Biblical times, but no Christian would advocate it today. Any christian denomination would find it abhorrent, yet the Bible contains no prohibition against it. Even St. Paul tells an escaped slave to return to his master. Biblical peoples, like other ancient folk, could hardly have imagined a sustained civilization that was not based in part on slavery. Yet today a Christian who tried to enslave another would be declared reprobate in any church and fellowship, which would almost certainly withdraw membership from such a person.

Of course, Gagnon reminds us, the Bible does not advocate slavery, and it might be argued that the principles of equality that the gospels enunciate led logically to its abolition in Christian countries. The Hebrew Bible, while not forbidding slavery, established laws for the humane treatment of slaves. Hebrews were constantly reminded that they, too, had been slaves in the land of Egypt, and millennia later the African slaves of North America were to find inspiration in the account of Moses' rescue of the Children of Israel from Egyptian bondage. In the New Testament when St. Paul sends the slave Onesimus back to Philemon, it is with a covering letter reminding the master that the slave is now his Christian brother, essentially his equal.

The changing position of women in the churches provides another example of positive social evolution since biblical times. Although there were some strong, audacious women in the Hebrew Scriptures, they were not members of the priesthood. In the early church, men were the clear leaders, the "bishops," although there is reference to women who were deaconesses and women who preached and prophesied generally with St. Paul's approval. Nevertheless, women have not been figures in the organization of the churches until recent times—although as saints they have been revered, and as queens and consorts of rulers they have sometimes been pious powers behind the throne. Today most mainline Protestant denominations accept the full ministry of women.

Divorce and remarriage is a third area in which most churches today often differ in practice from scriptural teaching. The words of Christ condemning divorce and remarriage seem to be as unequivocal as the Levitical prohibition of homosexuality, going far beyond the Law of Moses, which did make provision for "a bill of divorcement." Today, rather than face vacant pews and sit in judgment on the most personal and intimate matters, most Protestant denominations, however reluctantly, tolerate divorce and remarriage. Long ago the Eastern Orthodox Church made its adjustment to this human fallibility. Even Roman Catholics, who officially do not recognize divorce, have been generous in recent years in granting annulments. If the Archbishop of Canterbury, presiding over a communion that (while historically born in a divorce) has most consistently condemned divorce, could bless the second marriage of the Duchess of Cornwall, then surely some moderation of ancient rules has taken place.

So, if the church in modern times can reject its ancient and medieval tolerance of slavery and liberalize its views on women in church leadership, if it can even tolerate a practice seemingly so destructive to family values as divorce, why can it not find a way to allow two devoted persons of the same sex to pledge their loyalty and love for one another in a proper church ceremony? Why not same-sex marriage?

Homosexuality, Gagnon feels, is an issue different in nature from slavery, the status of women, or the problem of divorce. The role of women is a social rather than a religious issue today. The Scripture is not uniform in its condemnation of remarriage after divorce, and Christian laws have dealt with divorce in different ways through the centuries. Slavery was never mandated by divine command, and there were always Biblical rules mitigating its evils. There has been, however, over thousands of years, a consistent Jewish and Christian repudiation of homosexuality.

Religious advocates for traditional marriage fear "the slippery slope" at least as much as secular opponents of same-sex marriage. Will incest not be the next taboo to fall, if the sexual prohibitions of over two thousand years continue to be abandoned by the faithful?

In order to show how irrational he finds religious arguments in favor of regularizing gay relationships, Gagnon turns these arguments on their heads, reducing them to absurdity by applying them to incest:

A person cannot be held morally accountable for acting on innate incestuous passions?

The Bible's proscriptions of incest should be treated as out-dated purity rules?

The Levitical imposition of the death penalty on incest is reason enough to disregard the proscription?

Since Jesus said nothing explicit about incest he did not think incest was a major offense?

If a parent and adult child, or two adult siblings, love one another, it is none of the church's business?

Intense opposition to incest makes one an "incestphobe?"[32]

Gagnon answers those who contend that Jesus must surely have looked with favor upon homosexual lovers because he never said anything against them during his earthly ministry. Gagnon demonstrates the fallacy of the popular image of Jesus as a "meek and mild" ethical teacher especially lenient in matters of sexuality. Although Jesus did pardon the woman taken in adultery, according to that disputed passage in the Gospel of St. John, which is probably based on a valid Christian tradition, he then exhorted her to "go and sin no more."[33] In general, Jesus held to a stricter sexual code than did Moses. Gagnon rejects the pro-gay argument from Jesus' silence with the following observations:

the reason that Jesus did not speak explicitly against same-sex intercourse is obviously the same reason why he did not speak explicitly against incest and bestiality: the position of the Hebrew Bible on such matters was so unequivocal and visceral, and the stance of early Judaism so undivided, and with the incidence of concrete violation so rare, that nothing more needed to be said. There was no reason for him to spend time addressing issues that were not points of contention and on which he had no dissenting view. Jesus could turn his attention to sexual issues that were problems in his society: the threat posed by divorce and by sexually errant thoughts to the one valid form of sexual union—that between a man and a woman. Jesus did not loosen the restrictions on sexual freedom; he tightened them, albeit in the context of an aggressive outreach to the lost.[34]

Most Christians agree that Jesus replaced the Hebrew law with a covenant of grace. Yet the abolition of Mosaic Law was not intended to usher in an era of licentiousness. In fact, the new law, written on human hearts, is even more demanding of love and decency than was the old. Though God never required Gentiles to follow every letter of the Law of Moses, He expects an even higher standard of moral conduct of those who accept Christ.

Religious advocates of homosexuality often observe that there are only four occasions in which the Hebrew Bible condemns the practice, and some challenge the meaning of these.[35] Certainly, they feel, this suggests that while same-sex behavior may not be God's first choice for humans, it is less serious than Sabbath breaking and other offences singled out repeatedly in Scripture. However, Gagnon finds a "web of interconnecting texts" in the Bible that make quite clear the distaste of the Hebrew writers for homosexuality. Passages in the Bible in addition to those usually cited may well imply a rejection of homosexual practice. Gagnon cites the story of Ham's violation of Noah's nakedness, along with passages in Ezekiel and in the New Testament books of Jude and Second Peter.[36] There is a further problem; if homosexuality, which appears to have been practiced to some extent throughout human history, is so neutral an act, why is there not a single favorable reference to it in the entire Bible, either Old Testament or New?

The Creation story in Genesis is further corroboration of the divine intention that male and female be complementary. Two sexually differentiated humans are commissioned to complete God's plan of creation, to replenish the Earth. According to Gagnon: "To convey the legitimacy of homoerotic unions a different kind of creation story is needed—the kind of story spun by Aristophanes in Plato's *Symposium* (189c–193d), where an original male-male, female-female and male-female are split."[37]Although it might seem too obvious to point out, anatomy and psychology make the case for exclusive heterosexuality. Human bodies may be deformed and forced to perform certain acts for which they are not designed , but there is always a difficulty, a certain awkwardness, and sometimes physiological damage. Male and female bodies fit. Two male bodies may misuse physical parts, or they may attempt pale imitations of male-female contact. Yet a member of one's own sex, no matter how much he or she tries to imitate the opposite sex, can never supply the missing complementarity of its opposite.

Gagnon is sensitive to the contention that the Levitical proscription is limited in time and place because its primary motive was to promote procreation among a threatened people in an underpopulated world. His answer is clear:

Some scholars pinpoint to the procreative dimension as the primary motive behind the Levitical proscriptions (N47). This is tantamount to contending that, if not for procreation problems, sex with one's mother or another man's wife or one's sheep would have been acceptable. At stake are broader category issues, not having sex with too much of an "other" (bestiality) or too much of a "like" (incest, male-male ntercourse) and not disrupting the one-flesh bond of a legitimate sexual union (adultery; N48).[38]

Although Gagnon acknowledges the personal and professional risks involved, fully aware that "the knives of the politically correct are out" in the academic world, he feels compelled to speak not only because of the consistent and clear Biblical warnings of the dangers of the homosexual agenda but because reason itself rejects the ramifications of that program.

## St. Paul's Stance

Conservatively religious Jews and Christians are in basic agreement on homosexual conduct and same-sex marriage. Yet for Christians, the definitive word on homosexual conduct comes less from Hebrew Scripture than from the Epistles of St. Paul, who is often designated as "the second founder of the faith." Although Paul, contrary to his popular reputation, was a forgiving, charitable man, who well understood the dictates of the human heart and was, within the context of his time, respectful to the talents of women, he supported without compromise the strictures of Hebrew Scripture against homosexuality. Speaking in a cultural environment that demonstrated an unusual degree of tolerance for sexual behavior, he addressed the subject directly in Romans 1:24–27 and more cryptically in I Corinthians 6:9, as well as in I Timothy l:10. Attempts have been made to explain away this authoritative Christian source. First, it has been suggested that Paul was thinking only of the exploitative forms of homoerotic behavior that were common in the ancient world; such relationships were rarely conducted between equals. Usually it was a master exploiting a slave or an older man who was the lover of a young boy, an offense that today would land the senior participant in prison. Because slavery is rejected by civilized society today, our nearest equivalent to the former case would be a sexual relationship between an employer and employee, a potentially degrading situation that may violate several ontemporary laws. So naturally, it is alleged, Paul would have condemned the homosexual relationships that existed in his own day.

The second argument that seeks to weaken the objections of Paul claims that he could have known nothing of a homosexual "orientation" that is loving, permanent, and unchangeable. Surely he was speaking of the homoerotic relationships that existed in Greek and Roman communities, which were not exclusive but were either stages in the development of young men or supplements to more formalized marital relationships.

Finally the alleged misogyny of St. Paul comes again into play to disqualify his words. Paul is here accused, however falsely, of further subordinating women. He is said to have opposed homosexual love because he feared it would upset the proper dominance of men over women, when men were relegated in relationships to the status properly reserved for women, thus violating the great chain of being in which every creature knows its place and every woman knows that she is inferior to man.

The response to these attempts to mitigate the objections of St. Paul is simple, according to the defenders of traditional marriage. While Paul clearly would have known nothing about genes and how they influence our behavior and would not have engaged in debates about the existence of a "gay gene," he was a keen observer who would have recognized that a few men have a permanent sexual preference for their own gender. He would also have distinguished as readily as can we consensual relationships from those that are coerced. Had he intended, he could have easily made this distinction clear in his writing. People live with many desires that are destructive, and most strive to overcome them. The task is to tame our desires when they are harmful to society or abhorrent to others. Certainly the ancient world recognized deficiencies of nature. Paul spoke eloquently of perverted human nature, the result of being born into a world corrupted by the Fall. Furthermore, Paul mentions lesbian relationships and proscribes them in Romans 1:26. Paul ministered in cities where the goddess Aphrodite was worshipped. Although lesbian relationships in antiquity, unlike those of male homosexuals, were infrequently discussed and were probably not as exploitative, they certainly existed and did not win Paul's favor.

In conclusion, the traditionalist Christian approach to homosexuality affirms that it is a dishonoring of the design of God's creation, frequently an exercise in self-absorption and narcissism, when a physical nature like one's own is adored, and it evades the chief reason for the existence of sexuality, the perpetuation of the species. In fact, it makes a mockery of God's creative plan. Gender integrity is rejected, and God is informed that his design in creating two sexes is meaningless.

What is the proper approach of Christians to homosexuality? Most Christians today who examine the issue agree that the enlightened policy is not to condemn a person for having impulses beyond conscious control. Christians, like devout Jews or Muslims, seek to conform behavior to God's will. It is the behavior and not the innate desire—whether this comes from a gene, from unfortunate childhood experiences, or from some mixture of heredity and early environment—that is at issue.

What is the task of the Christian who has homosexual inclinations? Some psychologists affirm that it is the rare homosexual who has never experienced some heterosexual urges, however faint. Numerous people exist on the continuum, and perhaps they could function reasonably well as either homosexual or heterosexual. A few other people may be changed by so-called reparative or conditioning therapy, though the reported results have not been generally promising. For the majority of homosexuals, the proper Christian answer is celibacy. And it should not be forgotten that in Christian history it is the celibate state, no matter how unpopular today, that has been glorified above all others.

## Challenges to Boswell's Thesis

Because it has received such widespread acceptance, it becomes necessary for Christian opponents of homosexual recognition to provide a response to the thesis of John Boswell. Yale historian Boswell employed his vast scholarship in an attempt to establish that same-sex marriage was not new in Christianity but had been blessed by the Church in moving ceremonies before the fourteenth century. Although book reviewers who were not specialists in ancient and early medieval Christianity were initially impressed, it was not long before other scholars of ancient and medieval history were examining his theses and translated materials. They quickly discovered fallacies in his reasoning and major errors in his research. Boswell had let the urgency of his desire to justify christian homosexual conduct override his scholarly objectivity.

One of the most decisive responses to Boswell has been that of Dr. Marian Therese Horvat, whose extensive review of *Same-Sex Unions in Premodern Europe* appeared in *Catholic Family News* in October 2001. Horvat saw Boswell's work as a prime example of a pernicious trend in academia, what she called "the wholesale practice of historical revisionism," the inevitable result of advocacy scholarship. The academic world has been beset with books written from incomplete or questionable historical scholarship that has sought not to discover information but to promote a particular agenda—whether feminist, Afrocentrist, Marxist, or another ideological perspective.

While some books written from acknowledged platforms have been valuable contributions to scholarship, focusing attention on neglected historical information—for example, feminist studies examining private lives in the past—others have distorted facts to reach false conclusions. This "academic gobbledygook" has resulted in books such as *Constantine's Sword,* which uggested that Christianity's primary aim through two thousand years was the persecution of Jews. Horvat places Boswell's best known works in this same category. She carefully examines his central thesis that homosexuality was accepted in Eastern and Western Catholic tradition from the beginning of the Christian era until the fourteenth century. She discovers that this is not the work of an objective historian attempting to discover what actually happened in the past. Rather, Boswell is an activist working hard to find facts to promote a gay rights agenda and bring about a change in the doctrine of the Catholic Church.

Boswell's arguments are based on highly subjective readings of 80 manuscripts from libraries in Italy, France, England, and Greece—accounts and records of *adelphopoiesis* ceremonies. These were sealing ceremonies, once used in church liturgies to confirm loyal brotherhood between men. They appear to have been most common in the Eastern churches. Although the language is more ardent than we would expect today to find in expressions of fraternal love, this language is not out of keeping with the tenor of its time. Horvat finds these ceremonies completely different from those that united men and women in matrimony in ancient times. She also discovers that Boswell's translations are suspect in many particulars, because his choice of English equivalents for words used in the ceremonies often have gay connotations that the originals lack.

Horvat reminds us that Boswell ignores the consistent and frequently expressed disapproval of homosexuality by early and medieval Christian teachers. St. Augustine labeled sodomy a sin against nature, deserving the most serious punishments. According to St. John Crysostom, "there is nothing, absolutely nothing, more mad or damaging than this perversity." St. Albert the Great and St. Thomas Aquinas agreed that homosexual acts were disgusting, obscene, and contrary to the natural order of creation. Popes and saints in their writings and reported utterances consistently maintained this view.

Other documents from approximately the same period from which Boswell takes his supporting materials make clear that the Church imposed two or three years' penance on anyone found engaging in homosexual acts. The Church would hardly, at the same time, turn around and conduct ceremonies sanctioning this conduct on a permanent basis. Canon Law codes consistently and unequivocally proscribed homosexuality.

Horvat finds Boswell particularly objectionable when he implies that language used to describe "the most controversial same-sex-couple, Jesus and St. John, "the beloved Apostle" was "intimate, if not erotic." Boswell also implies some "libidinous relationships" between Sts. Peter and Paul, Sts. Perpetua and Felicitas, and Sts. Serge and Bacchus. Any friendships that are mentioned in Scripture or sacred tradition, if between individuals of the same sex—and opportunities for close friendships between persons of opposite sex without scandal were more difficult in past times—are likely to be given a libidinous interpretation by Boswell. Because of the association of homosexuality with military service in ancient Greece and Rome, Boswell is very quick to assume the same sort of relationship when he finds Christian soldiers paired in either service or martyrdom. Boswell also ignores the Christian stress on the brotherhood of all believers, in the Fatherhood of God, which further colors the language of early records.

Horvat finds it especially distressing that some other medieval historians have been so cowed by the gay rights movement and political correctness orthodoxy that they do not come forward to correct the evident excesses of books like Boswell's; rather, these historians heap praise on such books and give them prestigious awards. As a medieval historian, she objects:

Like bogus Marxist, feminist and black histories "homosexual" histories such as Boswell's are intent on "politics," and the scholastic works have become instruments in the struggle for influence and right of citizenship. What they are intent upon top-ping, however, is the whole code of ethics and morality of Christian Civilization.[39]

Another scathing answer to Boswell came from Robin Darling Young, Associate Professor of Theology at the Catholic University of America, who reviewed Boswell's second book in *First Things,* November 1991.[40] Young began her review by acknowledging that she has taken part in a bonding ceremony such as Boswell describes in his books. This was to seal a friendship with an Eastern church historian she met while on research in the Holy Land. Their friendship was blessed by a priest of the Syrian Orthodox Church in an ancient ritual from a collection of ceremonies designed to affirm friendship or adoption. Such ceremonies were never intended to sanction homosexual relationships, which have always been forbidden by the Church. Young points out that early Byzantine law codes contained extremely harsh punishments for proven homosexual offenses. Christianity, which promoted an austere sexual code, would never have developed ceremonies to be used as Boswell implies. Like Horvat, Young concludes that no genuine precedents for such permissiveness have ever been found.

Boswell's reading of ancient documents does not fully acknowledge the metaphoric language so commonly found in writings of their period, whether sacred or secular. For example, the word *adelphos,* brother, for Boswell all too often denotes a homosexual lover. For him the city of Philadelphia would be "the city of gay partners." Boswell also seems oblivious of the nature of Roman marriages, which were always clearly heterosexual—even if Romans sometimes entertained themselves on the side with the favors of slaves of their own gender. Boswell seems to regard Roman marriages strictly as property arrangements, as opposed to homosexual unions, which he believes were ardent, chosen, and morally superior. Although ancient marriages, not all that different from modern ones, were contracted for a variety of practical reasons, Young reminds us that they did not exclude mutual affection. Boswell's slanted use of materials gives the impression that homosexual marriage was acceptable and legal, even preferable to heterosexual unions, in the world into which Christianity came, and he dismisses those who disagree as blinded by their "homophobia."

Christians of all persuasions defer to Christian antiquity, because they believe that early Christians were close to the apostolic source of doctrine, which may since have become diluted by transmission. All try to establish "the sanction of antiquity" for their beliefs and practices. Boswell, in attempting to justify a contemporary attitude toward a universal but proscribed practice, has "invented an historical precedent." His book is filled with "unwarranted a priori assumptions, with arguments from silence, and with dubious, or in some cases outrageously false, translations of critical terms," according to Young.[41] He has created a false history in his attempt to find a usable past. His books, despite their elaborate scholarly apparatus, are ultimately embarrassing failures.

## NOTES

1. Richard G. Wilkins, "The Constitutionality of Legal Preferences for Heterosexual Marriage," in Lynn D. Wardel et al. *Marriage and Same-Sex Unions: A Debate* (Westport, CT: Praeger, 2003), 232.

2. John Witte, Jr., "Reply to Professor Mark Strasser," in Wardle, 43.

3. Ibid., 45.

4. Plutarch, "The Dialogue of Love," in *4 Plutarch's Moralia,* sec. 7690770 (Edwin L. Miner et al. trans., T. E. Page et al. eds., 1961).

5. Musonius Rufus, fragments 12, 13A, 15, reprinted and translated in Cora E. Lutz, ed., *Musonius Rufus: The Roman Socrates* 89 (1947).

6. Robert H. Bork, *Slouching Toward Gomorrah: Modern Liberalism and American Decline* (New York: HarperCollins, 2003), 369.

7. Lynn D. Wardel, "Image, Analysis, and the Nature of Relationships," in Wardle et al., 116.

8. Bork, 368.

9. Alan P. Bell and Martin S. Weinberg, *Sexual Preference, Its Development in Men and Women* (Bloomington: Indiana University Press, 1981).

10. In Sweden in the year 2005, a Pentecostal minister was charged with hate speech for teaching in his church that homosexuality is against the will of God. He is currently defending himself in court. Meanwhile, in British Columbia a man is in the same legal difficulty for quoting Leviticus in a newspaper advertisement.

11. After his gambling habit was revealed by the press, Bennett vowed to give up gaming, acknowledging that it sends a wrong message. While he reminded his public that gambling is not contrary to his Roman Catholic religious beliefs and that his family did not experience deprivations from his losses, he did understand how an advocate for the American traditional family needed to present a healthier example and should not be a fixture in gambling dens. He has not yet fully regained the trust that his many Protestant admirers previously had for him.

12. Quoted in William J. Bennett, *The Broken Hearth: Reversing the Moral Collapse of the American Family* (New York: Doubleday, 2001), 1.

13. Ibid., 106.

14. Gay Shame San Francisco, "Against Gay Marriage," in Greg Wharton and Ian Philips, *I Do I Don't: Queers on Marriage* (San Francisco: Suspect Thoughts Press, 2004), 136–137.

15. Tammy Bruce, *The New American Revolution* (New York: William Morrow, 2005), 230.

16. Ibid., 239.

17. Numerous historical and sociological books have presented the thesis that men without women are prone to crime, sickness, and early death. Of special interest is David T. Courtwright, *Violent Land: Single Men and Social Disorder from the Frontier to the Inner City* (Cambridge, MA: Harvard University Press, 1998).

18. Paula Ettelbrick, "Since When Is Marriage a Path to Liberation?" in Andrew Sullivan, ed., *Same-Sex Marriage Pro & Con: A Reader* (New York: Vintage Books, 2004), 123.

19. Ibid., 124.

20. Ibid., 128.

21. Frank Browning, "Why Marry?" in Sullivan, 133.

22. Chiefly the following: Gen. 19:1–9; Judg. 19:22–25; Lev. 18:22, 20:13; I Cor. 5–7; Rom. 1:24–27; 1 Thess. 4:3–8.

23. Two angels arrive in Sodom in the evening and receive hospitality in the home of Abraham's nephew, Lot. Soon the degenerate townsmen of Sodom, "from the youngest to the oldest," surround the house and demand that Lot send forth his visitors "so that we may know them." Lot, who does not want to violate desert rules of hospitality, offers his virgin daughters instead. The Sodomites, undeterred in their pursuit, try to break down his door and are struck with blindness. This episode confirms the Lord's determination to rid the world of such abominable people. He rains down ruin on the cities, though he spares Lot and his family.

24. Nathaniel S. Lehrman, "The Selling of Homosexuality," http://www.jewsformorality.org/aaaw148.htm (accessed February 9, 2005).

25. Ibid., 1.

26. Ibid., 2.

27. "Judaism's Sexual Revolution: Why Judaism (and then Christianity) Rejected Homosexuality!" http://www.orthodoxytoday.org/articles2/PragerHomosexuality. shtml (accessed winter 2005).

28. Ibid., 7.

29. Ibid., 12.

30. Robert A. J. Gagnon, *The Bible and Homosexual Practice: Texts and Hermeneutics* (Nashville, TN: Abingdon Press, 2001), 267.

31. Paul rejected the faction in early Christianity that wanted to make converts first Jews, subject to the Mosaic Law. He affirmed that neither observance of kosher food laws nor circumcision were required of Christians.

32. Dan O. Via an d Robert A. J. Gagnon, *Homosexuality and the Bible: Two Views* (Minneapolis: Fortress Press, 2003), 49–50.

33. The episode of Christ's pardon of the woman taken in adultery is not present in the oldest records of the Gospel of St. John. However, the narrative is a favorite in Christian lore, much celebrated by poets and artists, and may derive from an authentic tradition.

34. Via and Gagnon, 73–74.

35. Only the accounts of the destruction of Sodom, the narrative of the Levite at Gilbeah, and the two Levitical proscriptions appear to deal with the subject (Gen. 19:1–9; Judg. 19:22–25; Lev. 18:22, 20:13).

36. Gen. 9:20–27; Eze. 16: 49–50; Jude 7; II Peter 2:7, 10.

37. Via and Gagnon, 61.

38. Ibid., 65.

39. "Rewriting History To Serve the Gay Agenda," http://www.traditioninaction. org/bkreviews/A_002br_SameSex.htm (accessed fall 2004).

40. "Gay Marriage: Reimagining Church History," http://catholiceducation.org/ articles/homosexuality/ho0069.html (accessed September 12, 2004).

41. Ibid., 2.

# 6

# Life-style Choices: Alternatives to Traditional Marriage

Although some social theorists have recommended that governments get out of the business of regulating marriage, leaving individuals to fashion their own living styles and family patterns, most people agree that the state has an essential interest and role in protecting vulnerable persons in relationships and the children who may be dependent on these relationships. Whatever their attitudes toward same-sex marriage may be, almost everyone acknowledges that radical shifts in social and moral attitudes in the last three decades have led to the decline of the traditional family. Among the forces heading this decline are increased individualism; the rising expectations of Americans frantically pursuing happiness; the sexual revolution, which has included the birth control pill and legalized abortions; and multitudes of women joining the workforce. Changes in consumer patterns, the popular culture, and affluence also share responsibility. Some options to traditional marriage continue from the past, including single life, so-called Boston marriages, and nonsexual marriages. Others options include open marriages, cohabitation without legal status, communal marriages, group marriages, and socially approved but not legally certified same-sex unions. The law has assisted by allowing limited-commitment marriages with no-fault divorce, as opposed to the more restrictive covenant marriages, which are now available in a few states. Increasingly, more status is extended to domestic partnerships and civil unions. Some sociologists have advocated a revival of polygamy, in addition to trial marriages, term marriages with the possibility of renewal, and weekend marriages, all with some legal standing.

The view of marriage as "a permanent haven in a heartless world" began to change in the last half of the twentieth century. The popular idea of marriage as "something one just does" as a necessary rite of passage started falling into decline as well. Instead of an anchor amid the flux of uncertain existence, many people started defining marriage as an oppressive legal status that hindered the full realization of personality, especially for women. The divorce rate soared, and, curiously, it was highest in the American South, known as the conservative Bible Belt. Although divorce rates increased in all ethnic groups across the United States, they were highest among African Americans, who were more oppressed by economic conditions, and lowest among Asian Americans, who prospered in America and maintained their extended family concepts.

The media, too, played a part in the decline of traditional marriage in the last decades of the twentieth century. The Ozzie and Harriet early television model of family life became a standing joke, while Donna Reed and Myrna Loy were ridiculed as film models of the restricted conventional wife. First Lady Hillary Clinton made light of Tammy Wynette's hit song, "Stand By Your Man." Models of family life different than those acclaimed by television in the 1950s now attracted attention. In one popular situation comedy, Murphy Brown had a child out of wedlock and was widely congratulated for her audacity.

Despite decades of negative propaganda and a marriage failure rate in some states at 50 percent by the end of the century, Americans still remained basically a marrying people. After divorces, most Americans remarried rather quickly. Even when marriage seemed no longer socially obligatory, and as family pressures to marry declined and women in the work force were no longer economically dependent on husbands, most Americans were still seeking companions and the blessing of state and church on their relationships.

Yet marriage as experienced in the United States at the beginning of the third millennium was not marriage as it had been conceptualized for the past two thousand years in the West. It was far from the Jewish or Christian ideal. According to psychologist and would-be sexual mentor Albert Ellis, "today marriage is only technically or theoretically monogamous, . . . it is more often than not monogynous or pluralist; and . . . it is becoming, in many different ways, more marital (that is, companionable and partnership like) but less exclusive."[1]

What sociologists designated serial monogamy seemed clearly in place by the end of the twentieth century, with the high divorce rate and frequent remarriage. Some preferred to speak of progressive monogamy, suggesting that Americans "married up" each time, taking a complicated web of children, stepchildren, in-laws, and former in-laws along with them into new relationships. Although many people were living together before marriage, somewhat surprisingly, when they did marry, they had higher divorce rates than those who had not previously cohabited. With more people living longer than ever before, some sociologists suggested that long-term monogamy had become an unrealistic or impossible ideal to maintain. In the past, when so many women died in childbirth, a man who lived three score and ten might easily have three wives during the course of his life. Now the need for novelty in intimate relationships for many people had to be satisfied by either term marriage or accepted adultery.

As marriage became less a social, family, and religious obligation, people who embraced it demanded more of the institution. They took seriously the fairy tale and Hollywood happy ending, marrying to "live happily ever after." Yet reality had always been quite different. Marriage, especially for the middle class, was caught in a crisis of rising expectations. A spouse was expected to be more than any person, religion, or community ever before reasonably demanded. He or she was to be helper, friend, provider, confidante, counselor, and stimulating intellectual companion. This spouse would also be romantic, sexy, and emotionally enhancing. If children came, then expert parenting was further expected. A successful career, community status, and a good income were desirable now for both spouses. With such grandiose expectations, it is not surprising that so many people have found marriage disappointing.

With the married state in trouble, one might wonder why many gays and lesbians want to participate in the institution. Does the prestige of marriage remain, even with all its failures? And why do so many people who could legally marry without any problem still look for alternatives?

## SINGLE LIFE

Swimming against the current are those individuals who, through choice or circumstances, remain single. They are often stigmatized and sometimes legally disadvantaged. They have been the object of unkind jokes. Even today they generally shoulder more than their share of the tax burden and the work load, yet they have sometimes been the most creative and socially valuable people.

When Americans discuss rights, equality, fair treatment, diversity, choice, and public concern for the preferences of sexual minorities, one fact is sometimes overlooked. When legal benefits are extended to yet another group—benefits that are in part economic and affect work loads and tax codes—some benefits are taken away from another group. For every gift that government bestows, somebody pays. When employers extend family health and retirement benefits to dependents of more and more workers, these benefits are paid in part by the labor of those with fewer dependents. People who remain single are in some ways dismissed by a society intent on pairing. Does the government have a vital interest in this matching of citizens, and can it be proven that married people are healthier, more law abiding, more socially responsible, and more productive than single individuals?

Proponents of marriage for everyone frequently cite studies that show the gains in health and life expectancy that married people enjoy, but other studies have suggested that single women fare better in all these respects than married women. Some studies also have suggested a greater degree of happiness among single women.[2] Sir Francis Bacon—notably a single man and recently claimed, on highly contested evidence, by the gay community as one of their own—wrote a famous essay contrasting married and single men. He observed: "Unmarried men are best friends, best masters, best servants . . . a single life doth well with churchmen, for charity will hardly water the ground where it must first fill a pool." And then came his even more frequently quoted words: "The best works . . . have proceeded from the unmarried and childless men."[3]

At one time in England, as elsewhere, men who chose to remain single were subjected to a special tax; no attempt was made to disguise this tax on bachelorhood. Apparently spinsters were not believed to have enough income to tax. Today single people in the United States sometimes feel that they are unduly pressed. When they work in businesses and professions that provide an array of family perks, for which they do not qualify, their contribution is out of proportion to the remuneration they receive. Their labor helps pay for the family benefits others enjoy. A single female professor at Vanderbilt University suggested, perhaps facetiously, as she contemplated the free tuition the children of her married colleagues received: "To be fair, they should send my whippet to obedience school!"[4]

The claim made by couples for special access to lodging and certain types of tax relief places an unfair burden on single people, who must make provision for their own care in sickness and in old age, who must often live in places that provide additional security, and who, because of their freedom from family responsibilities, often contribute additional hours and fuller attention to their jobs and professions.

And single Americans are constantly increasing in numbers. In 1960, 1 in 10 American women aged 25 to 29 was single. By 1998, nearly 40 percent of women in this age group remained single, although it is unclear how many were living with partners. In the 1950s, married couples represented 80 percent of all households in the United States, but by the beginning of the twenty-first century they comprised less than 51 percent, while married couples with children represented 25 percent of all households. For the first time ever, there were more single-person households than those comprised of a married couple with children. Married persons were still a majority of the workforce and of home buyers in 2001, but unmarried individuals were gaining fast, accounting for 42 percent of the workforce and 40 percent of home buyers. The earlier contention of merchants and advertisers that nuclear families are the best consumers has been replaced by the discovery that single people today often have more disposable income and may be the best market for entertainment and luxury commodities.[5]

It is not known how many single people would be ready to take part in domestic partnerships or civil unions, but the trend toward true solitary living seems to be substantial. And this trend is not simply American. In 1950, 10 percent of all households in Europe contained only one person. Five decades later, one-person households made up a third of all British homes and 40 percent of Swedish ones. Even in Greece, which had the lowest percentage of one-person households in Europe at the end of the twentieth century, such households still represented almost 20 percent of the total, twice the 1950 average for Europe as a whole. The rights of single people, who may themselves eventually organize as a minority and political pressure group, would be compromised by a government that extended matrimonial benefits even further than it presently does.[6]

## THE BOSTON MARRIAGE

There are numerous reasons why two or more unmarried women might choose to live together. Usually they work at less lucrative jobs and are paid less than men even when performing the same jobs. Especially in cities, personal safety is an important consideration. Two people living together usually feel safer than one living alone. It is comforting, as well, to have a housemate in case of sickness or emergency. The need for companionship and affection, without the complications of marriage and children or the long-term commitment that marriage has traditionally entailed, has motivated many career-minded women to live with housemates.

Some women who might have accepted marriage but found no man who met their specifications choose to remain single rather than lower their expectations. These women, who frequently channel their energies into work, a profession, or volunteer work, sometimes choose to make their home with other congenial women. With the increased awareness of lesbianism in recent years, it has become more difficult for two women to live or room together over an extended period without arousing suspicion or generating assumptions. In the past such relationships were accepted even in the most conservative circles, and they were often encouraged. Accusations of lesbianism were rarely made, whether this toleration was the result of innocence or sympathetic understanding.

These relationships are sometimes referred to as *Boston marriages.* The term is derived from the Henry James novel *The Bostonians,* which depicts an affectionate bond between two women and states that such attachments were common in Boston society by the late nineteenth century. James described his 1885 novel as "a very American tale . . . [about] one of those friendships between women that are so common in New England." [7] Some creative artists—Amy Lowell, for example—left poetic accounts of their love affairs with the women whose residence they shared. Less prominent women sometimes left hints in diaries and journals of relationships that were more intense than friendship. Otherwise, it cannot be known which or how many of these relationships were overtly or covertly lesbian.

Students of the Boston marriage phenomenon, such as Kathleen A. Brehony, lament the deficiency of language for discussing and therefore validating relationships of this kind, whether sexual or nonsexual. Once such a companion would have been referred to as "a household member." Today, the preferred terms have an awkward flavor. "Significant other" and "gal pal" are too cute, while "partner" sounds like someone's business or law associate. "Mate" is too clinical, or perhaps nautical, in its connotations, while "lover" reveals more than necessary. Lillian Faderman, a major writer on lesbian and female relationships, has highlighted the problem of language ambiguity:

It may be useful to resurrect from history the term "Boston Marriage" as a description of long-lasting love relationships between women that are seldom or never sexual. That term might give women another way to look at their relationships that transcends twentieth century pressures to seek an elusive sexual passion, which often accounts for the breakup of the couple. The re-creation of that category would permit many women to explain their relationships to them-selves and others not as problematic because they lack what has been socially constructed in more recent times to be seen as essential, but rather as viable unions with honorable histories. [8]

Even before the Boston marriage was identified and named, there were "romantic friendships" that existed between women. Often these had their start in high school, in the girlish cliques, and flourished in boarding schools. Lesbianism seems not to have been assumed, and the word was not used before 1870. Not only were these deep friendships widely accepted; they were idealized. Almost every young girl had an official "best friend." For many, these friendships were a prelude to marriage and quickly dissolved after that; for others, the "best friend" relationship lasted into marriage, yet was not perceived as a threat to what then became the dominant relationship with the husband. Female associations were, at least in theory, asexual.

The Boston marriage achieved an informal social status; two women living together were acknowledged as companions by their associates. Openly lesbian Boston marriages existed more freely in artistic and bohemian circles. Ernest Hemingway in *A Movable Feast* speaks of being entertained in the elegant Paris salon of Gertrude Stein and Alice B. Toklas. While Stein discoursed on art and letters with the men, Toklas took care of the wives, shrewdly managing the likes of Zelda Fitzgerald. But most Boston marriages did not have such clear role differentiations and were based on an equal sharing of responsibilities, without mimicking heterosexual relationships.

Until the middle of the twentieth century, it was still difficult for a woman to maintain a home and a major career. High-achieving women usually remained single, either because their work left little time for courtship or their achievements intimidated likely suitors. In the early years of the century, the majority of Vassar graduates, the women whose names appeared most frequently in *Who's Who Among American Women,* remained single. And for any or all of the reasons suggested, many of them chose to make homes with other successful women of comparable sensibilities. Today in the American states and foreign countries that recognize domestic partnerships, these women might choose to so register their living arrangements. They probably would not, however, call their association "marriage."

## OPEN MARRIAGE AND COHABITATION

Significant numbers of people in the last decades of the twentieth century started searching for ways to liberate themselves from the restraints of traditional marriage without renouncing its legal and social advantages. Open marriage became the subject of some books and was acknowledged in a limited way as a social experiment. In open marriages, couples agree to live together and share responsibilities to the extent that it pleases them, at the same time accepting all the available perks of marriage. While presenting a united front to the community, each party reserves the right to experiment sexually and socially outside the marriage, conducting sexual encounters and even more sustained love affairs as they see fit. Each couple in an open marriage works out their own agreement. Some permit only recreational sexual encounters, stopping short of serious affairs in which there is emotional involvement and the fear of undermining the marriage. In practice, most couples find open marriage difficult to sustain and eventually reject the arrangement as unsatisfactory.

Cohabitation has proven a more lasting alternative to traditional matrimony for larger numbers of couples; in fact, it is often almost indistinguishable from marriage. Cohabitation today differs from the old common law marriages that are still recognized in at least two U.S. states. In common law marriages, the couples regard themselves as permanently united, and they present themselves as such to family and community. For whatever reasons—because of the expense and inconvenience of purchasing a marriage license, distrust of public officials, legal complications, or lack of opportunity—they do not register their union. However, in states that recognize common law marriage, the courts have upheld inheritance and other family rights and obligations.

Living together without formal or lasting commitment, still technically illegal in some states, is widely accepted. It is not always clear why such couples—especially when they are rearing children, as they are increasingly doing—choose not to obtain a marriage license. Some come from broken homes and distrust traditional matrimony. They may have seen bitter divorces with legal complications they do not wish to experience if and when they choose to sever their current relationships. They may want to make sure they have a quick way out of a relationship if they are unsure of its permanence. Or they may be philosophically opposed to marriage.

In the past it was largely the lower classes that chose this family style, but today it is a middle-class pattern as well. A middle-class couple is likely to cohabit until they decide to have children or become fully convinced that their relationship is permanent. At this point they may bring in the clergy, the records clerk, and their respective families and become legally married.

Breaking up can be just as painful, or more so, when there are no legal forms to complete, no social expectations to meet, and no in-laws to protest, as more and more couples are discovering. In Scandinavia, where unmarried families are more common than in the United States, a vast network of social services exists to mitigate the problems faced by unmarried couples who break up. In countries without these supports, severing ties may be economically devastating as well as emotionally wrenching.

## POLYGAMY

Some radical sociologists advocate a return to polygamy, particularly in places where women outnumber men. Polygamy has the sanction of antiquity, of having been tried even in the American past, and it is still practiced in many parts of the world. It may even be more in line with human nature. Humans appear not to be among the instinctively monogamous species, such as the wolf or the Canada goose. Males seem especially prone to seek sexual variety. Polygamy still exists in small Utah towns and a few surrounding states in isolated communities among Mormon fundamentalists. The official Church of Jesus Christ of Latter-day Saints, centered in Salt Lake City, strongly disapproves of and excommunicates those who commit polygamy, although the practice was a much-discussed part of Mormon history and is believed by Mormons to be a feature of the world to come. Polygamy was tolerated by the biblical Hebrews, and some of the most honored patriarchs had plural wives. Today in Islam a man is allowed to have four wives, provided he treats them impartially; European countries with large Islamic populations are experiencing legal challenges to their monogamous laws. It is possible within the next few years that there will be a constitutional challenge to monogamy in the United States, on the principle of separation of church and state. One Supreme Court justice, Ruth Bader Ginsberg, has examined the possibility tolerantly in her writings. If plural marriages were to be accepted in Western Europe or North America, women would have to be given the same privileges of multiple spouses as men, although it is unlikely that many would choose polyandry. And considering the supply of eligible men in the United States today, women would most likely have to import their plural husbands from countries with excess male populations.

The Mormons instigated a novel form of marriage when they decided that single women could be "sealed" to dead Mormon patriarchs. In an unrelated but similar development, French law recently recognized, under special circumstances, as legal a marriage contracted by a living person to one recently deceased.

## COMMUNES

Communes generated much curiosity in nineteenth-century and early twentieth-century America. The Oneida community of New York, remembered for its silverware industry, has been one of the most analyzed and discussed of these communal societies, in large part because it was not merely an economic commune but attempted innovative social experiments, most notably in group marriage. The commune's goal was to eliminate the jealousies, frustrations, possessiveness, and sentimentality that the group's founder, John Noyes, found so painful in conventional marriage. The eminent British sexologist Havelock Ellis studied the commune and gave it a favorable report. However, after 40 years of weathering the disapproval of the outside world, which was fed by lurid tales of life in Oneida, this commune, like others before and after it, collapsed. One problem, which was to resurface in practically every commune, was the autocratic control of the founder and leader and the fact that innovation eventually proved less satisfying than the established institutions of society.

Almost all American communes have sought to control the sex lives, or lack thereof, of people within them. The most successful and lasting of all American communal arrangements, with the exception of the religious orders of the Roman Catholic Church, were those of the Shakers. With flourishing Shaker villages located in strategic places in the East, Midwest, and South, men and women lived in the same buildings, yet maintained separate quarters and celibate lives. They were sustained by their unique form of Christianity, founded by a woman Mother Ann Lee who disdained sexual relations and emphasized a feminine as well as masculine face of divinity. Shakers developed exquisite crafts, and maintained flourishing farms. Their communes eventually closed, more because of industrialization than any disillusionment with the style of life or the celibacy of committed Shakers. For years they had sustained their numbers by adopting orphans and attracting converts. Interestingly, communes have been most successful and enduring when celibacy has been the rule.

Communes experienced a revival of popularity in the late 1960s and early 1970s. Although of appeal to only a small minority, they were again the objects of widespread and often prurient curiosity. Some were religious cults; those led by Charles Manson and Jim Jones were the most sinister. Others, whether religious or secular, were often built around idealistic beliefs that people could live together simply, be nourished by Mother Nature, maintain self-sufficiency, protect the environment, and rear children without the neuroses of a corrupt society or possessive parents. The Farm, a commune in Tennessee, attracted nationwide attention, both for its drug use and its polygamous common law marriages. Yet the inhabitants of the commune lived peacefully and generally maintained calm relations with their Bible Belt neighbors.

Most of the communes that appeared briefly in the United States during the 1960s and 1970s have long since dissolved and left too little data to make any convincing analysis of their success. Some of their inhabitants collapsed from drug use, other excesses, and mental illness. Most commune inhabitants simply vanished into the general population, some merging successfully with the middle class. Among the more successful communal experiments still functioning outside the United States are the Israeli kibbutzim, where conventionally married couples pool their efforts and resources in the rearing of children and maintain a self-sufficient life-style in a pioneer environment.

The idea is entertained by some people, at least in theory, that, with social acceptance, group marriage in a communal setting would offer certain advantages and solve some of the problems that numerous individuals face in traditional marriages. But many people who have lived in communes assert that in every such organization there is a chief who is an absolute dictator, who often arbitrarily determines who sleeps with whom and whose desires, after his own, are the first to be met. Most, though not all, cult leaders have been men.

## LIMITED COMMITMENTS

The anthropologist Margaret Mead, who tried several sexual and marital styles herself, decades ago proposed a two-tiered marriage model. In the first stage, which she called individual marriage, a man and woman would be legally tied but without the necessary expectations of permanence. The couple would not expect to have children. If the marriage survived and the couple decided to have a family, they would then move to the second stage— called parent marriage—which would have the expectations of permanence and be difficult to dissolve. However, this marriage might well be terminated without rancor in middle-age, after the children were grown, when a couple might feel it time to move along. Mead also advocated a type of legalized premarriage, in which young people could safely explore their sexuality and would, in effect, be in training for later mature marriage. Although without the terminology or the precise legal status she recommended, Mead's ideas have essentially come to fruition, both in the current custom of cohabitation and, with some modifications, in the Louisiana and Arkansas innovative practice of offering two grades of marriage.

The idea of trial marriage has been around for almost a century and did not originate with Margaret Mead. Early in the twentieth century, Judge Benjamin Lindsey lectured throughout the country as a proponent of such arrangements, which he called companionate marriages. He frequently debated religious leaders (most of whom were horrified by his proposals). Companionate marriage did not catch on with the masses of people in what was still a country with conservative bourgeois values.

The idea was once again introduced midway into the century by the social critic and popularizer, Vance Packard. He believed that young people should live together for a two-year "conformation period." If that were successful, they would be allowed to take formal wedding vows, which would commit them to a lifetime together. Today Packard's ideas seem a little conservative. Many couples who cohabit allow themselves something closer to a seven-year trial period. If they are still together by that time, the general perception is that they should have a good prognosis for matrimonial success. Unfortunately, this has not proven to be a very successful system; couples who forgo a trial period of living together have a lower divorce rate than those who lived together several years before marriage.

Lawrence Casler, a social psychologist, has proposed an alternative to traditional marriage that he calls "quaternary marriage,"[9] in which two couples and any children they may have live together, sharing responsibilities and bringing into the home a greater diversity of survival skills. The two couples may choose to be faithful to their primary spouses or they might choose alternating sleeping arrangements. Casler foresees no problem with either arrangement and thinks that few jealousies or personality clashes would mar the program. At this point, any couples who may have followed Casler's suggestions have not been forthcoming in sharing their experiences, so it is impossible to evaluate the success of his proposal.

"Contractual monogamy" is another alternative that has been proposed by social scientists. This usually refers to a marriage made as a civil contract only, which can be terminated without complicated legal haggling or religious stigma. Such marriages might be contracted for limited time spans,—much as college roommates agree to be together for one, two, or four years. Term marriage could be renewed by mutual consent or could be dissolved without rancor at the end of the contracted time. Such marriages, lasting typically five years, are reported to have been common in ancient Japan. The term contract, if recognized by law, could include any stipulations the partners agreed upon.[10]

A few sociologists have suggested the possibility of legally recognized weekend marriages, not unlike the one-day marriages said to take place, with religious sanction, in some parts of the Middle East. These, however, would seem to offer few advantages over casual encounters or prostitution and would be beset with many problems if instigated in Europe or North America.

Another form of limited-commitment marriage is the one conditioned by a prenuptial contract. Marriage contracts have long existed (they were, in fact, an ancient custom), but until recently, these contracts were difficult to enforce legally in the United States. In the past, the courts attempted to stay out of family affairs as much as possible.

Most religious organizations have assumed that marriage is a lifetime covenant based on the sharing of wealth, affection, and various responsibilities. Young, idealistic, and inexperienced people have often been reluctant to state conditions under which they would wed, considering any expressed reservations a damper to romance. Prenuptial agreements reduce marriage, in the eyes of many young people, to little more than a business transaction.

Yet with economic changes, longer life expectancies, and the possibility of multiple marriages in one's life, prenuptial agreements are making sense to more and more couples. In second marriages, there are often complications of inheritance and other problems inherent in blended families. A woman may come into a marriage with a great deal of money she has earned or inherited from an earlier husband. A man may have extensive obligations to children by former spouses. Today marriage contracts, which the courts are increasingly honoring, have come to be regarded as reasonable in second marriages and even acceptable in first ones. These contracts, in fact, have become so popular that they are sometimes renewed and amended every few years that a couple live together. They have become increasingly more elaborate, covering every conceivable feature of married life. But it is hard to deny that they have, in effect, generated a category of "conditional marriage."

Lenore J. Weitzman has listed several legal advantages of marriage contracts, including the following:

Escape from outmoded legal expectations
Promotion of an egalitarian relationship
Privacy and freedom in ordering personal relationships
Legitimation and structuring of cohabiting, homosexual, and other nontraditional
    relationships.[11]

In the past, the law recognized the obligation of a husband to support his wife, but it was generally unwilling to determine the level of support that should be required. There were cases of wives of wealthy men who could receive what they regarded as adequate support only by divorcing their husbands and then being granted substantial alimony by the courts. The legal expectations of wives were that they should maintain a home and care for a family—in other words, provide domestic service. In return, basic necessities were to be provided by their husbands. This distinction in sex roles makes little sense with the change in economic circumstances that has taken place, as more and more women have joined the work force and become self-supporting. The law continues to lag behind this social change. Family law as developed in the past was further predicated on the assumption that all marriages were first marriages between young, white, middle-class people who would rear children and live together for the rest of their lives, sharing everything. This no longer describes the majority of American marriages. Women consider themselves independent persons, frequently ready to establish conditions and limits to their matrimonial contracts. Same-sex marriages, if and when they become established, will necessitate further developments in family law.

## COVENANT MARRIAGE

No-fault divorce seemed like a good idea to many Americans when states started liberalizing their divorce laws a few years ago. People would not be legally bound after their marriages ended They would no longer have to establish residence in liberal states or falsify "grounds" in states that permitted divorce only in certain circumstances—for example, in the case of adultery. Yet the ease and rapidity with which people can now obtain divorce in almost every state has become troubling to some. There is no longer a "cooling off" period. Divorces, like marriages,, may be granted almost on a whim.

To discourage divorce, Louisiana, a heavily Roman Catholic state, introduced in 1997 a policy that has since been copied in two other states. "Covenant marriage" was enacted into law in Louisiana, with Arizona following in 1998 and Arkansas in 2001. Although the legal details differ slightly in each state, covenant marriage is an attempt to provide more stability for the institution by establishing what two grades of marriage. Regular marriage with no-fault divorce is available, but couples determined to make their marriage a lifetime bond may contract a covenant marriage. Unlike general marriage, it requires a longer waiting period before a license can be granted. Premarital counseling is additionally required. Although divorces may still be granted for adultery, abandonment, or abuse, there is a mandatory counseling period before any such decree may be given.

In the first five months after the law went into effect, only 1 percent of couples marrying in Louisiana chose the covenant form. Most couples understood their commitments to be permanent without the necessity of hardening the expectation into further law. Almost all religious ceremonies presupposed an intention to live together until death. Since no provisions were made for counseling at public expense and couples were expected to pay out-of-pocket for the service, many people concluded that only the legal and counseling professions were benefiting from covenant marriage. Others expressed a distaste for the implied distinction between first- and second-class marriages. Ultimately, whatever good intentions lawmakers had in setting up the law, it has had little impact. Arizona, in particular, has been accused of watering down its covenant marriage until it has become meaningless.[12]

## DOMESTIC PARTNERSHIPS AND CIVIL UNIONS

While a large number of people continue to oppose the concept of same-sex marriage, a general tolerance toward gay persons is evident throughout Western society. Even people with religious objections to same-sex marriages are often ready to acknowledge that we live in a secular society where individual sexual choices must be tolerated as long as they take place between consenting adults and no other person's rights are violated. The idea of legally recognized unions, which may have most or all of the legal benefits of marriage but are not so labeled, was initially proposed as a possible response to court decrees favoring homosexual partners. These arrangements were designed to give gay and lesbian couples civil protections without formally altering the institution of marriage. But the gay community has largely rejected this "separate but equal" solution as another attempt to keep homosexuals second-class citizens. Also finding them unsatisfactory, William Bennett has labeled civil union "a distinction without a difference." Numerous gay publications have attacked domestic partnership and civil union as reminiscent of the Jim Crow laws once passed in the American South.

Still, numerous benefits are assured with registered partnerships: inheritance rights without lengthy and costly legal proceedings; proper custody of children; and arrangements for the orderly supervision of medical care and provision for medical decisions in time of crisis. Not only may couples in civil unions be extended the protections that married couples enjoy, but society may be relieved of many responsibilities, because these couples will now be legally obligated to care for one another.

Domestic partnerships are designed for two unmarried people living together. Although they are tailored to help gay families, it will be difficult to limit benefits only to homosexuals. Strictly speaking, two people seeking a domestic partnership do not necessarily have to be in a sexual relationship, nor do they have to be of the same gender. By 1997, over 44 U.S. companies had already recognized domestic partnerships in offering some perquisites. Their definitions of "domestic partnerships" have varied, as have the benefits bestowed.[13]

First developed in Denmark and Sweden and called registered domestic partnerships (RDPs), laws establishing RDPs were enacted in Denmark in 1989; in Norway in 1993; in Sweden in 1995; in Greenland and Iceland in 1996; in the Netherlands, Belgium, and Spain in 1998; and in France in 1999 (where they are known as *pacte civil de solidarite*). The Danish legislature set the pattern for RDPs that has been generally followed, with some modifications, in several European countries. When North American governments have enacted such laws, it has been in response to gay activism and court rulings declaring current marriage laws discriminatory. These compromises, however, have not succeeded in pleasing either the gay rights movement or the general public.

In Denmark a clear distinction was drawn between marriage, for heterosexuals, and RDPs, for same-sex couples. The differences between the two programs were clearly set forth, and an RDP was not to be regarded as a form of marriage. RDPs would be registered by public authorities, while marriages could take place with religious ceremonies. Individual clergy could decide whether to bless RDPs, but they were not required to do so. Because RDPs were civil relationships solely, such couples could not claim mediation by clergy when problems arose, a service readily available to married couples. Only citizens or legal residents of Denmark could avail themselves of RDPs. Perhaps the most controversial part of the initial legislation addressing homosexuals in Denmark was the stipulation that lesbian couples could not use reproductive technologies to have children, and gay couples could not jointly adopt. If they wanted children, such couples had to use established stepparent adoption procedures or regular adoptions. Activists were outraged by these provisions of the law and, as the result of their agitation, adoption laws were liberalized in 1999.

U.S. state legislatures have attempted to learn something from the European plans. In response to court decisions that the denial of the right to marry amounted to unconstitutional discrimination, lawmakers in Hawaii, Vermont, and Massachusetts devised alternative structures that they hoped would satisfy the courts as well as gay activists. Only the Vermont civil union bill gave gay couples most, but still not all, the benefits of marriage. Several laws permitting RDPs were enacted at the municipal level throughout the United States, notably in cities where gays and lesbians formed substantial voting blocks.

Meanwhile, some liberal churches devised new, more powerful commitment ceremonies and continued to bless what they sometimes called "holy unions." But ultimately these efforts succeeded in pleasing no one for very long. Opponents of same-sex marriage were not impressed by what they regarded as hypocritical compromises. And in the gay community pressure was on for same-sex unions to receive the full prestige, benefit, and name of holy matrimony.

## NOTES

1. Albert Ellis, a psychologist and therapist, became an important influence in psychology during the late 1960s and 1970s, with many books, most of a countercultural nature, both academic and popular. See Windy Dryden, *The Essential Writings of Albert Ellis* (New York: Springer, 1990).

2. While the studies have been contradictory, the most recent ones suggest a high degree of satisfaction with the single life. As with gay individuals, single people have suffered more from social stigma than from inherent problems of solitary living. Lawrence Casier's *Is Marriage Necessary* (New York: Human Sciences Press, 1974) examines data from studies carried out at mid-century, the peak of matrimonial popularity. Many advantages of single status are suggested. Lucile Duberman's analysis in *Marriage and Other Alternatives* (New York: Holt, Rinehart, and Winston, 1977) is less positive. Stephanie Coontz in *Marriage, a History* (New York: Viking, 2005) documents the growing popularity of single living.

3. Bacon's famous essay "Of Marriage and Single Life" is frequently anthologized. This quotation was taken from the edition of Alexander M. Witherspoon and Frank J. Warnke, eds., *Seventeenth Century Prose and Poetry,* 2nd ed. (New York: Harcourt, Brace and World, 1963), 42.

4. For this pertinent comment I wish to thank Professor Ljubica Popovich, renowned Byzantine art historian of Vanderbilt University.

5. Coontz, 264, 276.

6. This data comes from official census figures from Europe and the United States.

7. F. O. Matthiessen and K. R. Murdock, eds., *The Notebooks of Henry James* (New York: Oxford University Press, 1947), 47.

8. Lillian Faderman, "Nineteenth-century Boston Marriage as a Possible Lesson for Today," in Esther D. Rothblum and Kathleen A. Brehony, eds., *Boston Marriage* (Amherst: University of Massachusetts Press, 1993), 40.

See Maggie Gallagher and Linda J. Waite, *The Case for Marriage: Why Married People Are Happier, Healthier, and Better Off Financially* (New York: Broadway, 2001).

9. Casier, 153.

10. Lenore J. Weitzman, *The Marriage Contract* (New York: Free Press, 1981), 227–254.

11. Ibid.

12. For recent discussions of covenant marriage, see Dave Ranney, "Covenant Marriage Called 'Next Step,'" http://www.gaypasg.org/GAYPASG/PRESSClippings, accessed winter 2005, and Michael J. McManus, "The Marrriage Debate: More than a Gay Issue," http://www.marriagesavers.org, accessed winter 2005.

13. For a full discussion of what he calls "marriage lite," see Jonathan Rauch, *Gay Marriage: Why It Is Good for Gays, Good for Straights, and Good for America* (New York: Henry Holt, 2004), 6, 31, 43–46, 49, 53, 90, 190–91.

# 7

# Same-Sex Marriage Today

It is now almost impossible to open a newspaper or listen to a television newscast without hearing something about same-sex marriage. Mainstream motion pictures and television dramas now routinely feature same-sex couples. Some wonder if same-sex marriage is the inevitable wave of the future. Will romantic billboards and magazine advertisements soon feature same-sex couples in tender poses?

Certainly, the same-sex marriage movement has made rapid gains that few would have predicted two decades ago. The analyses of these gains, along with the recognition that they have not been finally consolidated and that the worldwide struggle is just beginning, engages gay theorists and historians of the movement. Several reasons for this rapid and revolutionary social change seem evident. One is the human rights movement, which became an important feature of life in the Western world during the last half of the twentieth century. Former colonies in Asia and Africa were able to throw off the European yoke without much violence. European countries have granted many of their former colonies in Asia and Africa independence. There has been a growing recognition that all humans have definite rights of privacy and choice, even if their habits and customs seem peculiar or even perverse to most citizens. In the United States, African Americans mounted a successful Civil Rights movement led by eloquent and charismatic figures such as Dr. Martin Luther King, Jr. Encouraged by the success of the Civil Rights Movement, other groups have demanded equality and have employed some of the techniques that were developed by the architects of the original Civil Rights Movement.

Among the groups seeking equal rights have been Native Americans, Hispanics, Asian Americans (especially those of Japanese ethnicity whose parents and grandparents were interned during World War II), and women of all classes. It could not have been long before homosexuals also decided to come out of the closet and demand recognition. One of most effective arguments for gay rights became the analogy with other disadvantaged groups.

Studies of nineteenth- and early twentieth-century European sexologists influenced intellectuals, but it was the Kinsey Report of the 1950s that had real impact in the United States. The report suggested that manifestations of human sexuality are much more diverse than had previously been acknowledged. Homosexuality, Kinsey's research concluded, is not rare. Far from being an infrequent aberration, it appears to be a constant for a significant minority in all times and places. Attitudes toward what was acceptable sexual behavior started changing.

The sexual revolution that began in the 1960s—stemming from the Kinsey reports, economic developments, Hollywood, urbanization, the development of effective contraceptives, and the decline of religious influences—gave further impetus to the gay rights movement. In the anonymity of large cities, away from family and church members, people could do more or less as they chose. After Vatican II, the Irish American hierarchy of the Roman Catholic Church in the United States lost its tight grip on the faithful. School and university officials were no longer allowed to function in loco parentis. Even conservative families were obliged to tolerate, if not approve, their members who adopted more libertine life-styles.

As lives became more complicated in many ways, people started valuing their privacy more than ever and agitated for more laws to protect it. Self-expression, individuality, and the opportunities for exploration and discovery of new sensations were accepted as a right. With the increased economic power of women came, inevitably, more freedom for them. Miserable marriages no longer had to be tolerated, and a variety of family structures had to be accepted. All these changes taking place before the end of the century paved the way for the freer expression of homosexuality.

Consider what existence was like before the sexual revolution for those whose lives did not conform to the nuclear family structure. In small-town America, homosexuality seemed inconceivable. Certainly there were men who did not marry, the proverbial "confirmed bachelors," who were exceptionally attached to their mothers, who were particularly gifted in music and the other fine or decorative arts. There was always some truth in the stereotypes, which still did not take into consideration cruising truck drivers on the road, prison guards, priests, boy scout troop leaders and married men with hidden adventures. There were attractive and unmarried women with good jobs. People speculated on tragic love affairs with distant, mysterious men. Not infrequently, single women made homes with each other, and it was understood that they did so for companionship, security, and sometimes economic necessity. While there were numerous reasons why people did not marry, their single state was regarded as an aberration, though a respectable one.

While young people were abundantly admonished by parents, teachers, and clergy to be wary in the presence of the opposite sex, few parents thought to caution them about possible seduction by members of their own sex, so great was the innocence—or repression—of the time. As Tallulah Bankhead, the actress from Alabama who made her international reputation first in England in the 1930s, is reported to have said: "My family warned me about the boys, but they did not think to warn me about the girls."

In the past, in small-town America, there was little prejudice against people who were closeted homosexuals, as long as they were discrete, possibly because there was little overt acknowledgement that they existed. Some homosexuals chafed under their anonymous existence, longing to assert their sexual identities openly and be accepted for themselves. This was only possible, even in limited ways, if they chose to leave farms and small towns for the anonymity of the city. Even in the cities, they were largely confined to the gay ghettos.

The Netherlands has a long history of social tolerance and has for centuries been a place of refuge for oppressed peoples. As early as 1811, homosexuality was decriminalized there under French domination and the influence of the Napoleonic Code. Even after liberation from French influence, the Dutch did not choose to change this. In the 1980s, in response to changing social customs, the Dutch government took a look at unmarried cohabitants, including, but not exclusively, gay and lesbian partners. And in 1983 the government passed legislation to protect all citizens from unfair discrimination, including that based on sexual orientation. In April 2001, the Netherlands became the first country in the world to allow same-sex couples to wed. This was the culmination of progress over a period of almost twenty years, during which the Dutch government had extended many benefits to unmarried cohabitants and proscribed discrimination. The law also echoed public opinion in the Netherlands, where, despite objection from churches, the people were generally approving. The Roman Catholic Church, once a strong influence in the country, did not agree and neither did the conservative wing of Dutch Protestantism. But secularism was too far advanced in liberal Dutch society for these objections to be decisive. The laws made quite clear that legal gay and lesbian unions were marriages receiving state recognition on a par with more traditional heterosexual unions. Recently the Dutch government allowed a *ménage à trois*, composed of two bisexual women and a heterosexual man, to register their household as a civil union, though they could not yet call their relationship a marriage.

There was, however, one area where the law did not equalize. While legal paternity is determined by the man to whom a birth mother is married, the Dutch Supreme Court concluded that paternity could not be extended in the same way in same-sex marriages. It became necessary for the lesbian partner of a mother to adopt the child that both regarded as their own. There were similar problems when two men wished to parent a child. The intricacies of birth certificates for children in gay families have not yet been fully straightened out.

The Dutch marriage bill, amending Article 30, Book I of the Civil Code, defined marriage as a union contracted by two persons of different sex or of the same sex. The law considers marriage only in its civil applications and, of course, has no relevance to church definitions in Holland as elsewhere. Church officials are not required to perform marriage ceremonies or other-wise bless same-sex unions. The courts have also upheld the right of registrars with religious objections to refuse a certificate to an applicant. Many willing officials remain to carry out these legal tasks, so the conscientious objection of some has not presented an obstacle.

Belgium, in close proximity to the Netherlands, followed suit a short time later. In 2003, the second house of the Belgian Parliament passed a new marriage bill in favor of same-sex marriage. Almost all marriage benefits and responsibilities were extended to same-sex couples, though there were two important exceptions. Same-sex couples could not adopt children, and all those receiving marriage certificates had to be citizens or legal residents of the country. Significantly, in both Belgium and the Netherlands, it was the people's representatives, the authorized lawmakers, who instituted same-sex marriage, in recognition of changing social situations. The courts did not, in these unique instances, impose new measures upon a reluctant population.

Meanwhile, across the ocean in Canada, events were moving rapidly. Appellate courts in Ontario and British Columbia handed down decisions permitting gay couples to marry in the summer of 2003. In the spring of 2004, the Quebec Court of Appeal concurred with the rulings in Ontario and British Columbia. While the provinces were liberalizing, the govern-ment of the Canadian federation had reservations. Significant groups in the Canadian population were outraged by the changes. Nevertheless, the first civil marriages of lesbian and gay couples in North America were performed in Ontario and British Columbia beginning in 2003. British Columbia, the most U.S.-leaning of all Canadian provinces, redefined marriage as "the lawful union of two persons, to the exclusion of all others."

As had been anticipated, when same-sex marriage became available in British Columbia, couples from 22 foreign countries and every province in Canada came to take vows and receive legal certificates, even though their unions would not generally be recognized in their home provinces and countries. The Ontario honeymoon industry at Niagara Falls moved into full swing. U.S. officials voiced concern that many Americans would seek Canadian marriage licenses and then be upset when their unions proved invalid at home.

After about a year, pollsters were reporting shifts in Canadian public opinion toward acceptance. Nevertheless, there was still strong public outcry. Now a further difficulty faced Canada's federation. By 2005, with only three Canadian provinces recognizing same-sex marriages, there were still awkward complications. Canadians value their right to move freely from one province to another, and they feared some legal marriages (and the associated inheritance rights, parental obligations, and employment benefits) would not be recognized in every province. In the summer of 2005, the federal government of Canada solved a few of these problems by making same-sex marriage legal throughout the land.[1]

Not all Canadian problems, however, had been solved. Since Canadians frequently travel to the United States, have American extended families, and escape their harsh winters in the American South, some wonder what difficulties would await married same-sex couples south of their border, and what additional immigration problems might arise.

The progress of same-sex marriage in the United States has been more complicated than in Western Europe and Canada. Most, though by no means all, of the objection to same-sex marriage has been articulated by religious people. Roman Catholicism is the largest single religious persuasion in the United States and, though torn apart by scandals and challenged by its own gay activist groups, the Church has officially maintained a precise definition of marriage that excludes homosexual unions. At every level of the Church hierarchy, those who speak officially for the Church, maintain uncompromising opposition to homosexuality and same-sex unions. The most populous and powerful Protestant denomination in the United States, the Southern Baptist Convention, is equally vocal in its opposition to the gay life-style, same-sex marriage, and the ordination of practicing gay ministers. Other conservative denominations and independent churches oppose the gay life-style. With the Protestant Episcopal Church in schism over the issue and only the Unitarian-Universalist Fellowship, the United Church of Christ, and Reformed Judaism fully "inclusive," the final decision is not yet in.

Because the liberalization of laws affecting same-sex unions has been done by the U.S. courts rather than by elected officials, against the wishes of the majority of American people, there is widespread resentment of "courts that legislate." In late summer of 2005, the California legislature voted in favor of same-sex marriages, a first. Everywhere the matter has been put to popular vote, it has been defeated.

After decades of agitation, progress in the gay agenda was made in Hawaii in 1991. Two lesbian couples and one gay male couple filed suit against the state for discrimination after they had been denied marriage licenses. Although the state made a motion to dismiss the case as without merit, it was not successful. The Hawaii Supreme Court eventually rejected an appellate court's argument that hundreds of years of tradition supported marriage only between a man and a woman. The high court appealed to "changing customs" and an "evolving social order" in rejecting arguments based on tradition and religion. The state Supreme Court sent the case back to the trial court, demanding a full and proper hearing. The Baehr decision, as the result of this litigation is called, remains a landmark for several reasons—chiefly because of the convincing evidence presented by a host of witnesses in favor of regularizing same-sex unions. The presiding judge, Kevin Chang, made clear that, unless the state could demonstrate compelling interest in denying matrimony to any category of its citizens, the denial would be unconstitutional.

Because many of the legal provisions and benefits of marriage are based on concern for the welfare of children, and married couples are the anticipated custodians of these children, it made sense to examine the status of minors being reared in same-sex families. The Hawaii court took careful note of child welfare. State witnesses established to the satisfaction of the court that children were being responsibly reared by gay and lesbian parents and were entitled to the same benefits that the state makes available to children of heterosexual couples. Judge Chang released his decision in 1996 and in it made several important pronouncements that have wide resonance:

Same-sex couples can, and do, have successful, loving and committed relationships.

Lesbians and gay men share the same reasons for seeking to marry as heterosexual couples: emotional closeness, intimacy and monogamy, and to establish a framework for a long-term relationships that has personal significance for them, is recognized by society, and to have and to raise children.

Lesbian and gay parents and couples have children as foster parents, natural parents, adoptive parents, and through alternative conception.

Gay and lesbian parents and same-sex couples have the potential to raise children that are happy, healthy and well-adjusted.

Children of gay and lesbian parents and same-sex couples develop in normal fashion.[2]

The judge was unconvinced by arguments that same-sex parents presented an obstacle to the healthy development of children. He concluded that disallowing the marriage of gay couples violated Hawaii's state constitution and the state's reputation for tolerating diversity.

The majority of people in Hawaii, however, did not accept the judge's findings or his order to issue marriage certificates to same-sex couples; his order was stayed until an appeal could be heard. For three years the appeal was pending, but in the meantime legal action was taken. In 1997 the Hawaii legislature passed an amendment to the state constitution, giving the legislature power to "reserve marriage to opposite-sex couples." The amendment was accepted by a majority of voters in a state referendum, despite Hawaii's liberal reputation. Further attempts were made to pacify the courts with a number of proposed strategies. Alternatively, a severely limited domestic partnership arrangement was legally accepted, a compromise that satisfied almost no one.

Following Hawaii's lead, by 2000, 35 American states and the federal government had moved to "protect marriage" with similar legislation. The passage of "defense of marriage" laws became a major preoccupation of voters in numerous states.

The focus of attention in the United States next moved to Vermont. After much legal maneuvering, that state enacted what was acclaimed at the time as the most thorough non-marital legislative protection for same-sex couples that had ever existed in the United States. The status of civil union was established and open to both same-sex and opposite-sex couples, though it was designed primarily to accommodate homosexuals. This civil union law extended all "statutory, regulatory, common-law, equitable and policy features of civil marriage to parties to a civil union." Going one step beyond the liberal European laws, Vermont allowed couples in any civil union to adopt children. Although this legislation appeared generous, gay rights groups were not satisfied, complaining that the law still stigmatized same-sex couples.

In 2001, the Goodridge case was filed in Massachusetts; it would eventually result, after some initial disappointment, in the first granting by an American state of full matrimonial rights to same-sex couples. The Massachusetts Supreme Court determined that prohibiting gay couples from marriage violated the state constitution in two ways: it denied equality to all citizens, and it denied specified citizens the basic right of marriage, which all other citizens enjoyed. The court, consequently, decreed that the traditional definition of marriage as the union of "man and a woman" no longer applied in the face of contemporary reality. The decision contained the following declarations:

We construe civil marriage to mean the voluntary union of two persons as spouses, to the exclusion of all others. This reformulation redresses the plaintiffs' constitutional injury and furthers the aim of marriage to promote stable, exclusive relationships.

Extending civil marriage to same-sex couples reinforces the importance of marriage to individuals and communities. That same-sex couples are willing to embrace marriage's solemn obligations of exclusivity, mutual support, and commitment to one another is a testament to the enduring place of marriage in our laws and in the human spirit.[3]

The Court's order of remedy was as follows:

We declare that barring an individual from the protections, benefits, and obligations of civil marriage solely because that person would marry a person of the same sex violates the Massachusetts Constitution.[4]

Although many people in that heavily Roman Catholic state were outraged by this decision (and even the governor objected), the timing was such that same-sex marriages became legal before it was possible for the state legislature to amend the constitution or submit the question to referendum. The Massachusetts Senate, at odds with the court, immediately drafted a bill to extend all "benefits, protections, rights, and responsibilities of marriage" to same-sex couples, hoping to substitute civil unions for full-fledged marriages. The strategy did not work. The state's Supreme Court was asked to accept the substitute bill rather than proceed with its demand that full matrimonial status be extended to gay couples. The appellate court rejected the substitute as designed to make second-class citizens out of one segment of the population. The court stated its findings as follows:

The government aim [of marriage] is to encourage stable relationships for the good of the individual and of the community, especially its children. The very nature and purpose of civil marriage . . . renders unconstitutional any attempt to ban all same-sex couples, as same-sex couples, from entering into civil marriage.

Segregating same-sex unions from opposite-sex unions cannot possibly be held rationally to advance or "preserve" . . . the Commonwealth's legitimate interest in procreation, child-rearing, and the conservation of resources. . . . It continues to relegate same-sex couples to a different status. . . . The history of our nation has demonstrated that separate is seldom, if ever, equal.[5]

The Court further acknowledged that the only reason to differentiate "civil marriage" from "civil union" could be to stigmatize the latter, to make of it a definite secondary status.

With fully recognized matrimony, at least by law, now possible in Massachusetts, it will be interesting to see and instructive to observe the results. Will the optimistic predictions of gay advocates be achieved, or will the warnings of their opponents prove correct? The state's governor, like most citizens and lawmakers of Massachusetts, is still unconvinced and feels that a dangerous experiment has been imposed upon the people. The issue will, lawmakers promise, soon be submitted to referendum.

Mayor Gavin Newsom of San Francisco, on his own authority, started issuing marriage licenses in his city in February of 2004, defying state law. As the gay mecca of the United States, San Francisco caught the spotlight. More than 3,400 gay couples flocked to the city from all parts of the country to be married, and city hall became the site of what was essentially an extended gay demonstration and celebration. California's Supreme Court in the next month ordered a halt to this violation of state law, and the marriages performed in San Francisco were thus legally null and void. The state's governor, Arnold Schwarzenegger, came out against same-sex marriages, despite earlier gestures toward the gay community, and thus joined George W. Bush in opposition to the movement.

The issue, however, is far from dead. On March 14, 2005, a judge ruled that California state law had breached a constitutional right that demanded equal treatment of all citizens, regardless of their sexual preferences. The ruling came as the result of a case brought by Mayor Newsom and 12 same-sex couples who had married in his city. The issue was to return to the state Supreme Court. In the meantime, the state legislature became the first elected body in the country to vote in favor of same-sex marriage, changing everything.

A short time after San Francisco began issuing marriage licenses to homosexual couples, some officials in Sandoval County, New Mexico, attempted to do the same. About two dozen couples were "married," before the state's attorney general stopped the operation. In March 2005, to make sure there would be no further misunderstandings of the law, the New Mexico Senate approved a bill defining marriage as the union of a man and woman only.

Somewhat earlier in March 2004, Multnomah County in Oregon—an urban center that includes Portland—decided to issue same-sex marriage licenses. About three thousand licenses were issued, and neighboring counties were ready to begin issuing their own. However, a judge froze the action until a court decision could be rendered. In November, the issue was placed before the people of the state in referendum. Oregon, like the other nine states that faced referenda on the issue, voted solidly to reject same-sex marriage. Nevertheless, Oregon is a liberal state, and the governor, Ted Kulongoski, is widely believed to have been expressing the common will when he promised to support a new law giving gay couples the right to form civil unions providing most of the benefits, if not the name of, marriage.

Despite all the court action, the compromises offered by legislatures, and a constant bombardment from the media, the American public remains overwhelmingly opposed to same-sex marriage. Whenever the issue is put to a direct vote it still is soundly defeated. At the same time, the widespread willingness to tolerate civil unions and domestic partnerships suggests a readiness to be fair and to countenance a variety of family configurations. Polls further show that young people are more inclined to support same-sex marriage than their elders, which bodes well for its future.

Western Europe appears to be moving toward a general acceptance of homosexual marriage. During the Franco era, Spain was regarded as one of the most repressive countries of Western Europe, with little tolerance for any sort of diversity and with the Roman Catholic Church exerting a strong influence on conduct. Today Spain is a constitutional monarchy rather than a dictatorship and is one of the most liberal countries in Europe. On June 30, 2005, the Spanish government cleared the way for same-sex marriage to become legal in that country, beginning in July. Polls indicated that this law was passed with 62 percent of the population concurring, while 30 percent, including many members of the influential Catholic Church, opposed.

Same-sex marriage is rarely an issue in most of the countries of Africa. The one exception to the general disapproval of homosexuality throughout the continent is the Union of South Africa. The country's post-apartheid constitution includes a clause making discrimination based on sexual orientation illegal, and gay couples there have already been allowed to adopt children. In 2004, South Africa's highest court ruled in favor of a lesbian couple who asked that the official definition of marriage be changed to include same-sex couples. Although same-sex marriages have not yet been legalized in that country, it seems only a matter of time before they will be. The nation's best known cleric, Anglican Archbishop Desmond Tutu, has favored gay rights for a number of years. Evert Knoesen, a leader of the Lesbian and Gay Equality Project of South Africa, told radio audiences via BBC News:

We have to go ahead with legal action to fix up these somewhat more minor problems and we foresee that within the next twelve months or so, same-sex couples will indeed be married. The principle has been won.[6]

Other countries that appear to be moving in the same direction include Norway, Sweden, and Iceland, which all have "registered partnerships." Germany introduced "life partnerships" in 2001, but the provisions were limited to inheritance and tenancy rights. As early as 1999, France introduced much-discussed PACS, civil contracts that gave limited rights to registered cohabiting couples, regardless of gender. Full tax, inheritance, and adoption rights were not included, however. Although one French mayor conducted a same-sex marriage ceremony in 2004, a court soon nullified the union. Luxembourg, much influenced by neighboring France, instituted civil partnerships in 2004. Great Britain passed legislation in December of 2005 that gave registered partnerships the pension, property, social security, and housing rights normally reserved for married couples. Pop entertainer Elton John and his partner of many years were among the first to avail themselves of registered partnership, celebrating with a lavish celebrity-laden reception. At the end of 2004, New Zealand passed, not without the usual controversy, laws recognizing civil unions for gay people. Italy, too, is known for its sympathetic view of the plight of homosexuals and may be expected to attempt positive legislation in the near future.

At present in the United States, only Massachusetts offers legal marriage for same-sex couples. However, these marriages are not currently recognized in any other states. Americans prize their ability to move from region to region as good jobs, health, and other reasons motivate them. The "full faith and credit" clause of the U.S. Constitution has in the past meant that marriages made in one state, even common law marriages, were honored in others. With the advent of same-sex marriage, this no longer applies. Individual states have almost exclusive control over laws that apply to marriage within their borders. With some states recognizing civil unions and others recognizing domestic partnerships of varying definition, a bewildering network of laws will mean a legal nightmare when complicated cases reach the courts. These problems are already surfacing, as courts in different states attempt to adjudicate battles from disrupted same-sex unions made legal outside their borders.

Even if all North American and Western European states recognize same-sex marriages, there will still be problems of tourism in much of Asia and Africa. The United Nations seems unlikely at present to formulate policies that smooth such difficulties, considering the strength of many conservative African and Middle Eastern lands and the unwavering condemnation of same-sex relationships by Islam and the Roman Catholic Church. Just as the polygamous marriages of parts of Africa and the Middle East have not been legally recognized when these families have immigrated to the West, same-sex couples will continue to find their unions equally void in many parts of the world.

Many people worldwide believe that more liberal marriage laws are long overdue and are hopeful that they are the wave of the future. It must not, however, be forgotten that in all countries where laws favoring official recognition of gay couples have been enacted there remains strong opposition. In some lands this opposition has been well organized, frequently tapping the resources of the Roman Catholic Church, with a new pope as thoroughly opposed to same-sex marriage as his predecessors have been. Some pro-gay laws may yet be repealed by popular demand. It will be a few years before the results of the liberalizing actions are known. Legal kinks must be worked out, language must be expanded to reflect this changing reality, and the rights of children in same-sex unions must be further clarified.

Objections in places where same-sex marriage has been allowed, according to most reports, have softened. It may well be that as fears of the public are allayed and as gay couples blend more inconspicuously into the social mainstream, sharing the family values cherished by heterosexual families, many reservations will fade. If the attitudes of the more accepting young people do not change as they enter middle age, the future of same-sex unions seems positive. Still, experience has shown that legislatures cannot dictate the mores of people, and same-sex marriage has been too frequently imposed upon reluctant communities, either by courts or a slim plurality of voters. Basic moral and social views have not necessarily changed markedly. The problems arising from this conflict between social custom and imposed law remain to be resolved.

## NOTES

1. Daniel Cere and Douglas Farrow, eds., *Divorcing Marriage: Unveiling the Dangers of Canada's New Social Experiment* (Montreal: McGill-Queen's University Press, 2004) surveys Canadian objections to the new same-sex marriage laws.

2. Quoted in Kathleen A. Lahey and Kevin Alderson, *Same-Sex Marriage: The Personal and the Political* (Toronto: Insomniac Press, 2004), 52.

3. Ibid., 60.

4. Ibid., 61.

5. Ibid., 62–63.

6. "SA Ruling 'May Allow Gay Unions,'" BBC News World Edition, http://news.bbc.co.uk/2/hi/africa/4055549.stm (accessed summer 2005).

# 8

# The Future of Gay Rights and the Precarious State of Matrimony

Entire branches of the social sciences have been dedicated to predicting conduct, and the tabloid journals are filled with diviners holding crystal balls. Yet even the prophecies that seem most authoritative, that are supported by an impressive array of statistics, are never fulfilled in all their particulars. Unforeseen events occur daily, and public attitudes can change overnight. While the present impetus in the industrialized world appears to be in the direction of same-sex marriage, a less vocal majority continue their opposition for a variety of social and religious reasons. If the future of same-sex marriage is uncertain, the future of marriage itself, as we have known it, seems almost equally precarious.

A clear concern of both advocates and opponents of same-sex unions is the future of marriage of any sort. If it can be proven that same-sex marriage will strengthen rather than further debilitate the institution, then the argument of opponents will be decisively weakened. While marriage has become less popular with heterosexuals in industrialized countries, gays and lesbians have been clamoring for it. It is still too early to know whether the extension of legal matrimony to homosexuals will be to the advantage or detriment of marriage in general.

Marriage is clearly on the defensive in Scandinavia; its decline was first evident in Sweden and Denmark, but now the more conservative country of Norway reports similar statistics. Finland, which is Scandinavian in geography rather than ethnicity, has also followed the trend. Marriage has always been intertwined with religious imperatives, and its lessening in popularity has closely followed the decline and disestablishment of organized religion in these countries. In Sweden, sometimes identified as the world's most secular nation, more than half of all children are born out of wedlock, and illegitimacy has lost its stigma. While most parents in Sweden are together initially when their children are born, their loose unions make separation easy when problems arise. Such children will still be fed, clothed, and educated by the welfare state that modern Sweden has become. However, this blanket of welfare benefits from the womb to the tomb comes at a price that in numerous ways adversely affects families. Although Swedes have one of the world's highest standards of living, their tax burden is also extremely heavy.

Some Scandinavians have celebrated the changing family pattern and the gender equality it appears to represent. Others acknowledge a major social problem, pointing to the high suicide rates and other growing pathologies and wondering if long-term effects on children will be more than negligible.

While most Roman Catholic countries in Europe have been slower to relinquish traditional family patterns, changes are occurring in these countries as well. Ireland, recently secularized and newly affluent, now has as high a percentage of illegitimate children as has France, which for decades has taken its Catholicism more lightly. Social planners predict that Italy and Spain will soon follow suit. Switzerland, another prosperous country with both Catholic and Protestant populations, reports a similar decline in traditional family attitudes.[1] England, which still retains a substantial underclass and is beset with problems of immigration, suffers especially from the breakdown of family, because it lacks the extensive social welfare net that the Scandinavian countries have developed and maintained.

Family patterns remain strong in much of Asia and Africa, but these families can be oppressively controlling and severely limiting to the freedom of their members. Yet there is no immediate indication that these patterns will be reversed, except through immigration to the West and the gradual adoption of the values of the host countries.[2]

With the sexual revolution that came to the West beginning in the 1960s, social stability was sacrificed for personal freedom. Throughout history, periods of self-indulgence have alternated with times of stringent morality. Whether this pendulum will continue to swing is uncertain. What is evident is that attitudes change rapidly in the modern world. This change is seen vividly in the transformation within a few years of pious Quebec into a province so anticlerical that it could, at the beginning of the new century, defy the priesthood in support of a pro-gay government.

In the United States, a strong discrepancy between the theory of marriage and its actual practice is evident. Marriage is popular but very unstable, with divorce rates higher than in most other nations. One explanation is perhaps the habit of Americans to marry more frequently than citizens of most other industrialized nations. Marriage is more often a decision of the couples— often crossing ethnic, class, and religious lines—with less involvement from extended family. Despite the high divorce rate and the turmoil over same-sex rights, Americans still regard their marriages as the major life commitment they make. They are more likely than people elsewhere to tell pollsters that they value marriage highly. When their marriages do not work out, they are generally eager to try again.

While marriage is more fragile in the United States than ever before, it may also be more satisfying. A higher divorce rate does not necessarily mean a higher degree of dissatisfaction in marriage. Today poor marriages are relatively easy to leave, with no-fault divorce, little stigma attached to separation, and many women able to earn their own livelihood. Also, because marriages are more optional than ever before, those who enter them may place a higher value on the relationship.

In one respect marriage seems more necessary than ever before. Americans no longer live in the same communities for long periods of time, close to extended family and friends. Most people experience fluctuating patterns in their lives as they move from city to city, and living conditions may change enormously several times during a person's life. As people move to different locales—and through various professional and economic levels—their circle of friends changes. Many start a second or third career, with all the adjustments, realignments, and changes in locale and community this entails. Retirement may bring yet another environment and set of associates. Marriage, if it is successful through a lifetime, becomes the anchor in the midst of this impermanence.

As an expression of the value they place on traditional marriage—and in an attempt to prevent same-sex marriage as it is being imposed by the court system—the United States Congress passed, by an overwhelming margin, the Defense of Marriage Act, which was signed into law by President Bill Clinton in September 1996. There are two sections of this act. The first affirms the right of individual states to refuse recognition of same-sex marriages contracted in other states. The second part defines marriage for federal purposes. The text is as follows:

No State, territory, or possession of the United States, or Indian tribe, shall be required to give effect to any public act, record, or judicial proceeding of any other State, territory, possession, or tribe respecting a relationship between persons of the same sex that is treated as a marriage under the laws of such other State, territory, possession, or tribe, or a right or claim arising from such relationship.[3]

And the following is the federal definition of marriage:

In determining the meaning of any Act of Congress, or of any ruling, regulation, or interpretation of the various administrative bureaus and agencies of the United States, the word "marriage" means only a legal union between one man and one woman as husband and wife, and the word "spouse" refers only to a person of the opposite sex who is a husband or a wife.[4]

This act of Congress expressed the will of the people through their elected officials, regardless of what courts have decreed. It did not limit the right of individual states, however, to define marriage within their borders as they saw fit, and it did not invalidate the law in Massachusetts. During the 2004 presidential election, all major candidates proclaimed their view that marriage should properly be between a man and a woman only. And in every state where same-sex marriage was placed before the voters, it was again rejected. To protect the country further from what many designated as "runaway courts," a Federal Marriage Amendment to the United States Constitution was proposed, receiving strong verbal endorsement from President George W. Bush and numerous other elected officials. The following is the text of that proposed amendment:

Marriage in the United States shall consist only of the union of a man and a woman. Neither this Constitution or the constitution of any State nor state or federal law, shall be construed to require that marital status or the legal incidents thereof be conferred upon unmarried couples or groups.[5]

The President stated in his address of February 24, 2004, advocating the amendment that it in no way prevented state legislatures from enacting their own laws applying to arrangements other than marriage. Some critics complained that the proposed amendment did not go far enough. It did not specify that marriage would be between *one* man and *one* woman, thus leaving open the future possibilities of polygamy or polyandry, which are not currently issues of controversy but might become so.

Some opponents of same-sex marriage celebrated, concluding that these actions of government defined the American position for the foreseeable future. Advocates of same-sex marriage had lost. Opponents were heartened by the margins against same-sex marriage when it had been put to vote in Hawaii, Alaska, California, Nebraska, and Nevada. In percentages ranging from 61 to 70, voters were decisively against legalizing same-sex marriage. Legislative enactments in approximately two-thirds of the states have now further confirmed this decision. Only domestic partnerships and civil unions seemed still open for review.

Yet there are clear indications that the debate is far from over. California's 2005 vote in favor of same-sex marriage and growing acceptance by the younger generation bode well for same-sex marriage. Before the required number of states can have ratified the proposed constitutional amendment, public attitudes may change even more. Many conservatives who might be expected to oppose the push for gay rights still strongly resist any tampering with the Constitution.

One significant fact that cannot be ignored is the omnipresent influence of the American entertainment media, which condition attitudes and create desires here and around the world. And the entertainment industry is overwhelmingly gay friendly. Positive images of gay and lesbian people on television and video reach Americans as they relax in their living rooms. Even more significantly, these images also are seen throughout gay-resistant regions of Asia and Africa.

At the present, only the most venturesome clairvoyants should be ready to predict the future of same-sex unions or of the institution of marriage.

## NOTES

1. Especially pertinent are chapters 16 and 17 of Stephanie Coontz's *Marriage, a History* (New York: Viking, 2005).

2. Conservative Christian and Islamic views are widely held in most African countries, though tribal customs in many places mingle with the official stance. Some helpful information is available in William Femi Awodele's *Peculiar Conflicts: African Marriages in Western Cultures* (Longwood, FL: Xulon Press, 2003) and Carolyn Brown Heinz's *Asian Cultural Traditions* (Prospect Heights, IL: Waveland Press, 1999).

3. H.R. 3396. In the House of Representatives, May 7, 1996. Chapter 115 of title 28, United States Code, amended by adding after section 1738B.

4. For full discussion, see Andrew Sullivan, *Same-Sex Marriage Pro & Con; A Reader* (New York: Vintage Books, 2004), 207.

5. For a thorough analysis of legal actions and proposals, see Kathleen A. Lahey and Kevin Anderson's *Same-Sex Marriage; The Personal and the Political* (Toronto: Insomniac Press, 2004).

# Appendix A: Gay Acceptance and the Entertainment Media

No scrutiny of public opinion is complete unless it considers the influence of the American entertainment media, which condition attitudes and create fashion, not only in the United States but throughout the world. And the entertainment industry is overwhelmingly liberal. Considering the number of hours they spend watching television, American children are receiving media indoctrination at their most impressionable age. And because the United States leads the world as international purveyor of entertainment, these are the messages heard worldwide.

Only a few years ago, most major motion picture actors refused to play gay parts, despite the presence of numerous closeted actors, directors, and other artists and business people engaged in the film industry. Homosexuality was hidden, treated indirectly with jokes and double-entendre only insiders could understand. American movie audiences did not have the sophistication of Broadway audiences; neither were they ready to accept the complexities of human conduct as depicted in European art films. When adapted for the screen, gay stories from other media or from abroad were usually rewritten or handled so obliquely that their message was obscured.

Middle-class audiences were always slightly more comfortable with expressions of affection and sexual ambiguity in women than in men. Marlene Dietrich, a major sex symbol for both genders, was allowed to wear tuxedos and kiss another woman on the lips in one of her early films, and great androgynous actresses such as Greta Garbo and Alla Nazimova were considered "ethereal." Lesbian actresses, who were numerous during Hollywood's golden years, played straight romantic roles, which was not difficult since "butch" was generally recognized as aggressively seductive. In fact, the femme fatale, a sort of cinema dominatrix, became one of the stereotypes of the silver screen. Famous male players such as Clifton Webb—who escorted his mother to parties and was known to be gay by his associates—still played straight parts, though sometimes with undertones easily recognized by the Hollywood community. Webb's characterizations as the eccentric genius in the Mr. Belvedere films and as the obsessive murderer in *Laura* were clear to the knowledgeable, yet were not so blatantly gay as to offend the general public, which loved the films. Webb, a skilled comedian, had another success in *Cheaper by the Dozen,* a film that cast him as the father of a large family, to the amusement of his friends.

Almost all gay actors—Rock Hudson being an especially notable and ultimately tragic example—stayed officially in the closet, though their sexual preferences were known in entertainment circles and whispered beyond. To maintain a gay actor's cover, studios and publicity teams might arrange highly publicized dates for them with glamorous actresses. Sometimes marriages were forced on gay performers by their studios, especially in the postwar years when domesticity was favored in the fan magazines. Rock Hudson was paired with an innocently compliant secretary, Phyllis Gates, who, after his death, wrote a book about her three unhappy years of marriage to him.

Although New York theater audiences were more tolerant than film audiences throughout the country, several gay playwrights—notably Tennessee Williams, William Inge, and later Edward Albee—were accustomed to adding or substituting heterosexual intrigues to make their plot lines more widely acceptable. Even so, further changes were usually mandated when these plays were adapted for the screen. Tennessee Williams's New Orleans play *A Streetcar Named Desire* and his *Suddenly Last Summer* were prime examples. When it seemed impossible to disguise gay characters in films adapted from stage plays, homosexuality was implied rather than made explicit. Gay characters became either antic or disturbed personalities. Edward Everett Horton made a career of playing "fey" film roles, and Charles Laughton was particularly skilled at depicting pathological or eccentric personalities of ambivalent sexuality.

A few exceptions to the general trend appeared now and then. *The Children's Hour* (1962) featured two lesbian private school mistresses sympathetically and survived because it was based on a well-known play by Lillian Hellman and featured two respected actresses, Audrey Hepburn and Shirley MacLaine. *Advise and Consent,* a much-discussed film of the early 1960s, was adapted from a popular novel and dealt more openly with homosexuality in the Washington political establishment.

By 1982, changes toward more realism and inclusiveness were evident, and *Making Love* was heralded as a breakthrough for American films. One scene showed two men ardently kissing. Its treatment of gay characters who were upstanding, admirable citizens was generally accepted. Other films as well avoided the older stereotypes. The 1987 Merchant-Ivory production *Maurice* was the contribution of a respected cinema team who were life partners as well as creative collaborators. An adaptation of gay writer E. M. Forster's fictionalized autobiography, the film was memorable for its characteristically mellow Merchant-Ivory style and its elegiac mood. It skillfully captured the social environment of pre–World War I aristocratic England.

Today sexual ambiguity is experiencing a vogue in the mass media. Straight actors are willing to play gay roles, even when ardent love scenes with members of their own sex are required. There are several reasons for this change. One is the increasing availability on television, video, and DVD of foreign films, which, for several decades, have been less hesitant in dealing with controversial subject matter. Another is the conscious effort on the part of gay activism to establish legitimacy in the media. Realizing how important films and television have become in influencing American ideals and goals, it is not surprising that the gay-sympathetic entertainment world has been an accomplice in this activity. Actress Elizabeth Taylor has said that without homosexuals there would be no Hollywood.

Among the films of recent decades that have sought to reverse the unfavorable images of the past are the French and American versions of *The Birdcage (La Cage aux Folles)*. These films have shown gay people who are loving and lovable. They are part of a new genre, the "gay family story," which is increasing in popularity.

The "coming-out" narrative was the first of the gay subjects to become a favorite with filmmakers. It is now almost as popular as the standard *bildungsroman* or heterosexual coming-of-age tale, long familiar in both novels and films. Among recent films that have examined the problems faced by young gays and lesbians trying to accept themselves and be accepted by family and community are *All of Me, Beautiful Thing, Boy's Life 1* and *Boy's Life 2, Breaking the Surface: The Greg Louganis Story, The Hanging Garden, In & Out, Late Bloomers, Making Love, Maurice, Next Year in Jerusalem, Spitters,* and *The Toilers and the Wayfarers*. *All Over Me*, released in 1997, was the story of a 15-year-old girl's acknowledgement of her lesbianism while living in New York's Hell's Kitchen. *Beautiful Thing*, 1996, dealt with two London teenagers of working-class background, while *Boy's Life 1* and *Boy's Life 2* were set in the United States. *The Hanging Garden*, 1998, was a Canadian film set in Nova Scotia. In it, an awkward teenager emerged from the closet to become an attractive, confident man. *In & Out*, 1997, featured such well-known performers as Kevin Kline, Matt Dillon, Tom Selleck, and Debbie Reynolds and was billed as "a mainstream gay comedy," something that would have been unimaginable three decades before. *Late Bloomers,* also released in 1997, was a romantic lesbian coming-out story set in Eleanor Roosevelt High School, perhaps to capitalize on suggestions in the press that the late first lady had been a party to a "romantic friendship" with the daughter of Wild Bill Hickcock.

The AIDS crisis, which took a heavy toll in the artistic community, became a poignant and provocative subject for films. In the last years of the twentieth century, numerous scripts were based on AIDS affliction. *And the Band Played On,* 1993, claimed to be the first, and it remains the most notable. Based on journalist Randy Shilts's investigative account of the genesis of the epidemic, the film built suspense as it mirrored a subculture fearfully confounded by a mysterious malady. The movie's cast included Ian McKellen, a British gay activist who is one of the world's finest actors.

Numerous other motion pictures about AIDS have followed. *Citizen Cohn* is based loosely on the life of Roy Cohn, the lawyer deeply implicated in the excesses of the McCarthy era, who never came out of the closet and is widely regarded as a traitor and hypocrite by the gay community. *Breaking the Surface: The Greg Louganis Story* and *Longtime Companion* pays tribute to partners who lovingly cared for AIDS patients. Perhaps the most acclaimed of all the films centered on the AIDS crisis is *Philadelphia,* 1993, in which Tom Hanks plays a successful lawyer whose firm rejects him when he contracts AIDS and Denzel Washington plays an ambulance-chasing attorney who is the only one who will represent the Hanks character in his discrimination suit against his firm.

Other films have explored different issues of gay life. The conflict between religious repression and authentic sexual identity has merited particular attention. In *Latter Days,* a young Mormon missionary is "brought out" by a Hollywood party boy. Well-known actresses Mary Kay Place and Jacqueline Bisset starred in the film, which was commended by the *New York Times* and the *Los Angeles Times,* despite its highly negative portrayal of Mormonism and Mormon parents.

Two powerful films that demonstrated the public's fascination with gender ambiguity have been *M Butterfly,* 1993, and *The Crying Game,* 1992. The former, whose plot unfolds against a backdrop of the traditional Chinese theater, was based on the actual experiences of a French diplomat who was for several years the lover of a Chinese performer. He was presented with a child from this relationship. Deeply and devotedly in love, he worked hard to bring his lover and child to France, only to discover the painful reality of his situation in a French courtroom. His paramour was revealed to be a transvestite male, who had tricked him for many years, maintaining their relationship in order to spy on the French for the Chinese government. Preposterous as this plot may seem, the events really occurred, and the film presented them convincingly. *The Crying Game* takes place amid Irish political turmoil. IRA terrorism and violence sustain interest, but the impact of the drama comes from a surprising revelation of sexual identity that the public was placed on its honor not to reveal. Notably, this film introduced the dazzling actor/ actresses, Jaye Davidson.

The winter of 2006 saw the release of several gay theme films. The most discussed was *Brokeback Mountain,* a serious film about two cowboy lovers. Movie fans might contrast the openly sexual theme in the Academy Award–nominated *Brokeback* to the Westerns of long ago, when Roy Rogers was not allowed to kiss Dale Evans, who later became his wife, on screen. After the early-2006 release of Ol Parker's *Imagine Me & You,* about a woman who falls in love with another woman at her own wedding reception, no film seemed legitimate without at least one notable gay character.

While both popular and art films have been important, it is television that has had the greatest impact on personal beliefs and social interactions. The enormously popular prime-time serial *Dynasty,* which first appeared in 1981, included a prominent and highly sympathetic gay character. But the media event that brought gay love most forcefully and entertainingly to public attention was the HBO serial adaptation of *Tales of the City,* with its crew of zany characters and its convoluted though sustained story line. Based on the collection of stories by Armistead Maupin, which have been called "the most sublime piece of popular literature American has ever produced,"[1] the tales originally comprised six books and were initially serialized in San Francisco papers. The characters include gay male lovers, lesbian sweethearts, religious fanatics, prostitutes, madams, transsexuals, blackmailers, straight lovers, elderly paramours, and a peculiar assortment of people who come together to form an affectionate family. The original tales as well as the film adaptation are filled with details of San Francisco life in the 1970s and 1980s. The coming of the AIDS crisis is mirrored, as well as the horror of the Jim Jones People's Temple massacre, events that touched the city profoundly. Characters visit bathhouses and brothels, as well as cathedrals; they experience anonymous as well as committed sex. The principals, each with a different story and problem, are brought together through their residence in an apartment house on San Francisco's Russian Hill, presided over by a mother hen of a landlady, played by Olympia Dukakis, with her own secrets. Admittedly sentimental as well as pro-gay, the episodes are filled with too many coincidences, but they remain irresistible. They went a long way toward acclimating audiences to same-sex relationships. Before *Will and*

*Grace, Queer Eye for the Straight Guy,* and Showtime's gay-friendly dramas hit the small screen, *Tales of the City* created audience empathy for the joys and woes of same-sex lovers. It was not to be very long before television shows would explode with gay and lesbian characters.

Not only did numerous mainstream films and television programs begin presenting gay characters and issues with sympathy, but several popular entertainers who had been previously closeted found it safe enough to "come out" to their public. Rosie O'Donnell, Ellen DeGeneres, and K. D. Lang were among the best known. Even earlier, tennis pro Billie Jean King had been "outed," inadvertently revealing the extent of lesbianism in women's tennis. Honest biographies unmasked the homosexual and sexually ambiguous natures and activities of major entertainers of the past. While Rock Hudson, a popular film star of the 1950s and 1960s, had been the first major entertainment figure known to have died of AIDS, he was followed in a few years by pianist Liberace, Russian ballet dancer Rudolph Nureyev, and others. Much sympathy was generated by the very public plight of these artists.

The media are always a good gauge of what has become acceptable to Americans. Actors now freely accept homosexual roles. Performers who were earlier closeted feel more confident appearing in public with their partners, rearing children together, and acknowledging their gay identities. Bisexuality has become fashionable, to which the public exploits of Angelina Jolie and Anne Heche attest. Some celebrities such as Elton John have held "marriage" ceremonies. The stated goal of the gay liberation movement of employing the media to soften the public to its aspirations and demands has met with considerable success. Legalized same-sex marriage is relatively new, and the media have not yet fully explored its possibilities. It seems inevitable that movies— perhaps first from Holland, Belgium, and Canada—will show legally married same-sex partners raising children, coping with discrimination, and pursuing happiness in their own way. Well-known and well-liked actors will be employed, thus paving the way the way for wider acceptance of same-sex marriage.

## NOTE

1. Laura Miller with Adam Begley, eds., *The Salon.com Readers Guide to Contemporary Authors* (New York: Penguin Books, 2000), 245.

# Appendix B: Selected Motion Pictures

As the gay liberation movement has heightened its influence throughout Europe and North America, motion pictures have done much to make gay life and eventually same-sex marriage seem less startling. American films have now taken the lead in this endeavor from the pioneering European filmmakers. The following is a selection of mainstream movies that treat gay subjects seriously. Although few deal directly with same-sex marriage— a topic that has not yet been fully explored in film—they reveal much information about changing attitudes and the growing acceptance of homosexuality. Almost all are sympathetic toward gay persons and their aspirations, and a few go further by casting homosexuals in a heroic light. Some of the films show family scenes in which children are being intelligently reared. Because of these films, young people no longer find homosexual love scenes so arcane, and images of glamorous, successful gays and lesbians are put before the public. Quality films taking an opposing view are not being made at the present time.

The films listed here are recommended less for their consistent high quality (see the annotations) than for their easy availability in VHS or DVD formats. Pornographic gay films are not listed, although some of the films in this list do contain explicit scenes of a sexual nature. A full filmography would be immense; I have included here only films that I have personally examined.

*Advise and Consent* (1962, 140 min., United States, Otto Preminger)

This adaptation of Allen Drury's popular novel about Washington intrigue reflects the scandal that homosexuality of government functionaries could generate in the 1960s.

*Aimee & Jaguar* (1999, 126 min., Germany, Max Farberbock)

A holocaust background adds danger to this star-crossed romance between the wife of a Nazi officer and a member of the Jewish underground in wartime Berlin. The film, based on real events, provides a picture of the German lesbian subculture that flourished under the Weimar Republic but was targeted for extermination by the Nazis.

*All over Me* (1997, 90 min., United States, Alex Sichel)

This serious and sensitive film was the joint effort of two sisters; Alex directed and Sylvia Sichel wrote the screenplay. Set in New York's Hell's Kitchen, two painful events unfold in the life of a teenage girl. She must contend with her first love, an unrequited passion for her best friend, at the same time she acknowledges her lesbian sexuality.

*And the Band Played On* (1993, 140 min., United States, Roger Spottiswoode)

Based on an acclaimed book by Randy Shilts and featuring a distinguished cast, this medical thriller traces the scientific discoveries that finally brought understanding of the causes and progress of the HIV virus. Criticized in some quarters for the impression it leaves that straight scientists finally brought awareness to a befuddled gay population, *Band* nevertheless presented an important health message to the gay community.

*Angels in America* (2003, 352 min., United States, Mike Nichols)

Based on an award-winning play and featuring a cast of major actors, *Angels* first surfaced as a major production for HBO. Mingling realistic fiction and fantasy with historical fact, this overlong and somewhat cluttered dramatization of the AIDS crisis nevertheless sustains interest throughout. Included is a deathbed visitation to attorney Roy Cohn, of McCarthy-era notoriety, by a ghostly Ethel Rosenberg (played by Meryl Streep), whom he was instrumental in sending to the electric chair. Crooning a Yiddish song to him, she becomes a prototypical Jewish mother hovering over his bedside. A wayward angel played by Emma Thompson reveals herself, from time to time, to another AIDS sufferer, a WASP aristocrat who has been abandoned by his Jewish partner. A third figure important to the drama is a young Mormon attorney from Utah who must struggle with religious repression of his homosexuality.

*Beautiful Thing* (1996, 90 min., United Kingdom, Hettie MacDonald)

A story of teenage awakening, *Beautiful Thing* is set in a working-class English neighborhood. Some critics have labeled this the best "coming out" film in many years. A relationship between two boys from culturally deprived families works itself out in positive fashion.

*Les Biches* (1968, 104 min., France/Italy, Claude Chabrol)

Although an example of the greater openness of European cinema, Chabrol's treatment of lesbian characters is not especially favorable. This is a suspenseful study of sexual domination and bisexuality by the director frequently (and not very accurately) referred to as "the French Hitchcock."

*The Birdcage* (1996, 100 min, United States, Mike Nichols)

Despite a notable cast that includes Robin Williams, Gene Hackman, and Dianne Wiest, this remake of a famous French film lacks the charm of the original. Nevertheless, it sustains some interest as it relates the amusing plight of a likeable same-sex couple faced with the approaching marriage of the son they have reared. They prepare with much apprehension to meet the bride's conservative family. In this remake, the setting is shifted from Paris to Palm Beach.

*Boys Don't Cry* (1999, 116 min., United States, Kimberly Peirce)

This highly acclaimed film featured Hilary Swank as a transsexual convincingly living, working, and carrying on a romance as a boy. Based on a true story, the movie ends tragically with a senseless murder. The plight of the transsexual is sympathetically presented.

*La Cage aux Folles* (1978, 91 min., France/Italy, Edouard Molinaro)

This delightful French farce, the source of *The Birdcage* is said to have made drag stars respectable in France. While the movie shows little insight into the serious problems facing homosexuals, the good intentions and likeability of the principal characters, two gay men with a son, humanizes same-sex couples and creates empathy for their families with general audiences.

*The Children's Hour* (1962, 107 min., United States, William Wyler)

A courageous film for its time, *The Children's Hour* was based on a play by Lillian Hellman. Two school mistresses, played by Shirley MacLaine and Audrey Hepburn, discover their attraction to each other after their careers have been ruined because of a spiteful—and false—accusation of lesbian activity.

*Chutney Popcorn* (2000, 92 min., United States, Nisha Ganatra)

This "chick flick" is a family story that concentrates on the adaptation of first-generation Indian youth to the North American milieu. Lesbian lovers and artificial insemination provide special tensions in the Indian American family depicted.

*Citizen Cohn* (1992, 112 min., United States, Frank Pierson)

Made for HBO, this drama portrays the life of Roy Cohn, the McCarthy-era witchhunter, brilliant divorce lawyer, and deeply closeted gay who died of AIDS in 1986. His story has generated several films and fictionalized biographies. This one is entertaining, though cruel and possibly unfair to the memory of Cohn.

*Conspiracy of Silence* (2005, 87 min., United Kingdom, John Deery)

Exploiting the scandals in the Catholic Church at the end of the twentieth century, this rather ugly film attacks the Church's rules on clerical celibacy and homosexuality and suggests widespread corruption and hypocrisy at all levels of clergy. Pope John Paul II is shown briefly as a feeble old man, out of touch with reality. Deery is credited as both scriptwriter and director.

*The Crying Game* (1992, 112 min., United Kingdom, Neil Jordan)

One of the outstanding films of the 1990s, *The Crying Game* is a sympathetic study of transsexuality with a startling conclusion. Glamorous performer Jaye Davidson was introduced. With its background of IRA terrorism, this first-class thriller makes a serious statement while providing major entertainment.

*Edward II* (1992, 90 min., United Kingdom, Jerek Jarman)

This retelling of Christopher Marlowe's play employs Elizabethan language but stresses the gay theme indirectly implied in the original. Period scenes are juxtaposed with contemporary footage of gay rights demonstrations. The scenes are artistically rendered.

*Far from Heaven* (2002, 107 min., United States, Todd Haynes)

This beautifully filmed tribute to director Douglas Sirk, is in some ways a modernization of an old Rock Hudson movie. It is brought up to date by the addition of an interracial romance (between Julianne Moore and Dennis Haysbert) and a same-sex adulterous affair. Dennis Quaid plays one of the gay lovers.

*Fire* (1998, 108 min., India/Canada, Deepa Mehta)

Not surprisingly, *Fire* was banned in India, where lesbianism, its subject, is barely acknowledged to exist. It also aroused considerable controversy when first shown in the United States. The film may also be regarded as an exposé of the dangers of marriages that are arranged without the true consent of the participants by brokers who seek religious enlightenment through celibacy. The central character strives to liberate herself from her loveless marriage through a relationship with her sister-in-law, with sad consequences.

*Four Weddings and a Funeral* (1994, 116 min., United Kingdom, Mike Newell)

This rambling romantic comedy features a homosexual as a member of a large circle of friends. A significant feature of this appealing and popular movie is that the homosexual friend is treated like any other, with full acceptance without making any special issue of his orientation.

*Further Tales of the City* (2001, 223 min., United States, Pierre Gang)

In this final installment of the dramatization of Armistad Maupin's engrossing tales, an important series is brought to a close. Not as interesting as the previous two installments, *Further Tales* becomes a bit overwrought even for an already campy series. Gay, lesbian, and transsexual lesbian lovers are still searching for and finding one another, but into the mix are added a suicidal millionaire, a foreign adventure, and Jim Jones.

*Gay Weddings* (2004, 210 min., United States, Kirk Marcolina and Douglas Ross)

This documentary follows the paths of two male and two female gay couples through their commitment ceremonies and into their lives for about six months. Interactions with friends and family members are especially revealing. While three of the couples are shown to be happy with their choices, one couple discover that their "marriage" was a mistake. All are thoughtfully and compassionately presented.

*The Hanging Garden* (1998, 91 min., Canada, Tom Fitzgerald)

Set in Nova Scotia, a troubled family is brought together by a wedding. A son returns after a 10-year absence, now a sophisticated, openly gay man. His schoolboy lover, who is now marrying his sister, finds that long-buried emotions are reawakened. This is a clear example of the openness of contemporary Canadian cinema.

*The Hours* (2002, 114 min., United Kingdom, Stephen Daldry)

In this Academy Award–winning film (Nicole Kidman as best actress), an interestingly nonlinear plot features Kidman as the British bisexual author Virginia Woolf. A poet dying of AIDS is played by Ed Harris. *The Hours* is what used to be known as "a woman's film," with elements of melodrama but devoid of excessive sentimentality.

*In & Out* (1997, 92 min., United States, Frank Oz)

A comedy with an all-star Hollywood cast, *In & Out* toys with gay stereotypes. A schoolteacher, played by Kevin Kline, is accidentally outed on national television right before his wedding, with amusing rather than tragic results.

*The Journey* (2004, 107 min., Malaysia, Ligy Pullapully)

The atmosphere is dense in this story of troubled, forbidden love.

*Kissing Jessica Stein* (2001, 96 min., United States, Charles Herman-Wurmfeld)

According to one of its actors, this comedy about bi-sexual women aspired to alert audiences to the range of sexual possibilities. Although some scenes are funny, the film is ultimately tedious and preachy.

*Late Bloomers* (1997, 104 min., United States, Gretchen Dyer and Julia Dyer)

This lesbian coming-out story is set in Eleanor Roosevelt High School. The plot is a bit different, in that the lovers discover their orientation in later life. One is a middle-aged basketball coach, and the other is the school secretary, married and the mother of two. Love, however, conquers all in an ending reminiscent of old Hollywood, even if the inclinations of the characters are not.

*Latter Days* (2003, 107 min., United States, C. Jay Cox)

Even though *Latter Days* (written and directed by Cox, the noted screenwriter of *Sweet Home Alabama*) was praised by critics of the *New York Times* and *Los Angeles Times* and features two attractive actresses, Mary Kay Place and Jacqueline Bisset, it is offensive in its depiction of middle-class Mormons as hate-filled bigots. Viewers may wonder whether Mormons are chosen for special ridicule because of their reputation—ironic in view of their history—as strong promoters of traditional family values. A further problem is the intense realism of the homosexual love scenes, which move the film almost into the category of pornography.

*Longtime Companion* (1990, 96 min United States, Norman Rene)

One of the first films to treat the AIDS crisis realistically and compassionately, *Longtime Companion* accurately reflects the loving concern with which numerous partners of AIDS victims have attended their lovers' last days.

*M Butterfly* (1993, 100 min., United States, David Cronenberg)

This is the screen version of a hit play based on the real-life experiences of a French diplomat. Jeremy Irons, as the diplomat, falls in love with a Chinese opera singer and conducts a long affair before he learns that the object of his passionate affections is really a transvestite male sent to spy on him for the Chinese government. While the events seem preposterous, we are assured that they really happened. *M Butterfly* remains effective drama, a moving study of obsessive love and delusion.

*Making Love* (1982, 113 min., United States, Arthur Hiller)

Although resembling a soap opera, this film was a breakthrough for U.S. movie makers. For the first time, two men were seen kissing in a film designed for general audiences. *Making Love* is also regarded as a first in its positive treatment of gay characters who are neither sick nor maladjusted.

*Maurice* (1987, 140 min., United Kingdom, James Ivory)

This Merchant and Ivory film is a skillful adaptation of E. M. Forster's semi- autobiographical novel. The setting is pre–World War I England, in which a university student, after much self-doubt, comes to terms with his homosexuality and class prejudices.

*Michael* (1924, 86 min., Denmark, Carl Dreyer)

A masterpiece of cinema by a legendary director, *Michael* is a 1924 adaptation of a decadent novel. It recreates in a more modern setting the love triangle between the Roman god Jupiter, his wife Juno, and the lad Ganymede. The fin de siècle sets and the cinematography alone make this film worth viewing.

*Midnight in the Garden of Good and Evil* (1997, 254 min., United States, Clint Eastwood)

Based on the best-seller that put Savannah, Georgia, on the tourist map, *Midnight* tells a story inspired by a real murder in which homosexuality was a motivating factor. Although the film was a box office disappointment, it retains considerable merit, with actor Kevin Spacey, the songs of Johnny Mercer, and the humorous and sympathetic portrait of The Lady Chablis, a memorable transvestite performer.

*More Tales of the City* (1998, 330 min., United States, Pierre Gang)

This sequel to *Tales of the City* has been described as "more relaxed" than the initial HBO feature. Armistead Maupin's collection of interesting gay and straight characters in San Francisco form a circle around the mysterious Mrs. Madrigal, a transsexual admirably portrayed by Olympia Dukakis.

*My Beautiful Laundrette* (1985, 98 min., United Kingdom, Stephen Frears)

After a substantial run in art houses, *Laundrette* became a staple in cinema societies. It tackles both British racism and gay prejudice in a comic narrative of an English-born Pakistani and his Anglo lover who successfully operate a laundry emporium in London's East End.

*My Life on Ice* (2002, 100 min., France, Olivier Ducastle and Jacques Martineau)

Set in Rouen, this film follows the developing awareness of a 16-year-old boy who discovers his homosexuality through his interest in photography and ice skating. This is a cheerful, accepting film, composed in the more leisurely style characteristic of the French cinema.

*Myra Breckinridge* (1970, 94 min., United States, Michael Sarne)

Based on the novel by Gore Vidal, *Myra Breckinridge* has a reputation for being one of the campiest movies ever made, with its transsexual rape scenes and its odd casting. Remembered as a classic of absurd films, the movie is now a cult favorite.

*Philadelphia* (1993, 120 min., United States, Jonathan Demme)

The City of Brotherly Love has been appropriately chosen as setting for one of the most acclaimed films to treat AIDS sympathetically. Tom Hanks won an Oscar for his portrayal of a successful Philadelphia lawyer whose career is wrecked when his associates learn he is HIV positive. *Philadelphia,* which claims to be the first Hollywood film about AIDS, suffers from some preachiness but has genuine historical and dramatic interest.

*Priest* (1995, 97 min., United Kingdom, Antonia Bird)

Father Greg, a young priest, is assigned to a working-class parish in Liverpool. As he begins this ministry, he is attempting to reconcile his pressing homosexuality with his vow of celibacy. The most moving scene, possibly the emotional climax of the film, takes place when a tormented young man goes to mass and, looking up, discovers the priest giving him communion, Father Greg, is the man with whom he had anonymous sexual contact the night before.

*Sacred Silence* (1996, 115 min., Italy, Antonio Capuano)

In this well-scripted film, the Mafia attacks an activist priest through his relationship with an altar boy.

*Same Sex Parents* (2004, 86 min., France, Laurence Katrain)

The action of this film unfolds through the eyes of a teenage girl whose mother is a lesbian and whose father is gay. Though taunted by fellow students, the young woman comes to terms with her two loving parents and experiences her own first romantic encounter, with her boyfriend.

*Saving Face* (2005, 87 min., United States, Alice Wu)

This Chinese American film presents an ironic picture of a structured subculture confronting contemporary problems. An elderly Chinese professional couple, immigrants to America, must contend with a widowed, middle-aged but pregnant daughter, and a lesbian granddaughter. The situation is handled with humor and, ultimately, affirms family solidarity.

*Tales of the City* (1993, 360 min., United States/United Kingdom, Alastair Reid)

Based on the popular stories of San Francisco life in the 1970s by Armistead Maupin, *Tales* brings together an assortment of likable people who manifest varying degrees of sexual ambiguity. In many ways the film is a celebration of the emerging gay life-style that has come to characterize the city in the minds of many. One young man haunts the gay retreats of the city, hoping to find the perfect life partner. A transsexual woman finally finds her true love only months before his death.

*The Tempest* (1979, 95 min., Derek Jarman)

This reworking of one of Shakespeare's most mature plays has been greatly admired by many critics. It does eliminate the most striking feature of the Shakespeare's art, its language. Still the images are startling. As usual in Jarman films, a gay message, not present in Shakespeare, is blatant.

*those who love me can take the train* (1998, 122 min., France, Patrice Chereau)

Considered a landmark in French experimental cinema, this film was also praised for its depiction of the contemporary gay experience in Europe. The spiritual emptiness of much continental life today is also well demonstrated.

*Torch Song Trilogy* (1988, 117 min., United States, Paul Bogart)

Led by performer Harvey Fierstein, *Torch Song* is based on the Tony Award–winning play about a lovable drag queen in Brooklyn. Partly autobiographical, the narrative examines not only the career of the drag queen but explores his relationship with three significant individuals: his mother, his gay lover, and his bisexual companion.

*Trembling before G-d* (2001, 84 min., United States, Sandi Simcha DuBowski)

Although somewhat misleadingly billed as "the hidden lives of gay and lesbian Orthodox and Hasidic Jews," this is still the most important film to explore the conflicts between homosexuality and religious aspirations. Examining gay orientation within Orthodox Judaism, the director interviews several men and women who have struggled for years to reconcile their desire to be faithful Jews with their homosexual impulses. The most notable feature of this film is not its sympathy for the plight of gays but its respectful treatment of Hassidism and other forms of Orthodox Judaism that have been unequivocal in their historical condemnation of homosexual activity. *Trembling* shows how powerful and precious the rituals and ceremonies of Judaism are for faithful Jews. The DVD extra features include interviews with several orthodox rabbis; while they are sympathetic to the problems of gay Jews, they uphold *halakah,* the Jewish law. The participation of Rabbi Steven Greenberg is particularly noteworthy, because he convincingly claims to be the first openly gay rabbi in the history of Orthodox Judaism.

*Walk on Water* (2005, 103 min., Israel, Eytan Fox)

This is a well-made, engrossing thriller that clearly equates "homophobia" with Nazism and cultural bias. A macho Israeli assassin is sent to eliminate a sick, elderly Nazi in Germany "before God gets him." During his assignment he meets and falls in love with the granddaughter of the old Nazi, and he also comes to accept the homosexuality of her brother. The ultimate message of the film, which even expresses some sympathy for the Palestinian plight, is "make love, not revenge."

*The Wedding Banquet* (1993, 108 min., United States/China/Taiwan, Ang Lee)

Described as "a wholesome gay comedy," this film examines the cultural and generation gap between a successful businessman living in America with his same-sex lover and his Taiwanese parents, who are anxious to see him wed to a suitable Chinese bride.

*The Wedding Video* (2001, 84 min., United States, Norman Kerpi)

Instructive and informative, this film follows the preparations for a long-anticipated same-sex wedding.

*Yentl* (1983, 134 min., United States, Barbra Streisand)

Although not regarded as one of Streisand's better films, this one was evidently a labor of love. Based on a story by Isaac Bashevis Singer, with a turn-of-the-century Russian setting, Streisand plays a young woman who yearns to study Talmud. In order to be admitted into the yeshiva, she must disguise herself as a man. While the central focus of the film is not transsexuality or transvestism, but feminism, it remains one of the earlier attempts to explore the fascination with sexual ambiguity that would become a major preoccupation in the cinema of the next decade.

# Selected Annotated Bibliography

Abbott, Elizabeth. *A History of Celibacy: From Athena to Elizabeth I, Leonardo da Vinci, Florence Nightingale, Gandhi, & Cher.* New York: Scribner, 2000.

It is well to remember that throughout history, for various personal and social reasons, some individuals have chosen celibacy, frequently in the face of religious, family, and state disapproval. This sometimes frivolous but generally informative survey gives some perspective on contemporary claims of "sexual rights."

Adam, Barry D. *The Rise of a Gay and Lesbian Movement.* Boston: Twayne/ G. K. Hall, 1987.

Adam provides a clear account of the beginnings and development of the contemporary gay rights movement, which is currently demanding marriage equality. Surveying movements around the world, he demonstrates that the Stonewall riots in New York, from which some historians date the gay rights movement, are not as germinal as often suggested. He locates the first modern gay rights movement in Germany in 1897. The impact of the AIDS epidemic is further analyzed, along with the increasing acceptance of domestic partnership legislation. The book includes interesting anecdotal information as well as historical scholarship.

Archer, Bert. *The End of Gay: And the Death of Heterosexuality.* New York: Thunder's Mouth Press, 2002.

In one of the most provocative discussions on the market, Archer asks why contemporary humans are so obsessed with defining themselves by their sexual behaviors. He makes a powerful case for his contention that sexual orientation is more fluid, ambiguous, and indeterminate than current politics have led us to believe. The ramifications for same-sex marriage are many.

Bailey, D. S. *Homosexuality and the Western Christian Tradition.* New York: Longmans, 1955.

Although his book comes from the 1950s and surveys a very different social climate than today, Bailey still provides a good overview of Western attitudes, from the conservative viewpoint.

Baldizzone, Tiziana, and Gianni Baldizzone. *Wedding Ceremonies: Ethnic Symbols, Costumes and Rituals.* Paris: Flammerion, 2001.

In addition to helpful commentary, the Baldizzones provide a lavish photographic journey to distant lands—from Lapland to Indonesia, from Niger to Tibet . All over the non-European world, their camera documents lavishly celebrated marriages.

Bellis, Alice Ogden, and Terry L. Hufford. *Science, Scripture, and Homosexuality.* Cleveland, OH: Pilgrim, 2002.

Providing a clear discussion of issues from a conservative Christian point of view, this study is more likely to confirm opinions than to change them.

Benkov, Laura. *Reinventing the Family: Lesbian and Gay Parents.* New York: Crown Trade Paperbacks, 1994.

A clinical psychologist and instructor in psychiatry at Harvard Medical School, Benkov makes an earnest plea for society's support of gay and lesbian parents. She carefully outlines the obstacles these parents face as they try to rear their natural or adopted children.

Bennett, William J. *The Broken Hearth: Reversing the Moral Collapse of the American Family.* New York: Doubleday, 2001.

Bennett presents an eloquent lament for what he believes is the threatened traditional American family. This former "morals czar" strongly contends that marriage can exist only between a man and a woman, and alternative arrangements, such as same-sex marriages, can only be destructive for family and society. This is one of the strongest defenses of conventional marriage that does not rely primarily on religious arguments.

Berube, Allan. *Coming Out Under Fire: The History of Gay Men and Women in World War Two.* New York: Free Press/Macmillan, 1990.

In this insightful account of homosexuality during a period of world crisis, Berube examines the struggles of homosexual men and women in the U.S. military during World War II, a turning point in attitudes toward sexuality. He records, chiefly through interviews with survivors, the purges of both gay servicemen and lesbian women that took place in the army. He also credits military psychiatrists with an early defense of gays in service. Berube is clearly sympathetic toward gay servicepeople, but his well-documented study remains balanced.

Bidstrup, Scott. "Gay Marriage: The Arguments and the Motives" (2004), http://www.bidstrup.com/marriage.htm.

This is an impassioned, comprehensive defense of same-sex marriage, with useful resources cited at the end.

Blair, Ralph. *An Evangelical Look at Homosexuality.* Chicago: Moody Press, 1963.

Although this earlier discussion of homosexuality could not possibly anticipate all the developments in the liberation movement today, Blair still makes a valuable and thoughtful conservative statement. His argument continues to represent the thinking of millions of Americans.

Bork, Robert H. *Slouching Towards Gomorrah: Modern Liberalism and American Decline.* New York: Regan Books, 2003.

This is a carefully reasoned conservative analysis of the direction of American society, by one of the greatest legal minds in the United States today. Bork bemoans the corruption of popular culture, the politics of sex, and the decline of reverence for life observed in the increasing acceptance of abortion, assisted suicide, euthanasia, and same-sex marriage. He finds serious problems with American education and trouble in American religion. A section on the homosexual movement and Bork's evaluation of its claims is one of the finest analyses from a traditional point-of-view. Anyone seeking to understand why intelligent conservatives object to same-sex marriage must read this book.

Boswell, John. *Christianity, Social Tolerance, and Homosexuality.* Chicago: University of Chicago Press, 1980.

Although the conclusions of this study have been convincingly challenged by other scholars, Boswell's historical scholarship is impressive and his work must be considered by any student of religious attitudes toward homosexuality.

———. *Same-Sex Unions in Premodern Europe.* New York: Vintage Books, 1995.

Boswell is best remembered for his thesis, presented in this book and in other studies, that early Christianity blessed same-sex unions and developed ceremonies to sanctify them. While acknowledging Boswell's scholarship and the appeal of his presentation, most historians agree that he misread his sources and therefore presented a thesis that collapses under scrutiny.

Bouldrey, Brian, ed. *Wrestling with the Angel: Faith and Religion in the Lives of Gay Men.* Itasca: Putnam, 1995.

Twenty-one gay men from Hindu, Muslim, Jewish, Baptist, Lutheran, and Mormon backgrounds explore the perplexities of faith and gay identity. Some of the essays are especially poignant in the shadow of the AIDS crisis.

Bourassa, Kevin, and Joe Varnell. "Troy Perry at Halifax Marriage Celebration; Founder of MCC: 'Thank God for Canada'" (2005), http://www.samesexmarriage.ca/advocacy/shm170905.htm.

The Reverend Troy Perry's praise of Canada for pioneering same-sex marriage in North America is the subject of this highly favorable report.

Bowker, John, ed. *The Oxford Dictionary of World Religions.* New York: Oxford University Press, 1997.

Although this is a general reference book, the section on the status of marriage in the major world religions is particularly pertinent.

Boyd, Nan Alamilla, ed. *Wide Open Town: A History of Queer San Francisco to 1965.* Berkeley: University of California Press, 2003.

This collection of essays and oral histories provides a revealing narrative of the emergence of San Francisco as "the gay capital" of the United States. The chapters outlining the confluence of the gay bar culture and the social action groups is especially interesting.

Brooten, Bernadette J. *Love between Women: Early Christian Responses to Female Homoeroticism.* Chicago Series on Sexuality, History, and Society. Chicago: University of Chicago Press, 1996.

This work is of value chiefly because lesbianism has received much less attention than its male counterpart and has generally been the object of less hostility. Brooten's work is also a contribution to the broader field of women's studies.

Brownback, Sam. "Defining Marriage Down" (2004), http://www. nationalreview.com.

A Republican senator from Kansas, Brownback argues firmly that legalized same-sex unions will weaken the institution of marriage and the structure of society.

Browning, Frank. *A Queer Geography: Journeys toward a Sexual Self.* New York: Crown, 1996.

Browning's thesis is that gay activism has assumed a religious character in the United States. He compares coming-out experiences with the religious perception of being "born again." He contrasts the experiences of American gays with those in Italy, Brazil, and the Philippines and reviews anthropological information on tribesmen in New Guinea. Gay identity, Browning believes, is strongly shaped by national culture.

Bruce, Tammy. *The New American Revolution: Using the Power of the Individual To Save Our Nation from Extremists.* New York: William Morrow, 2005.

Highly readable if somewhat glib, Bruce is noteworthy as a lesbian conservative who supports traditional definitions of marriage. Her discussion of what she refers to as "the Gay Gestapo" and its pressure tactics is especially interesting.

Cantarella, Eva (translated by Cormac O'Cuilleanain). *Bisexuality in the Ancient World.* New Haven, CT: Yale University Press, 1992.

This is one of the most cogent and thorough historical studies of bisexuality. Bisexuality in the ancient world was much more common than homosexuality, which was rarely, if ever, acknowledged as a permanent orientation. Cantarella examines practices and attitudes in ancient Greece, Imperial Rome, and the Late Roman Republic. She concludes with a discussion of the changes in sexual ethics that took place near the end of the ancient period, particularly with the spread of Judeo-Christian ideals.

Caramagno, Thomas C. *Irreconcilable Differences?: Intellectual Stalemate in the Gay Rights Debate.* Westport, CT: Greenwood, 2002.

Noteworthy for his examination of the rhetoric on both sides of the gay rights controversy, Caramagno finds a stalemate in the debate because of stereotypes and the tendency to pathologize opposing views. Such attitudes and tendencies make any consensus presently impossible. Some issues, Caramagno feels, can be settled by appeals to science and historical scholarship, but some cannot.

Casier, Lawrence. *Is Marriage Necessary?* New York: Human Sciences Press, 1974.

A curiosity and seriously dated, this book is still readable. Casier represents an anti-establishment view from the early seventies. He advocates a variety of alternatives to marriage: modified monogamy, nonmonogamous matrimony, and an assortment of nonmarital relationships. He largely dismisses traditional matrimony as patriarchal and a poor setting for the rearing of children. He does not consider same-sex unions among the alternatives to traditional marriage that he recommends.

Catholic Answers. "Gay Marriage" (2004), http://www.catholic.com/library/gay_marriage.asp.

Expressing the official Roman Catholic position on same-sex marriage, this 15-page polemic is carefully reasoned and fully documented.

Cere, Daniel, and Douglas Farrow, eds. *Divorcing Marriage.* Montreal: McGill University Press, 2004.

Twelve Canadian scholars from different disciplines and different sexual orientations present their strong reservations about "Canada's new social experiment" in same-sex marriage. More than almost any other book on the market, this one isolates the chief problems in changing the definition of marriage. All contributors write with clarity, liveliness, and some characteristic Canadian wit.

Chasin, Alexandra. *Selling Out: The Gay and Lesbian Movement Goes to Market.* New York: Palgrave, 2000.

Chasin examines the emerging gay market in the United States, which is aggressively being targeted by advertisers and purveyors of goods and services. Not surprisingly, the elaborate wedding industry in this country has a vested interest in promoting same-sex marriage. This book is a good corrective to excessive consumerism, well researched and filled with pertinent information.

Chauncey, George. *Why Marriage?: The History Shaping Today's Debate over Gay Equality.* New York: Basic Books, 2004.

In this somewhat glib gay rights history, Chauncey asserts that marriage became a primary gay rights goal because of the AIDS crisis, which altered the life-style of many gay men. The problems gay couples faced in their efforts to adopt children were also crucial. Chauncey has insightful observations on religious objections to gay rights.

Coontz, Stephanie. *Marriage, a History.* New York: Viking, 2005.

*Marriage* is an informal, often anecdotal history by a sociologist and prolific writer on family life. Coontz holds the Victorians—who idealized, protected, and in many ways imprisoned women—responsible for many of the problems marriage faces today. For a short time in the 1950s, American marriage experienced a "Golden Age," she recalls, but the opening of marriage to equality of the sexes has also helped undermine its durability. Coontz believes that marriage has changed more in the last 30 years than in all previous recorded history.

———. *The Way We Never Were.* New York: Basic Books, 2000.

In an examination of the myths that surrounded marriage in the recent American past, Coontz contends that matrimony was never the blissful state that many people like to believe it was before the women's rights movements and gay liberation started making inroads. In a new introduction, Coontz examines events since the original 1992 publication.

———. *The Way We Really Are: Coming to Terms with America's Changing Families.* New York: Basic Books, 1998.

A provocative work of history and sociology, this study looks at the mythology of today's family. "Mothers are going to remain in the work force, family diversity is here to stay, and the nuclear family can no more handle all the responsibilities of elder care and childrearing." Coontz is often highly opinionated, but she demands that readers define exactly what they believe a family should be.

Cott, Nancy F. *Public Vows: A History of Marriage and the Nation.* Cambridge, MA: Harvard University Press, 2000.

In this valuable historical survey of American marriage, with much relevance to emerging models of same-sex unions, Cott examines a variety of marriage forms that have existed in North America. She elucidates Native American concepts of matrimony, the loose marriages necessitated by the institution of black slavery, common law arrangements as they existed on the frontier, Mormon polygamy, immigrant family styles, as well as communal movements such as Oneida, which attempted freer sexual arrangements.

Countryman, L. William. *Dirt, Greed, and Sex: Sexual Ethics in the New Testament.* Philadelphia: Fortress Press, 1988.

Countryman interprets biblical messages from a liberal Christian perspective. He examines Judaic purity laws and their relevance for Christianity and includes a pertinent perspective on homosexuality.

Crompton, Louis. *Homosexuality & Civilization.* Cambridge, MA: Belknap Press of Harvard University Press, 2003.

A work of vast scholarship, Crompton's study is probably the most comprehensive, up-to-date treatment of same sex relationships from a historical point of view. Attitudes and practices of homosexuality are examined throughout history and in every major culture, both Eastern and Western.

Decter, Midge. "Civil Unions: Compromise or Surrender?" (2004), http://www.hillsdale.edu/newimprimis.htm.

Decter, a noted author and social critic, sees the civil union compromise as unwholesome and unworkable. She warns of the social devastation she feels will result from the success of the gay agenda.

D'Emilio, John. *The World Turned: Essays on Gay History, Politics, and Culture.* Durham, NC: Duke University Press, 2002.

In this impassioned examination of events in the gay community during the 1990s, D'Emilio, a prominent activist, asserts that gay concerns, formerly regarded as peripheral, moved to the center of American life during this decade.

Dickson, Lovat. *Radclyffe Hall at the Well of Loneliness.* New York: Scribner's, 1975.

This biography of a minor British writer shows the social and personal impact of earlier theories of sexual orientation. It also provides an intriguing glimpse of urban Edwardian lesbian subculture in England.

Duberman, Lucile. *Marriage and Other Alternatives,* Second Edition. New York: Holt, Rinehart and Winston, 1977.

Duberman provides a sociological examination of suggested marital models, including monogamy, serial marriage, and group marriage. While 1977 was seemingly too early for Duberman to consider same-sex marriage, she does take a charitable view of the homosexual life-style. Of special interest are her predictions for the future of marriage.

Dumesnil, Cheryl. *Hitched!* New York: Thunder's Mouth Press, 2005.

Many couples were "married" in February of 2004 in San Francisco, upon the authority of Mayor Gavin Newsom. Although these unions were later declared invalid, the exuberance of the event is well captured in this book, which includes an introduction by Rosie O'Donnell, an essay by Phyllis Lyon and Del Martin, arguably the most famous lesbian couple in the world, and a collection of personal stories by people who received licenses at San Francisco City Hall.

Elliott, Dyan. *Spiritual Marriage: Sexual Abstinence in Medieval Wedlock.* Princeton, NJ: Princeton University Press, 1993.

Although not directly related to the issues of same-sex marriage, this well-documented study provides new insights into the meaning of marriage in the medieval world and suggests that there were more acceptable variations on Christian marriage than are usually acknowledged.

Faderman, Lillian. *Chloe Plus Olivia: An Anthology of Lesbian Literature from the Seventeenth Century to the Present.* New York: Penguin Books, 1995.

Some of Faderman's facts are open to different interpretations than those she provides, but she has brought together a vivid collection of writings by women.

———. *Odd Girls and Twilight Lovers: A History of Lesbian Life in Twentieth-Century America.* New York: Penguin, 1992.

In this readable account of lives of women who have chosen to defy social expectations and refrain from marriage, Faderman traces the development of the concept of "lesbian," emerging from the experiences of "romantic friendship" and "sentimental friendship." Particularly provocative is the connection made between the economic emancipation of women and the death of innocence about female relationships.

———. *Surpassing the Love of Men: Romantic Friendship & Love Between Women from the Renaissance to the Present.* New York: Perennial, Harper Collins, 1998.

This is a fine historical study of female friendships and lesbianism, but Faderman reaches debatable conclusions about the relationships she examines. Nevertheless, she has offered a readable survey of a topic not often explored and documented.

————. *To Believe in Women: What Lesbians Have Done for America—A History.* New York: Mariner Books, 2000.

Faderman has written a stimulating book with some questionable assumptions. She believes that many of the early leaders in the struggles for women's higher education and their right to practice the professions would be identified as lesbians today. While it was true that the early women's colleges were operated by spinsters, it is not appropriate to label so many of them lesbian. Faderman shows how it was necessary that these early struggles for rights be carried on by single women, relieved of family duties.

Foucault, Michel. *The History of Sexuality,* Volume I: *An Introduction* (translated from the French by Robert Hurley). New York: Vintage Books, 1980.

Foucault's work is germinal to philosophical discussions of sexuality in the modern world. His writing is difficult and his thought controversial, but his work remains essential for an understanding of the gay-straight confrontation today. While Foucault was reticent about his own homosexuality, he did put sexual practices and attitudes into thoughtful philosophical perspective.

Frum, David. "The Marriage Buffet" (2003), http://www.opinion journal.com/ac/?id+110004173.

Frum argues that same-sex marriage in the United States, following the precedent already established in a few European countries, would lead to chaos.

Gagnon, Robert A. J. *The Bible and Homosexual Practice: Texts and Hermeneutics.* Nashville, *TN*: Abingdon Press, 2001.

Gagnon provides the most fully reasoned and comprehensive statement of the orthodox Christian opposition to homosexual practice. This is a fine scholarly study, clear and readable, and essential for any understanding of religious thinking on the subject.

Gerstmann, Evan. *Same-Sex Marriage and the Constitution.* Cambridge, England: Cambridge University Press, 2003.

Gerstmann provides a clear examination of her subject from the legal and constitutional perspective. Although he understands the hesitancy of the majority of Americans to legalize, and therefore endorse, homosexual marriage, he feels their concerns are overwrought, their reasoning legally questionable. Especially illuminating is the discussion of court decisions that establish public policy as opposed to legislative action.

Greenberg, David F. *The Construction of Homosexuality.* Chicago: University of Chicago Press, 1988.

Greenberg's writings are among the most frequently quoted in discussions of the same-sex marriage issue. He provides a historical survey, examining gay subculture with an emphasis on economics and class values.

Greenberg, Rabbi Steven. *Wrestling with God & Men: Homosexuality in the Jewish Tradition.* Madison: University of Wisconsin Press, 2004.

*Wrestling* is one of the most significant books on religion and homosexuality, by the man who identifies himself as the first openly gay Orthodox rabbi in the history of Judaism. Rabbi Greenberg's spirituality and his love of the Bible are evident, though his reconstructions of passages in Genesis, Leviticus, and Deuteronomy will continue to be controversial.

Hall, Kermit L., ed. *The Oxford Companion to the Supreme Court of the United States.* New York: Oxford University Press, 1992.

Because the Supreme Court may ultimately determine whether same-sex marriage will exist in the United States, this thorough guide to the Court's history and workings is indispensable for anyone who wants to understand the legal ramifications of this and other important constitutional issues.

Hamer, Dean, and Peter Copeland. *The Science of Desire: The Search for the Gay Gene.* New York: Touchstone/Simon & Schuster, 1994.

In this clear account of his attempt to discover a gay gene that would prove the "normalcy" of homosexuality, Hamer provides a readable personal narrative. He is a clear, forceful scientific writer, though his "discoveries" are still hotly debated within the scientific community.

Hartog, Hendrik. *Man and Wife in America: A History.* Cambridge, MA: Harvard University Press, 2000.

Nineteenth-century law assumed that marriage was a permanent relationship defined by a husband's authority and responsibility for the economic welfare of his family. The wife was a dependent being whose duty was the care of the home. Yet this ideal of marriage was impossible to uphold in reality, and the result was a century of legal warfare. Hartog has no illusions about any golden age of marriage in the American past. The records he reviews speak of manipulative women, abusive husbands, crimes of passion, bigamy, and cold-blooded murder.

Helminiak, Daniel A. *What the Bible Really Says about Homosexuality.* San Francisco: Alamo Square Press, 2000.

Helminiak, a Roman Catholic priest, reexamines the biblical passages usually cited by opponents of gay liberation and concludes, on the basis of his historical readings that "the Bible supplies no condemnation of homosexuality!" He relies heavily on the work of Yale historian John Boswell. This is a readable popularization of pro-gay biblical scholarship, not endorsed by his church or by any noted biblical or secular historians.

Highwater, Jamake. *Mythology of Transgression: Homosexuality as Metaphor.* Oxford, England: Oxford University Press, 1996.

It is difficult to make sense of this confused, wildly eclectic statement. Written from an acknowledged gay Native American point of view, Highwater relates his concerns to the arts, literature, psychology, and anthropology, in a highly theoretical study.

Hogan, Steve, and Lee Hudson. *Completely Queer: The Gay and Lesbian Encyclopedia.* New York: Henry Holt, 1998.

Encyclopedias usually contain a wealth of useful information and, like this one, may even be readable. This illustrated lively reference for gay and lesbian resources covers historical developments, contributions to the arts, individual homosexuals of distinction, along with events and issues of concern to the community.

Horvat, Marian Therese. "Rewriting History To Serve the Gay Agenda" (October 2001), http://www.traditioninaction.org/bkreviews/A_002br_SameSex. htm.

In this review of *Christianity, Social Tolerance, and Homosexuality,* Horvat labels John Boswell's central thesis (that same-sex unions were blessed by early Christianity) wholesale "historical revisionism" and "advocacy scholarship" to serve a clear political agenda.

Ignatieff, Michael. *The Rights Revolution.* Toronto: House of Anansi Press, 2000.

Examining entitlement claims made by many contemporary groups, Ignatieff relates the demands of gays to those of other minorities. The material comes from Massey Lectures delivered by this popular Canadian novelist, professor, and human rights advocate.

Johnson, Toby, and Edwin Clark Johnson. *Gay Perspective: Things Our Homo-sexuality Tells Us about the Nature of God and the Universe.* New York: Alyson Publications, 2003.

Investigations of gay spirituality are welcome, and always speculative. The Johnsons believe that gay people, as outsiders, are able to provide unique insights into theology and religion. They contend that gay people are better able to see across boundaries of gender, helping society overcome ignorance. Homosexuals are also more open to mystical experience. These arguments, while not always convincing, are provocative.

Jones, James H. *Alfred Kinsey: A Public/Private Life.* New York: Norton, 1997.

This revealing study is probably the best biography of the man often des-ignated as the father of the sexual revolution. Kinsey is viewed not merely as a scientist but as a man whose obsessions influenced his research. His experi-ence included homosexual relations with his research assistants and others.

Jones, Stanton L., and Mark A. Yarhouse. *Homosexuality: The Use of Scientific Research in the Church's Moral Debate.* Downers Grove, IL: InterVarsity Press, 2000.

Although the authors make a strong case for the traditional Christian position on homosexuality, they impartially and honestly survey the latest scientific research on homosexuality. Both are qualified scientists as well as theological thinkers.

Kilbride, Philip L. *Plural Marriage for Our Times: A Reinvented Option?* Westport, CT: Bergin & Garvey, 1994.

A Roman Catholic who has lived and worked in African societies, Kilbride is Professor of Anthropology at Bryn Mawr College. He presents a favor-able case for plural marriage by examining family patterns in a cross-cultural perspective, with special attention to the doctrines and historical practices of Mormons. He also provides an overview of African polygyny, and what he calls "crisis polygyny" in the African American community. He looks with favor on plural marriage, which he refers to as "a reinvented option." Neither his Roman Catholic coreligionists, nor few others in America, support his thesis.

Kinsey, Alfred, et al. *Sexual Behaviour in the Human Female*. Philadelphia: W. B. Saunders, 1953.

More inflammatory than Kinsey's study of the human male, this report asserted that lesbianism was much more widespread than generally acknowledged.

————. *Sexual Behaviour in the Human Male*. Philadelphia: W. B. Saunders, 1948.

This controversial study is often alleged to have started the sexual revolution. Although a dry scientific report, it became a best seller and Kinsey's name became a household word. Among other findings was that homosexuality was widespread among men of all social classes

Kraft-Ebing, Richard von. *Psychopathia Sexualis: The Case Histories* (translated by Domino Falls). London: Velvet Publications, 1997.

Although his work is now dated, Kraft-Ebing remains the classic sexologist of the pathological.

Kurtz, Stanley. "Beyond Gay Marriage" (August 2003), http://www.weeklystandard.com/Content/Public/Articles/000/000/002/938xpsxy.asp.

Kurtz presents the thesis that same-sex marriage is a step toward the abolition of marriage in general. He takes strong issue with liberal sociologists who have proposed alternatives to traditional marriage.

Lahey, Kathleen A., and Kevin Alderson. *Same-Sex Marriage: The Personal and the Political*. Toronto: Insomniac Press, 2004.

Lahey and Alderson provide a good historical discussion of the political and legal struggle for same-sex marriage, with a close look at gains already achieved in Europe and Canada, as well as the conflicting legal maneuvers in Hawaii. Of special interest are the personal stories of the couples who have sought same-sex marriage.

La Huerta, Christian de, and Lam Kam Chuen. *Coming Out Spiritually: The Next Step*. New York: Tarcher, 1999.

The thesis of this New Age declaration is that gay people have a beneficial role to play in world culture. The authors examine Buddhism, Christianity, Judaism, Hinduism, Taoism, Sufism, New Thought, New Age, and various Earth-friendly sects to see what insights each might provide gay and lesbian people. Especially interesting are the speculations about roles homosexuals may have played as shamans and priests in traditional societies.

Leap, William L., and Tom Boellstorff, eds. *Speaking in Queer Tongues: Globalization and Gay Language.* Champaign: University of Illinois Press, 2004.

Linguistic analyses of "gay talk" have received little previous attention. Because language is a fundamental tool for shaping our understanding of ourselves and the world, the evolving and changing language of homosexuality is particularly significant. What words do gay and lesbian people throughout the world choose to designate themselves, and how are they referred to by their broader communities?

Lehman, Nathaniel. "The Selling of Homosexuality" (April 2004), http://www.jewsformorality.org/aaaw148selling_hs.htm.

Lehman, a distinguished physician, provides a strong traditionalist Jewish response to the gay agenda.

McBrien, Richard P., general editor. *The Harper Collins Encyclopedia of Catholicism.* San Francisco: Harper Collins, 1995.

This excellent, well-illustrated, and clearly presented volume is a compendium of Roman Catholic lore and general information. The section on the sacrament of marriage is especially pertinent.

Manji, Irshad. *The Trouble with Islam Today: A Muslim's Call for Reform in Her Faith.* New York: St. Martin's Griffin, 2003.

Manji, a Canadian Muslim of Pakistani heritage, presents a critical analysis of contemporary Islam. A journalist who hosts *Queer Television* in Canada, she is open in her lesbian identity while she practices an unorthodox form of Islam. Her book is half spiritual autobiography and half attack on what she regards as contemporary mistakes and distortions in her faith, by its own adherents rather than its antagonists.

Mann, William J. *Behind the Screen: How Gays and Lesbians Shaped Hollywood, 1910–1969.* New York: Penguin Books, 2002.

In this entertaining, well-researched book, Mann does not rely simply on gossip or salacious revelations but looks at the ways in which the gay sensibility has penetrated, sometimes subliminally, the American psyche through film. Most people do not realize how many gay actors, screenwriters, directors, costume designers, and producers have worked in the film industry. Even when strict censorship did not allow overt treatment of homosexuality, gays and lesbians injected subtle messages into the films they made. Mann also explores their participation in shaping the studio system.

Marco, Anton N. "Gay 'Marriage?'" (December 2005), http://www.leaderu. com/jhs/marco.html.

Marco is author of Colorado's Amendment 2 campaign against "protected class" status for gays and is active in family values causes. In this lengthy discussion of over 40 pages, he is especially interested in debunking the widely held view that gays and lesbians are the victims of discrimination.

Nissinen, Martii. *Homoeroticism in the Biblical World: A Historical Perspective.* Minneapolis: Fortress Press, 1998.

In one of the most informative historical studies of its subject, Nissinen provides helpful insights into the formulation of religious attitudes. Biblical denunciations of homosexuality are placed against Mesopotamian, Greek, and pagan Roman backdrops. Nissinen supports the widely accepted view that homosexual identity was not understood in the ancient world, which was concerned almost entirely with who had the active and who had the passive roles in sexual encounters.

Pawick, Edward J. *Libel by New York Times: Gay Marriage Don't Just Happen in Massachusetts, It Was Engineered by the New York Times.* Kennesaw: Mustard Seeds Publishing, 2003.

An amusing satire (I think).

Prager, Dennis. "Judaism's Sexual Revolution: Why Judaism (and then Christianity) Rejected Homosexuality" (September 1993), http://www. orthodoxytoday.org/articles2/PragerHomosexuality.shtml.

Prager presents a carefully reasoned defense of traditional marriage and heterosexuality from an Orthodox Jewish viewpoint.

Quinn, D. Michael. *Same-Sex Dynamics among Nineteenth-Century Americans: A Mormon Example.* Chicago: University of Illinois Press, 1996.

A highly controversial book. Quinn, contrary to most students of Mormonism, asserts that same-sex relationships were accepted by his Church well into the 1940s.

Rauch, Jonathan. *Gay Marriage: Why It is Good for Gays, Good for Straights, and Good for America.* New York: Henry Holt, 2004.

Rauch makes one of the most persuasive cases for the legal recognition of gay unions. While most advocates of same-sex marriage stress discrimination and the many inequities gay relationships face, Rauch concentrates on the obligations of marriage and the benefit to society when individuals take responsibility for one another, whatever their gender. He also presents a persuasive thesis that allowing homosexuals to marry would strengthen the entire institution of matrimony.

Rimmerman, Craig A. *From Identity to Politics: The Lesbian and Gay Movements in the United States.* Philadelphia: Temple University Press, 2002.

Rimmerman gives a fine review of the politics of the gay rights movement with concise discussions of the same-sex marriage issue, the opposition to it by the Christian Right, and criticism from within the gay and lesbian movement itself. Rimmerman identifies discriminatory policies and suggests strategies for dealing with them.

Ross-MacDonald, Jane. *Alternative Weddings: An Essential Guide for Creating Your Own Ceremony.* Lanham, MD: Taylor Trade Publishing, 1997.

This is an entertaining look at all sorts of tailor-made wedding ceremonies that depart from the traditional. Included is general instruction on planning an alternative wedding, making sure it is legal, and dealing with loved ones who may be a little shocked by the unconventionality of it all. There is information about traditional Protestant ceremonies, along with Quaker, Unitarian, Jewish, civil, interfaith, Buddhist, Baha'i, spiritualist, pagan, Druid, humanist, Viking, and pacifist rites. Almost all of these may be adapted for use by same-sex couples. There is, however, a special section on gay and lesbian ceremonies and the special issues they entail.

Rothblum, Ester D., and Kathleen A. Brehony, eds. *Boston Marriages: Romantic but Asexual Relationships among Contemporary Lesbians.* Amherst: University of Massachusetts Press, 1993.

This collection of essays examines the domestic alliances of numerous nineteenth- and twentieth-century women, most of whom were high achievers. There are personal stories as well as theoretical discussions from psychological and social perspectives.

Rubinstein, Helge, ed. *The Oxford Book of Marriage.* New York: Oxford University Press, 1992.

More readable than some of the other *Oxford Books of . . .* series, this is a charming anthology of poems, stories, and reflections on the varied experiences of matrimony.

Runzo, Joseph, and Nancy M. Martin, eds. *Love, Sex and Gender in the World Religions.* Oxford, England: One World Publications, 2000.

Although individual essays contain pertinent information, this book as a whole is a disappointment. It is far from comprehensive in the treatment of its subject, and the essays, some of which are highly eccentric, tend to be written in dry professional jargon.

Sailer, Steve. "Analysis: Gay Marriage around the Globe" (July 2003), http://upi.com/inc/view.php?StoryID = 20030714–073510–5671r.

Sailer, a United Press International national correspondent, has provided a brief but informative survey of attitudes and developments around the world regarding same-sex marriage.

Satinover, Jeffrey B. *Homosexuality and the Politics of Truth.* North Dartmouth, MA: Baker Books, 1996.

Satinover, a psychiatrist who rejects the doctrine that homosexuality is immutable, examines recent medical scholarship, as reported in leading journals and the press. He presents an interesting explanation of how psychology, biology, choice, and habit all contribute to sexual "orientation." Although his argument is presented from a Christian viewpoint and a belief that all humans operate within their fallen nature, he has much of general interest to say about habits, compulsions, and addictions and how they often determine sexual expression.

Sears, Alan, and Craig Osten. *The Homosexual Agenda: Exposing the Principal Threat to Religious Freedom Today.* Nashville, TN: Broadman and Holmar, 2003.

Sears and Osten provide a conservative Christian critique of the homosexual movement and its legal activism. Their findings are well documented and effectively identify the dangers of political correctness when its proponents promote an agenda by denying free expression to those who oppose their goals.

Signorile, Michelangelo. *Queer in America: Sex, the Media, and the Closets of Power.* New York: Random House, 1993.

A frequently quoted interpretation of the American scene near the end of the twentieth century, *Queer* is also an angry personal plea from the "pioneer of outing," a prominent activist-journalist. Signorile believes that homosexuals can only win if they courageously and openly accept themselves and reject the "hypocrisy" of those who remain closeted. His attack, passionate and sometimes careless, is aimed chiefly at the religious right, the New York City media, the Washington political establishment, and Hollywood.

Siler, Mahan, "Blessings Unforeseen" (November December 2001), http://www.theotherside.org/archive/nov-dec01/siler.html.

Siler is an established Baptist minister whose church has welcomed lesbian, gay, bisexual, and transgendered people for several years. He argues that it is time the churches rethought their objections to same-sex activity and marriage.

Slater, Philip. *Foot Holds: Understanding the Shifting Sexual and Family Tensions in Our Culture.* New York: E. P. Dutton, 1977.

Slater, a controversial social critic, examines the family crisis of the 1970s. Although he does not deal directly with gay issues, some of the questions he asks are pertinent. He contends that patriarchy stems from the simple fear men have of the "greater powers of women." Monogamy, he believes, is a greater threat to society than promiscuity.

Sobran, Joe. "The Amendment Strategy" (July 2004), http://www.sobran.com/columns/2004/040715.htm.

With racy, argumentative language, Sobran discusses the difficulty in obtaining a constitutional amendment to counter court decrees. He feels that judicial abuse is a central problem in America today.

Sprigg, Peter. *Outrage: How Gay Activists and Liberal Judges Are Trashing Democracy To Redefine Marriage.* Washington, DC: Regnery, 2004.

In this effective polemic by the director of the Family Research Council's Center for Marriage and Family Studies, Sprigg expresses outrage that judges rather than elected officials are now responsible for many of our most important laws. He suggests action to remedy this state of affairs and explains that many libertarians, democrats, and homosexuals oppose same-sex marriage for very legitimate reasons.

Sullivan, Andrew, ed. *Same-Sex Marriage Pro & Con: A Reader.* New York: Vintage Books, 2004.

Sullivan's excellent collection of essays expresses a variety of opinions. Included are everything from excerpts from Genesis and Leviticus to the latest discussions by Camille Paglia, William Safire, Barney Frank, and Sonny Bono.

———. *Virtually Normal: An Argument about Homosexuality.* New York: Vintage Books, 1995.

Most books on the gay rights movement are dated within one year, but Sullivan's work remains relevant. Here he examines the definition of "homosexual," along with attitudes of prohibitionists, liberationists, conservatives, and liberals. He evaluates the politics of homosexuality and concludes with a thoughtful epilogue entitled "What Are Homosexuals For?" This is one of the best introductions to the subject, written from the pro-gay point of view.

Swidler, Arlene, ed. *Homosexuality and World Religions.* Valley Forge, PA: Trinity Press International, 1993.

Swidler has compiled one of the few currently available books on her subject. A well-known Roman Catholic liberal, she is favorable to homosexual aspirations. She has brought together fine discussions of homosexuality from the following viewpoints: traditional religions of the Americas and Africa, Hinduism, Buddhism, Judaism, Roman Catholicism, Protestantism, Islam, and the historic Chinese and Japanese religions. Each chapter is contributed by a specialist, often a practitioner of the religion under discussion.

Thumma, Scott, and Edward R. Gray, eds. *Gay Religion.* Lanham, MD: AltaMira Press, 2004.

This unusual book examines the inventive ways homosexuals have found to express their unique spirituality. Special attention is given to gay Seventh-Day Adventists, Radical Faeries, and those who practice mixtures of pagan and animistic rituals. Some reviewers have complained that the material is seriously dated.

Toussaint, David, with Heather Leo. *Gay and Lesbian Weddings: Planning the Perfect Same-Sex Ceremony.* New York: Ballantine Books, 2004.

Toussaint and Leo's planning guide tackles the unique problems that gay and lesbian weddings encounter. Which father gives away which bride in a lesbian wedding? Which gay groom's father pays for the wedding? Does one invite disapproving relatives to the ceremony? How does one plot a religiously mixed same-sex ceremony? The authors survey the changing marriage laws in the United States and abroad, explaining differences between domestic partnership, civil unions, and marriage proper. Lively case studies of actual same-sex weddings are provided, along with useful information about the attitudes of different American religions toward homosexual unions.

Turner, William B. *A Genealogy of Queer Theory.* Philadelphia: Temple University Press, 2000.

This dense and philosophical but informative examination of the roots of "queer theory" as a tool of academic inquiry, relates the work of Michel Foucault to feminists and other investigators of race, ethnicity, class, gender, and sexual orientation.

Via, Dan O., and Robert A. J. Gagnon. *Homosexuality and the Bible: Two Views.* Minneapolis: Fortress Press, 2003.

This concise (117 pages including notes) but thorough discussion of biblical teachings on homosexuality, from two distinct points of view, is an essential source. Via, Professor Emeritus of New Testament at Duke University Divinity School, takes a revisionist position on Christianity and sexuality, while Gagnon, Associate Professor of New Testament at Pittsburgh Theological Seminary, is the most noted defender of the traditional Christian view.

Wardel, Lynn D., Mark Strasser, William C. Duncan, et al., eds. *Marriage and Same-Sex Unions: A Debate.* Westport, CT: Praeger, 2003.

A thorough examination of the basic issues involved in same-sex marriage, from responsible observers on both sides of the debate, this book provides a thorough review of legal decisions up to the point of its publication and remains one of the most useful books on the subject.

Weitzman, Lenore J. *The Marriage Contract: Spouses, Lovers, and the Law.* New York: Collier Macmillan, 1981.

Although Weitzman's legal information is dated, his argument still merits attention. He acknowledges that current marriage law is obsolete and is based on a social structure long gone and religious ideas no longer held by millions of Americans.

Wharton, Greg, and Ian Philips, eds. *I Do, I Don't: Queers in Marriage.* San Francisco: Suspect Thoughts Press, 2004.

This entertaining and informative anthology of poetry, reflections, and essays does not take itself too seriously. The book provides a good sampling of opinion within the gay community on the subject of marriage, including some contributors who clearly reject the idea.

Whisman, Vera. *Queer by Choice: Lesbians, Gay Men, and the Politics of Identity.* New York: Routledge, 1996.

Whisman examines the role choice plays in sexual identity, based on interviews with 72 people, about equally divided between men and women. Conscious choice in sexual orientation is not often discussed and is frequently not even acknowledged. Whisman also looks at the effects of race, religion, and level of education on sexual persuasion.

White, John. *Eros Defiled, The Christian and Sexual Sin.* Downers Grove, IL: InterVarsity Press, 1977.

White's examination of Christian sexual conduct places homosexuality in the broader context of general sexual ethics.

White, Mel. *Stranger at the Gate: To Be Gay and Christian in America.* New York: Plume Books, 1995.

White was formerly a ghostwriter for such Christians and political conservatives as Jerry Falwell, Pat Robertson, and Oliver North. He details his own troubling journey from suppression of his homosexuality to his official coming out, explaining how he eventually reconciled his gay orientation with his Christian faith, but not before a struggle that lasted over 25 years.

Wigoder, Geoffrey, editor-in-chief. *The Encyclopedia of Judaism.* Jerusalem: Jerusalem Publishing House, 1989.

An excellent source of Jewish information, this splendidly illustrated one-volume compendium of fact and lore includes especially good sections on Hebraic sexual ethics and marriage.

Wink, Walter, ed. *Homosexuality and Christian Faith: Questions of Conscience for the Churches.* Minneapolis: Fortress Press, 1999.

A liberal Christian thinker, Wink is frequently quoted in debates on homosexuality and same-sex marriage. In this anthology he brings together essays by prominent Roman Catholic and Protestant clergy, all demanding that Christianity abandon its traditional views on sexuality in the name of openness. This is not a dialogue but a symposium of statements by people who clearly agree. Contributors include Methodists, Northern Baptists, Evangelical Lutherans, Episcopalians, Franciscans, and others. Some, such as William Sloan Coffin, are well-known media personalities; others are lesser-known divinity school professors and bishops.

Witte, John. *From Sacrament to Contract: Marriage, Religion, and Law in the Western Tradition.* Louisville, KY: Westminster John Knox Press, 1998.

In this acclaimed study of concepts of marriage within basic Christian traditions, Witte provides a sound correction of earlier theoretical studies. He examines models of marriage in Roman Catholic, Lutheran, Calvinist, and Anglican teachings and relates these to later Enlightenment pronouncements. He is especially good at demonstrating how religious models of marriage have affected civil law.

Wolfe, Christopher, ed. Introduction by William Kristol. *Homosexuality and American Public Life.* Dallas, TX: Spence Publishing Company, 1999.

Eleven papers are included here from a conference sponsored by the American Public Philosophy Institute. The authors challenge commonly held notions about the genetic and immutable nature of homosexuality and examine the social consequences of homosexuality.

Wolfson, Evan. *Why Marriage Matters: America, Equality, and Gay People's Right to Marry.* New York: Simon & Schuster, 2004.

An attorney, Wolfson believes that the organization of the freedom-to-marry movement is one of the most important features of the early twenty-first century. He contends that marriage as the "highest expression of love, dedication, and responsibility, should be open to all." He supports his contention with legal arguments.

Yalom, Marilyn. *A History of the Wife.* New York: Harper Collins, 2001.

Writing in a popular style and not always documenting thoroughly, Yalom is still helpful in considering the different roles wives have been expected to perform from antiquity to the present. Relevant, too, is the examination of the changing expectations people, especially Europeans, have had of matrimony.

Young, Robin Darling. "Gay Marriage: Reimagining Church History" (1991),
    http://catholiceducation.org/articles/homosexuality/ho0069.html.

Young, who teaches early Christian history at Catholic University of
America, convincingly refutes the much-acclaimed thesis of John Boswell
that same-sex unions were sanctioned by the early Church.

# INDEX

*Adelphopoiesis* ceremonies, 144
Adi Granth, 23
*Aenead,* 44–45
Aeschylus, 40
Affirmation, 15
Alexander the Great, 41
Alighieri, Dante, 48–49
American Civil Liberties Union, 128
Antony, Mark, 47
Aquinas, St. Thomas, 12, 48, 144
Arinze, Francis Cardinal, 120
Aristophanes, 40
Arkes, Hadley, 117
Augustine, St., 144
Ayisha (wife of Mohammed), 19

Bacon, Roger, 49
Bacon, Sir Francis, 152
Baehr decision, 172
Bahaism, 29–30
Baha'Ullah (Mirza Husayn Ali Nuri), 29
Ball, Carlos A., 81
Balzac, Honoré de, 66

Bankhead, Tallulah, 169
Baudelaire, Charles, 66
Bazzi, Giovanni Antonio, 54
Beach, Frank, 79
Beauvoir, Simone de, 66
Belgium, 72, 78, 163, 170
Benedict XVI, Pope, 13
Bennett, William J., 120–24, 147n11–12, 162
Berdache, 60
Bernardino of Sienna, 52
Beth Chayim Chadashim, 7, 16
Bollywood, 21
Bork, Judge Robert, 117–20
Boston marriage, 153–55
Boswell, John, 12, 78, 108–10, 143–46
Boy Scouts of America, 70, 71
Brehony, Kathleen A., 154
Brethren/Mennonite Council for Gay Concerns, 15
Browning, Frank, 127
Bruce, Tammy, 117, 125–26
Buddhism, 23–25, 27, 28, 36n16
Buonarroti, Michelangelo, 53

Calvin, John, 13, 55
Canada, 78, 170–71, 180
Cantarella, Eva, 62n1
Casler, Lwrence, 159–60
Catullus, 45
Celibacy, priestly, 13
Cellini, Benvenuto, 54
Chang, Judge Kevin, 172
Charles, Prince of Wales, 2
Chasin, Alexandra, 71
China, 49–51
Christianity: argument against
    homosexuality, 134–46; concept
    of marriage, 7–17,
    101–10
Christian Science, 30
Christina, Queen of Sweden,
    55–56
Churches of Christ, 15
Church of England, 2, 10, 11, 14
Church of the Brethren, 15, 16
Cicero, 46
Civil union, 162–64
Cocteau, Jean, 66
Code of Manu, 49
Communes, 157–58
Confucianism, 25–26
Covenant marriage, 161–62
Crazy Horse (Lakota warrior), 61
Crete, 41
Crompton, Louis, 44, 61, 62

Daughters of Bilitis, 69
David, King of Israel, 100–101
Defense of Marriage Act, 181–82
Defense of Marriage Constitutional
    Amendment, 31
DeGeneres, Ellen, 122
Deism, 58
Denmark, 163, 179
Dietrich, Marlene, 65
Dignity/USA, 13
Divorce, 9–11, 18, 28, 138
Donatello, 53

Eastern Orthodox Churches, 9, 13,
    78, 109
Eddy, Mary Baker, 30
Elders, Dr. Jocelyn, 123
Elizabeth I, Queen of England, 57
Ellis, Albert, 150
Ellis, Havelock, 67, 157
England, 56–57, 66–68
The Enlightenment, 58–60
Eskridge, William, 79
Ettelbrick, Paula, 126–27
Euripides, 40
The European Union, 127
Evans, Arthur, 32

Ford, Clelland S., 79
Fademan, Lillian, 154
The Farm, 158
Farrakhan, Louis, 20
Florence, 52–54
France, 55, 66, 163, 176
Frederick the Great, 58
Freud, Sigmund, 65

Gagnon, Robert A. J., 135–41
Gallagher, Maggie, 117
Ganymede, 40, 54, 55
Garland, Judy, 63
Gay Shame of San Francisco, 124–25
Germany, 65–66, 131
Gibbon, Edward, 45
Gide, Andre, 66
Ginsberg, Ruth Bader, 157
Greece, 37–42
Greek drama, 40
Greenberg, Rabbi Steven, 35n3,
    92–101
Greenland, 163
Gregory IX, Pope, 48
Griswold, Bishop Frank, 14

Halakah, 15, 93, 99–101
Hay, Harry, 69
Hemingway, Ernest, 155

Henry VIII, 56
Hinduism, 20–23
Homer, 38, 116
Horace, 45
Horvat, Marian Therese, 143–45
Hubbard, L. Ron, 32–33
Hurston, Zora Neale, 60

Iceland, 163, 176
*The Iliad,* 38, 42
India, 49, 20–23
Integrity, 15
Iran, 19
Isherwood, Christopher, 65
Islam, 17–20, 47
Israeli Penal Code, 7

Jackson, Don, 69
James, Henry, 154
James I of England (James VI of
    Scotland), 56
Japan, 57–58
John, Elton, 177
John Crysostom, St., 144
Judaism: argument against homosexual
    marriage, 129–34; concept of mar-
    riage, 4–7. *See also* Greenberg, Rabbi
    Steven
Judea, 42–43
Julius Caesar, 46
Julius II, Pope, 54, 55
Juvenal, 45–46

Kabuki, 29, 57
Kama Sutra, 22
Kameny, Frank, 69
Kan, Hak Ja, 34
Keats, John, 39
Khadijah (wife of Mohammed), 18
Khomeini, Ayatollah Ruhollah, 19
King, Martin Luther, Jr., 167
Kinsey Report, 60, 168
Kirk, Marshall, 131
Knights Templar, 48

Knoesen, Evert, 176
Kraft-Ebing, Richard von, 65, 67
Krauthammer, Charles, 117
Kulongoski, Ted, 175
Kurtz, Stanley, 117

Landers, Ann, 117
Lawrence, T. E., 19
Leadbeater, Bishop Charles
    Webster, 16
Lee, Mother Ann, 158
Lehman, Nathaniel S., 131–32
Lenya, Lotte, 65
Leonardo Da Vinci, 53, 54
Lesbos, 39
Levenstrecht, 65
Liberal Catholic Church, 16
Lin, Yu-tang, 26
Lindsey, Judge Benjamin, 159
Log Cabin Republicans, 125
Lowell, Amy, 154
Luther, Martin, 10, 13
Lutheranism, 14
Lutherans Concerned, 14–15
Lyon, Phyllis, 69

Manji, Irshad, 91
Mao, Tse-Tung, 26
Marat, Jean-Paul, 59
Marlowe, Christopher, 56
Martin, Dale, 107
Martin, Del, 69
Mary, Queen of Scots, 57
Mattachine Society, 69
McKay, John, 117
McNeill, John, 12
Mead, Margaret, 60, 159
Medici, Lorenzo de', 53
Metropolitan Community Church, 7,
    16–17, 102
Middle Ages, 47–49
Milton, John, 11, 129
Mishima, Yukio, 27
Mohammed, 17, 18–19

Monroe, Marilyn, 63
Montesquieu, 58
Moon, Sun Myung, 33–34
Mormonism, 3, 30–31
Morocco, 19
Moynihan, Daniel Patrick, 120–21
Murasaki, Lady Shikibu, 28
Musonius, Rufus, 116

Nanak, 23
Nation of Islam, 20
Nazi party, 65
Neo-paganism, 31–33
Netherlands, 72, 78, 163, 169–70
Newson, Mayor Gavin, 124, 175
Noahide Law, 96
Norway, 163, 176
No theater, 57
Novak, David, 92, 97–98
Noyes, John, 157

*The Odyssey*, 38
Oneida community, 147
Open marriage, 155–56

Packard, Vance, 159
Paul, St., 11, 12, 134–38, 141–44
Paul IV, Pope, 54
Perry, Troy, 16, 102
Philip II of Macedonia, 41
Philo of Alexandria, 42
Piaf, Edith, 63
Pill, Erastes, 131
Plato, 39
Plutarch, 116
Polygamy, 156–57
Powell, Louis, 60
Prager, Dennis, 132–34
Presbyterianism, 15
Presbyterians for Lesbian and Gay
    Concerns, 15
Protestant Episcopal Church, 14, 120,
    171
Protestant Reformation, 9

Protestants and Other Americans
    United for Separation of Church
    and State, 128
Proust, Marcel, 66

Radclyffe-Hall, Marguerite Antonia, 67
Rauch, Jonathan, 85–91
Renaissance, 51–54
Renault, Mary, 42
Robinson, Bishop Gene, 14
Roman Catholic Church, 11, 13, 34,
    78, 91, 109, 128, 158, 171
*Roman de Fauvel*, 48
Rome, 42–47
Russian Orthodox Church, 2

Sade, Donatien Alphonse Francois,
    Marquis de, 59
Safire, William, 117
*Salome*, 67
Samurai warrior, 29
Sappho, 39, 42, 45
Schwarzenegger, Arnold, 175
Scientology, 32–33
Sekulow, Alan, 117
Seventh Day Adventists, 15
Shakers, 158
Shakespeare, William, 56–57
Shinto, 27–29
Sikhism, 23
Single life, 151–53
Situation ethics, 102–3
Smith, Joseph, 31
Society of Friends, 15–16
Socrates, 40
Sodom and Gomorrah, 19, 95, 130,
    147n23
Sontag, Susan, 64
Sophocles, 40
Southern Baptist Convention, 15
The Soviet Union, 2
Spain, 47, 54–55, 78, 163, 176
Spong, Bishop John Shelby, 15, 85
St. Augustine, 144

Stein, Gertrude, 66, 155
Stevenson, Edward Prime, 68
St. Francis Xavier, 57
St. John Crysostom, 144
Stoicism, 40
Stonewall riots, 69
St. Paul, 11, 12, 134–38, 141–44
Strauss, Richard, 67
Suetonius, 45–46
Sullivan, Andrew, 64, 69–70
*Summa Theologiae,* 48
Sweden, 55–56, 147n10, 163,
    176, 179
Swidler, Arlene, 35, 36, 62
*Syballine Oracles,* 133

*The Tale of Genji,* 28
Tantric Buddhism, 24–29
Theodore de Beze, 55
Toklas, Alice V., 66, 155
Trembling Before G-d, 6
Troubridge, Una, 67
Tutu, Archbishop Desmond, 176
Tyrannicides, 41

Unification Church, 33–34
Union of South Africa, 176
Unitarian-Universalist Fellowship, 16
United Church of Canada, 16
United Church of Christ, 16, 171

United States of America, 60, 68–72,
    171–75, 177, 180–83

Vasari, Georgio, 53
Vatican II, 8, 168
Venice, 51–52
Verlaine, Paul, 66
Via, Dan O., 103, 105–8
Virgil, 44–45, 48
Vittoria della Colonna, 53
Voltaire, 58

Wardel, Mark Strasser, 62n1
Weitzman, Lenore J., 161
*The Well of Loneliness,* 68
West, Mae, 124
Wilde, Oscar, 67
Wilkins, Richard, 114
Winkte, 61
Witte, John, Jr., 115
World Council of Churches, 17

Xavier, St. Francis, 57

Young, Robin Darling, 145–46

Zen Buddhism, 24, 27
Zeno, 40
Zenophon, 40
Zoroastrianism, 22–23, 98

**ALLENE PHY-OLSEN** is Professor of English at Austin Peay State University.